IMAGES
of America

WALTON-VERONA

On the Cover: This is a photograph of an early-1900s gathering of families from the Beaver Lick and Verona areas. Pictured from left to right are Lewis Ryle, Roy Kenney, Jeff Hutsell, John A. Roberts, Belle Taylor Hutsell, Anna Taylor Kenney, family friend Mariah Roach, and unidentified grandchildren. (Courtesy of Kathleen Wiley.)

IMAGES
of America

WALTON-VERONA

Melinda Sartwell

ARCADIA
PUBLISHING

ISBN 978-0-7385-6618-4

Published by Arcadia Publishing
Charleston SC, Chicago IL, Portsmouth NH, San Francisco CA

Printed in the United States of America

Library of Congress Control Number: 2009925181

For all general information contact Arcadia Publishing at:
Telephone 843-853-2070
Fax 843-853-0044
E-mail sales@arcadiapublishing.com
For customer service and orders:
Toll-Free 1-888-313-2665

Visit us on the Internet at www.arcadiapublishing.com

Contents

ACKNOWLEDGMENTS

I would like to thank the following people for their help and encouragement throughout this endeavor: Bridget Striker and Jennifer Gregory of Boone County Public Library; Dr. Rebecca Bailey and Lois Hamill of Northern Kentucky University; Bernie Spencer and his wonderful Web site, www.nkyviews.com; Asa Rouse; Matt Becher of Boone County Historic Preservation Review Board; Connie Goins and the City of Walton; Janice Grubbs; Charlie "Hunky" Holder; Russell Groger; Mary Berkemeier; Mary Lou Rice and Zion Baptist Church; Margaret Percival Armstrong; Tom Armstrong; Anne Leake; Kathleen Wiley; Jeff Renaker; Paul Webster; Suzan Pratt, Polly Neace, and Richard Robinson of U.S. Bank; Johnny Gault; Michael Patko; Ruth Meadows; Pat Scott; Kent County Public Library; Jim Poole; and Steve Cauthen. I would also like to thank my editor, Luke Cunningham, for his guidance and patience.

Introduction

When Boone County was established in 1799, formed from the western side of Campbell County, only about 200 men owned all of the land. These pioneers travelled west to settle that vast new wilderness known as Kentucky, choosing the rich, fertile land along the Ohio River as their new home. These men prospered, with the land providing a large surplus of goods and the proximity to shipping up the Ohio River.

Boone County was also home to numerous salt licks, and the buffalo that migrated through the area created paths, or traces, along the Dry Ridge Corridor in the eastern half of the county, providing access to inland areas for pioneers to expand their holdings. The Dry Ridge Corridor became the major north-south route, and by 1819, construction began on the Covington and Lexington Turnpike along this buffalo trace, connecting Covington on the Ohio River with Lexington, center of the Bluegrass State.

Along this corridor, on the southeastern border of the county, a man named Col. Abner Gaines purchased a large parcel of land in 1809. A man of considerable means, Gaines, a Boone County justice, quickly began establishing his home and business interests, building an imposing Federal-style mansion that served as both his residence and a tavern. In 1815, a post office was established for the tiny community that had grown up around the Gaines holdings, and James Matthews Gaines, Abner's oldest son, was named the first postmaster for Gaines Crossroads. Gaines also established the first stagecoach line between Covington and Lexington, carrying mail and passengers on a trip that took 34 hours. Gaines's other son, John Pollard, became a Mexican War hero, a Whig congressman, and the first governor of the Oregon Territory.

Three months after Abner Gaines's death in late 1839, the town was renamed Walton. Town legend says that it was renamed for a steamboat captain who had helped Gaines in the early years, but that claim has never been proven. The town grew up along the Covington and Lexington Turnpike, attracting German immigrants who found that the crossroads town provided economic opportunity and a congenial lifestyle. When the Louisville and Nashville and Cincinnati Southern Railroads came through town in 1869 and 1877, Walton experienced major growth in its economy and subsequently, the population. By the late 19th century, Walton was the largest town in Boone County, boasting several hotels, taverns, blacksmith shops, tobacco warehouses, mills, and stockyards. The railways carried workers and shoppers into the city and brought shipments of goods into town.

This influx of people into the community made it necessary to create a school system, finding that the small, private, and one-room schoolhouses around town were insufficient. At a time when education was still mostly an afterthought, Walton had the foresight to establish the first county high school in 1901, and students commuted by train from all over Boone County into Walton to attend the school.

As the 20th century progressed and the dependence on the railway system diminished, Walton's prominence in the county faded. The old turnpike had become part of the U.S. Highway System, with U.S. 25 (Dixie Highway), the major route of transportation throughout the eastern United States, passing through town. In the 1960s, the interstate system was created, and Interstate 75 ran parallel to Dixie Highway, just west of downtown. Even with these advances in transportation, Walton was left further behind as its neighbor to the north, Florence, became the hub of activity for Boone County. Content with its small-town atmosphere, Walton resisted further growth for much of the 20th century.

Verona, a sleepy little community about 5 miles southwest of Walton, established a post office in 1831, and a Baptist church, New Bethel, was created within the farming community. Irish immigrants who arrived in Kentucky in the mid-19th century flocked to Verona, with its rolling hills and peaceful lifestyle, and found it an attractive place to start a new life. These new residents established St. Patrick's Catholic Church and created a firm foundation in the community.

Verona has never incorporated, choosing to remain a small community built around the crossroads of Walton-Verona and Verona-Mudlick Roads. When the Louisville and Nashville Railroad came through in 1869, the Verona Depot became a busy place for shipping and passenger pickup, improving the quality of life both economically and socially for residents.

The advent of the railroad also improved education for Verona-area residents. A private high school run by Nannie Hamilton in the late 19th century and a public high school built in 1914 provided schooling to children not only from Verona, but also children from neighboring communities to the south in Grant and Gallatin Counties who were able to ride the train to Verona.

Like Walton, Verona remained a small community throughout the 20th century. Even though progress was literally in its backyard when Interstate 75 cut directly through the Walton-Verona Road to the northeast, and Interstate 71 cut across McCoy's Fork to the west, Verona was a step back in time for those who wandered off the interstate.

As Boone County has become one of the fastest-growing counties in Kentucky, inevitably that growth would extend towards Walton and Verona. Today the sprawling countryside of Verona is dotted with subdivisions tucked between the horse farms; Walton has taken steps to revitalize the city by building the Walton Towne Center, providing shopping and jobs for residents of the town and surrounding areas. Walton also has plans to restore the old Abner Gaines house to its original beauty and turn it into a museum, providing cultural and educational opportunities and attracting visitors to this historic town.

The Walton-Verona school system, one of the top districts in Kentucky and listed on *U.S. News and World Report*'s best schools, is a source of pride for both communities. Cincinnati, Ohio, is less than 25 miles away via Interstate 75, providing easy access for people wanting the ease of country living but also able to enjoy the amenities of a city. Walton-Verona's excellent location, along with its top-rated schools and revitalization efforts, make it a desirable place to call home.

One

The Early Years

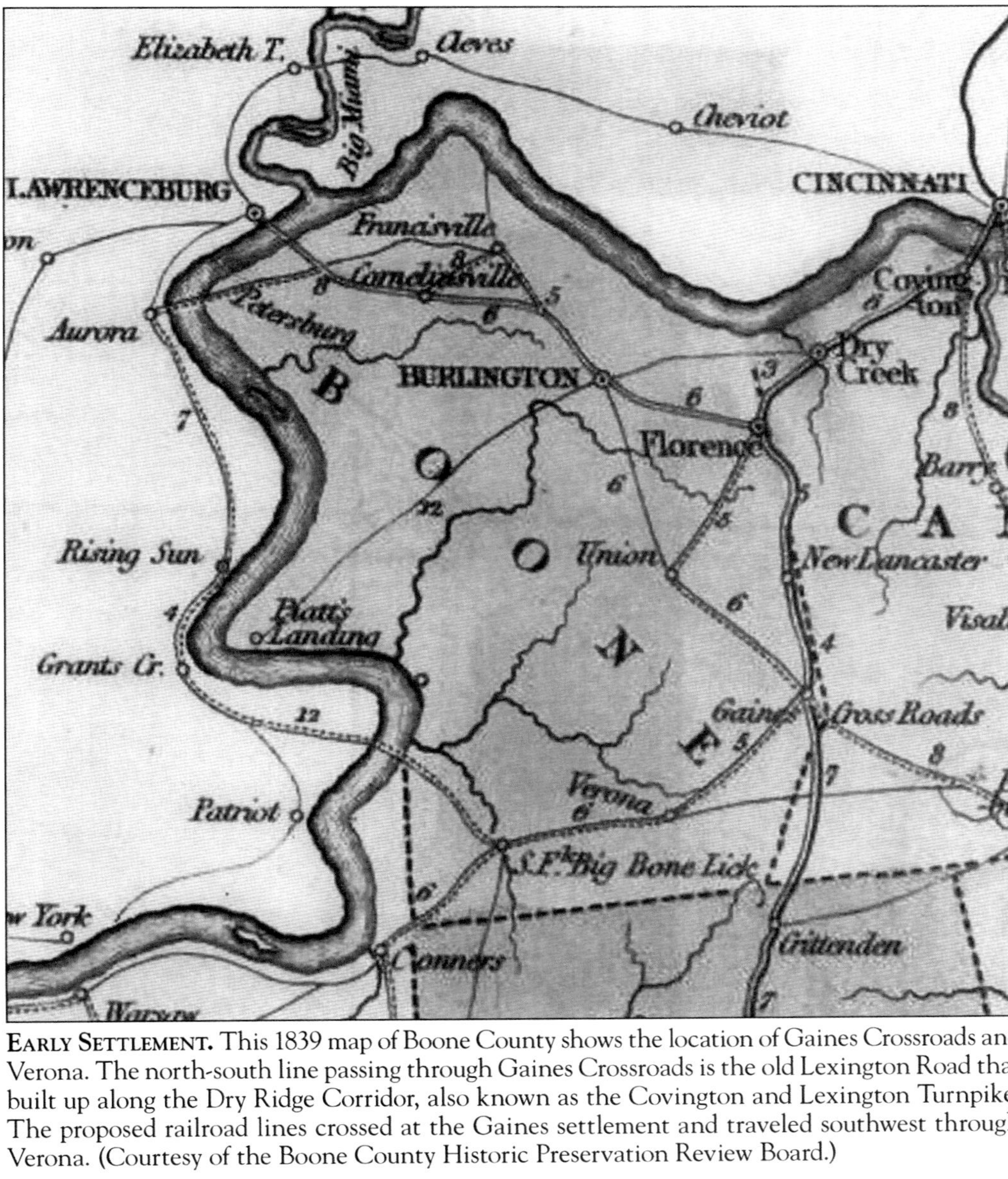

Early Settlement. This 1839 map of Boone County shows the location of Gaines Crossroads and Verona. The north-south line passing through Gaines Crossroads is the old Lexington Road that built up along the Dry Ridge Corridor, also known as the Covington and Lexington Turnpike. The proposed railroad lines crossed at the Gaines settlement and traveled southwest through Verona. (Courtesy of the Boone County Historic Preservation Review Board.)

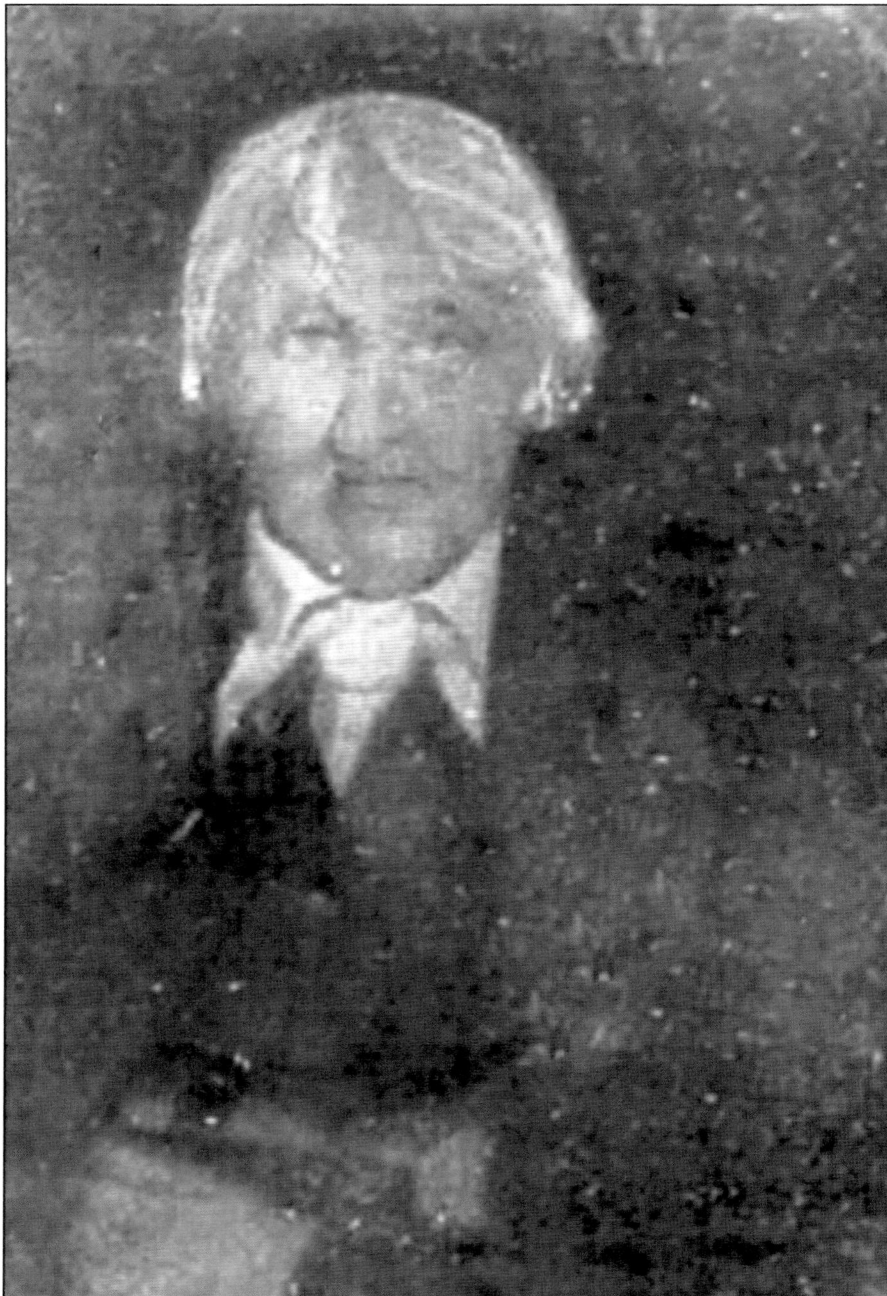

PIONEER LEGACY. Abner Gaines came to the area in around 1800, settling along the ridge road in southeastern Boone County. The settlement that grew up around his large landholdings became known as Gaines Crossroads, and a post office was established in 1815. Gaines was a Boone County justice and tavern owner, and he established the first stagecoach line between Lexington and Cincinnati, a trip that took 34 hours. Gaines died in 1839 and was buried in the family cemetery near the house. The cemetery was moved when the railroad came through, relocating to Highland Cemetery in Fort Mitchell, Kentucky. (Courtesy of the City of Walton.)

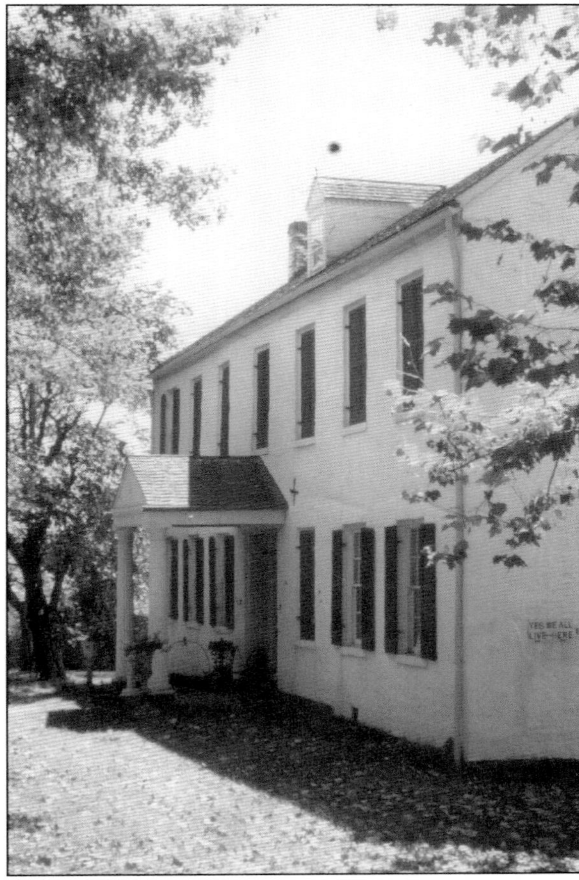

THE HOUSE THAT GAINES BUILT. Abner Gaines built this Federal-style dwelling in about 1810. It faced the Lexington Road, and being approximately the halfway point between Lexington and Cincinnati, Gaines found great success in running his stagecoach line and providing accommodations for weary travelers. The house remained in the family until after the Civil War, with subsequent owners using the property for apartments, an antique shop, and a private residence. The photograph at right shows the house when in use as an antique shop. The photograph below shows the current condition of the property. It is being restored by the City of Walton for future use as a museum. (Right, courtesy of Johnny Gault; below, courtesy of Polly Neace.)

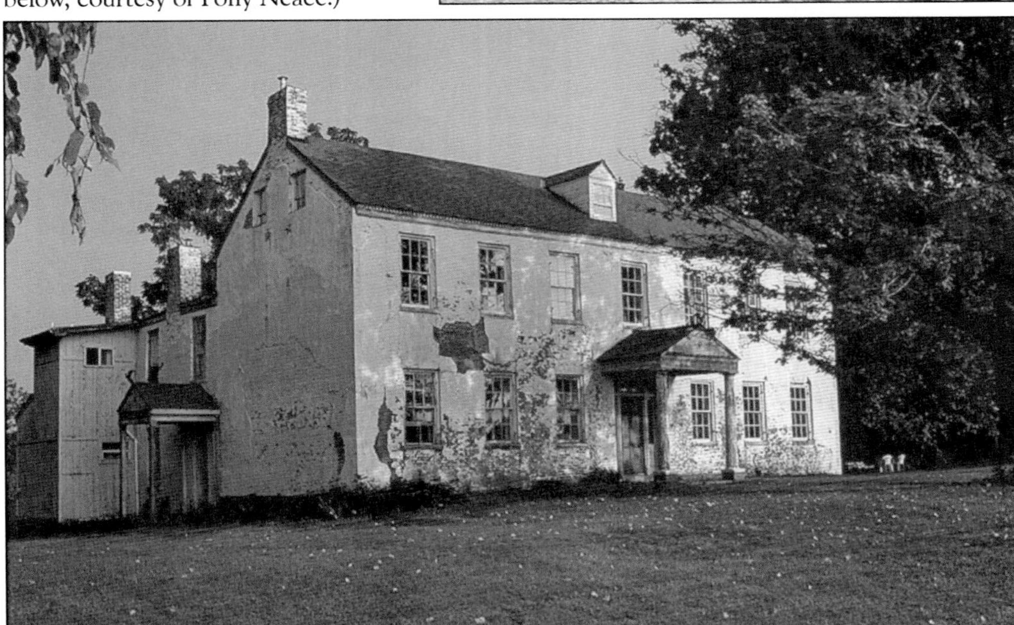

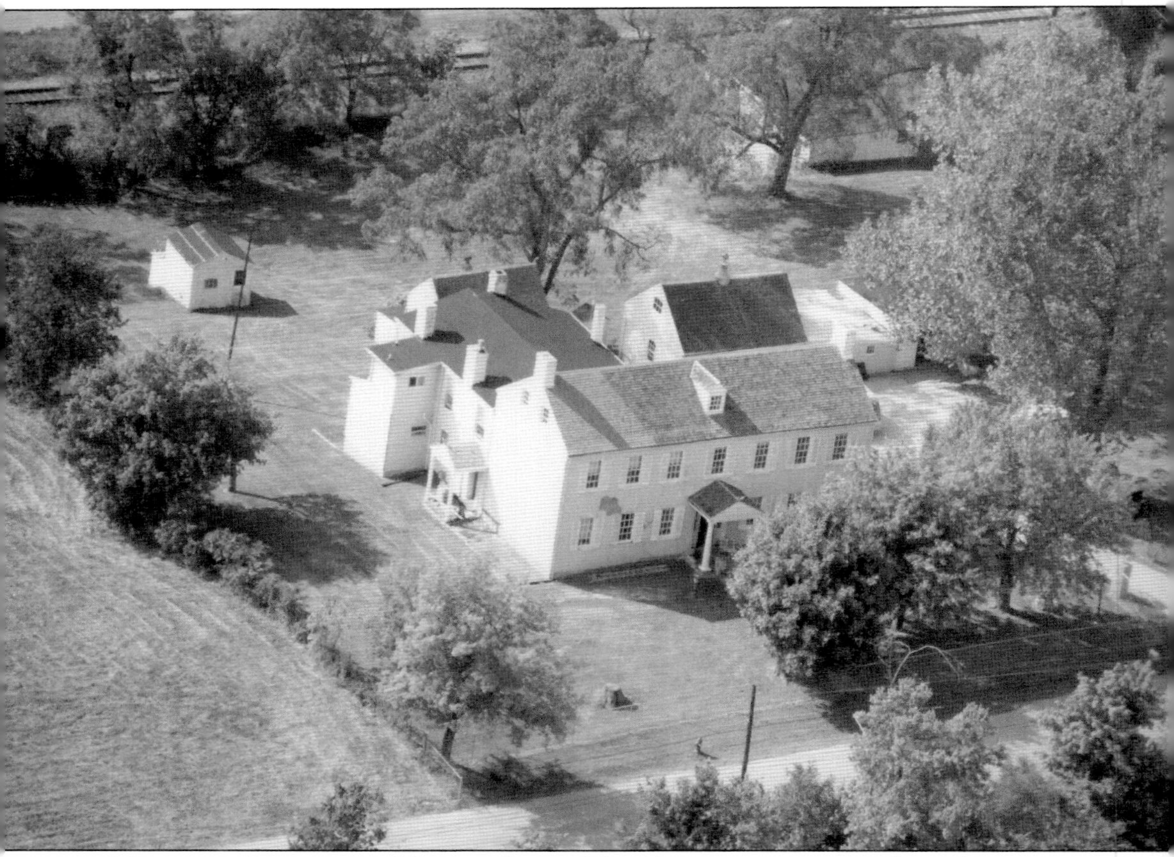

A Different Perspective. This aerial view of the Abner Gaines property shows the proximity of the old turnpike in front of the house, the Louisville and Nashville Railroad that was built directly behind it, and the Cincinnati Southern, located directly beyond the trees in the bottom corner in front. This photograph was taken during Col. John Gault's tenure as owner and operator of the Old Haunted House Antique Shop. Colonel Gault also added the outbuildings, a bathroom, and an elevator to the house. The addition is slated to be demolished, restoring the mansion to its original style. (Courtesy of Johnny Gault.)

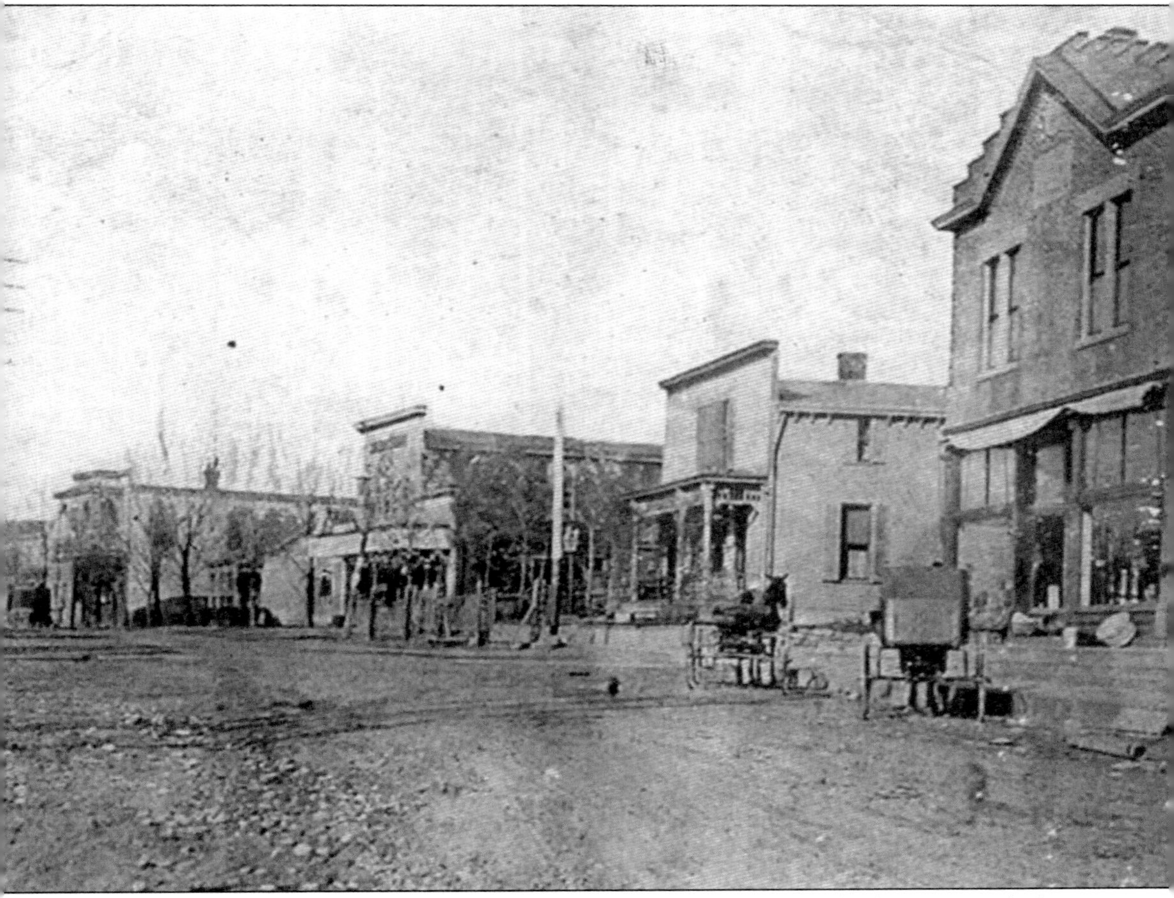

Main Street. Looking north along the Covington and Lexington Turnpike (Main Street), this photograph from about 1906 shows the business district of Walton. The building in the near right corner was at different times the Odd Fellows Hall, a grocery store, and a drugstore. Continuing north is Rosa King's boardinghouse next to the hall (now the Waltonian), and the largest building farther down the street is the Phoenix Hotel. The Phoenix was torn down in 1971. (Courtesy of Bernie Spencer, www.nkyviews.com.)

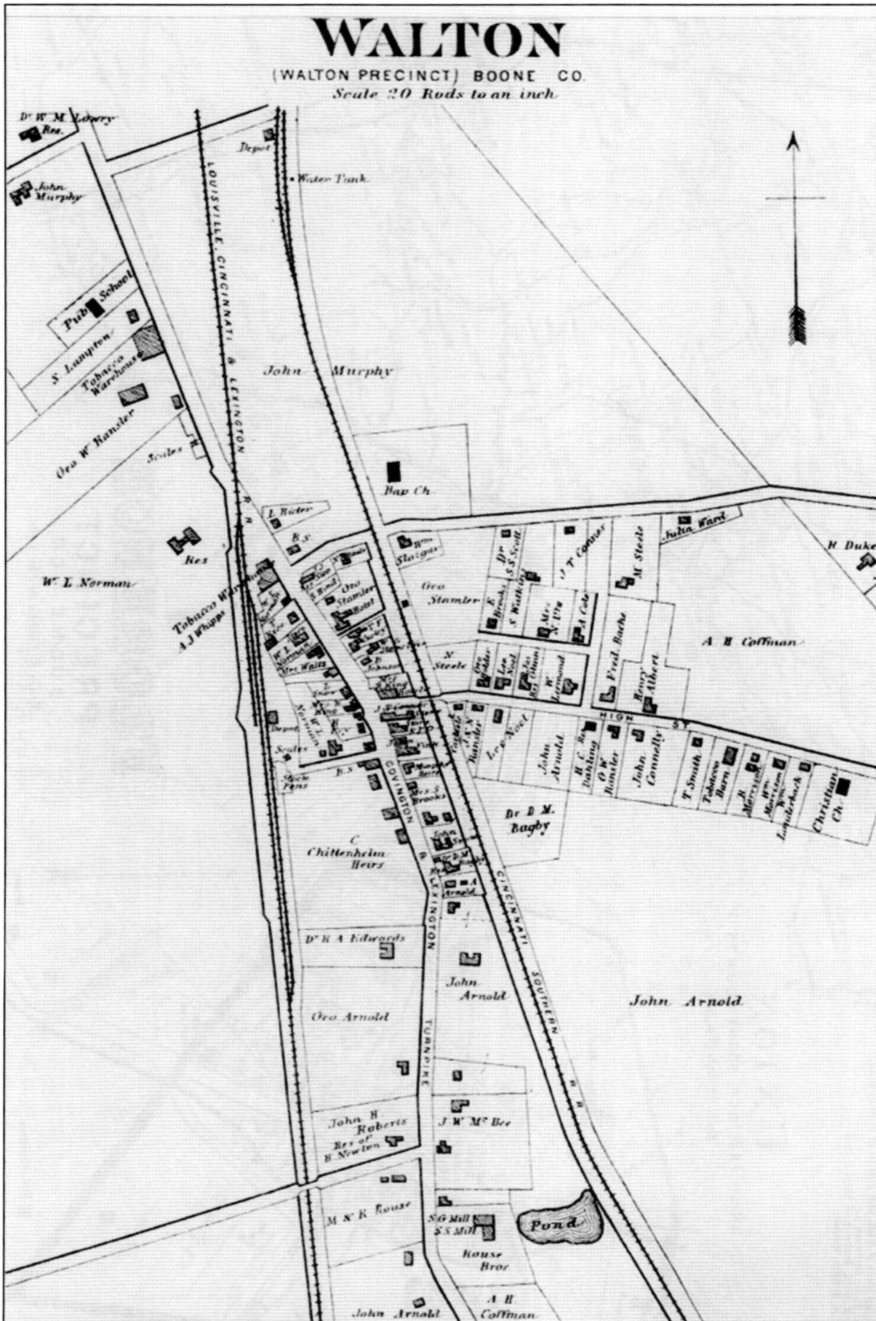

WALTON MAP. The 1883 atlas of Boone, Kenton, and Campbell Counties provides a detailed look at the economy of Walton in the late 1800s. The business district enjoyed a bustling economy due to the Louisville and Nashville and Cincinnati Southern Railroads, as well as the Covington and Lexington Turnpike. The larger residential estates lined the turnpike on the north and south ends of town, and the in-town residents clustered around the High Street and Cruises Creek Road areas. (Courtesy of Boone County Public Library.)

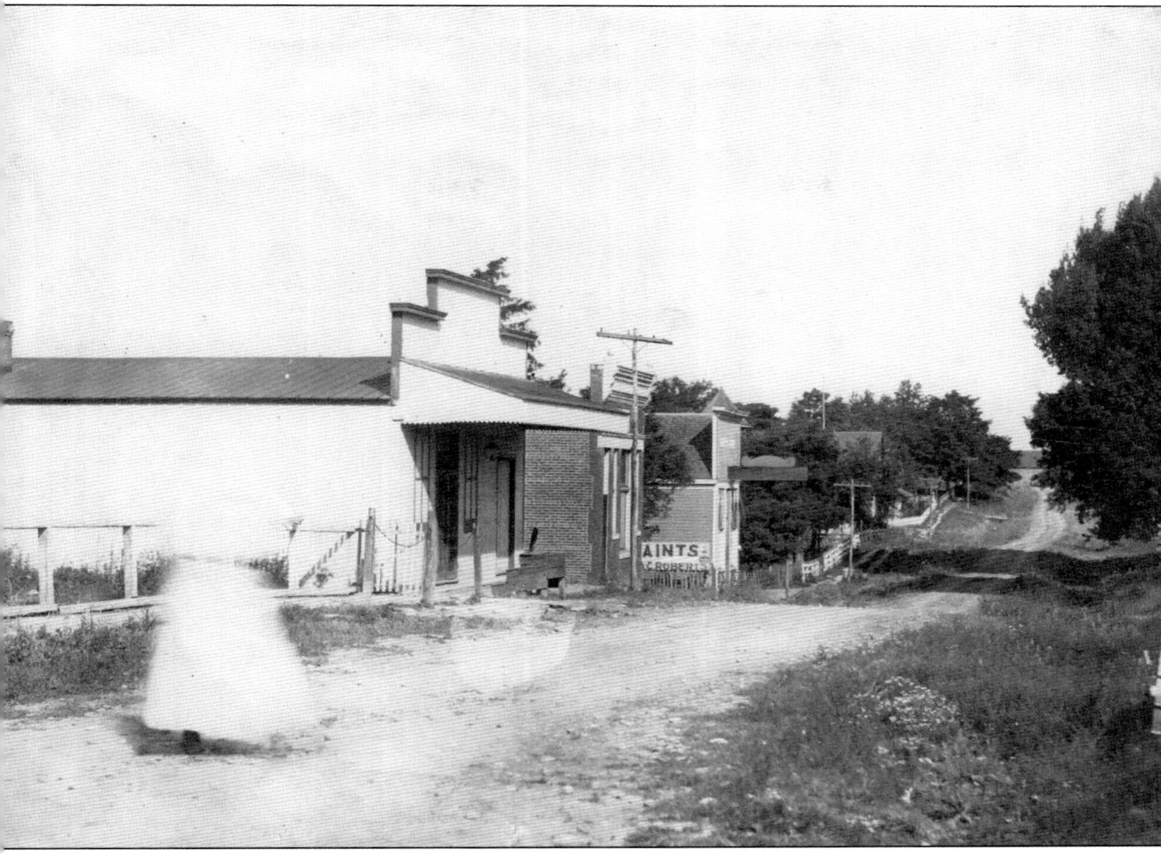

Looking West in Verona. This rare photograph shows the Verona-Mudlick Road facing west *c.* 1900. The photographer stood just past the intersection of this main road through town with the Walton-Verona Road. The white building was used as a funeral parlor (later the Verona Garage), the brick structure next door is the Verona Bank, and the old hardware store is the third building on the left. (Courtesy of Jeff Renaker.)

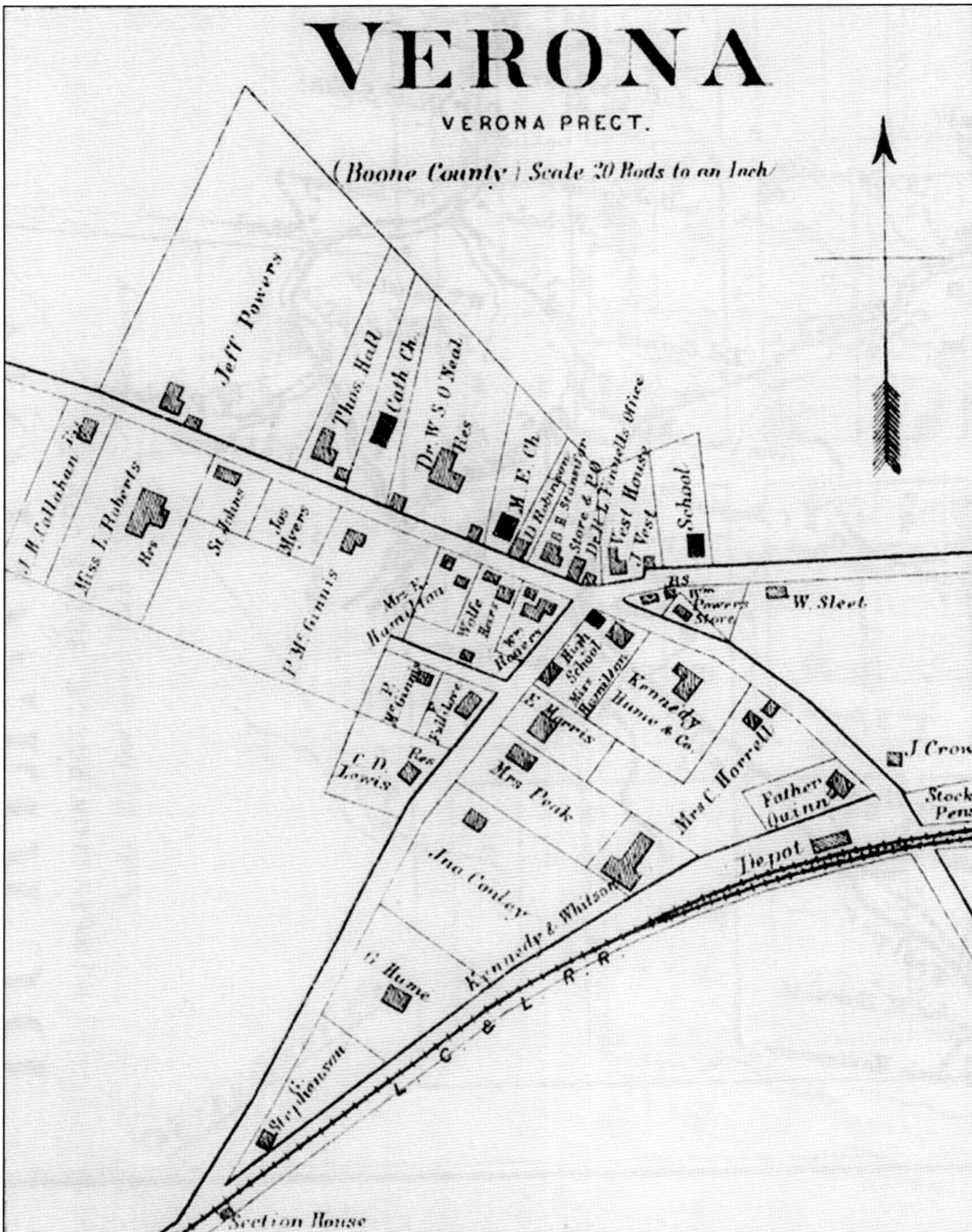

Verona Map. Verona, as shown in the 1883 atlas of Boone, Kenton, and Campbell Counties, was a small community at the crossroads of Verona-Mudlick Road and Walton-Verona Road. It boasted several stores, churches, a private school, and a busy Louisville and Nashville Depot. (Courtesy of Boone County Public Library.)

Two

A Bustling Economy

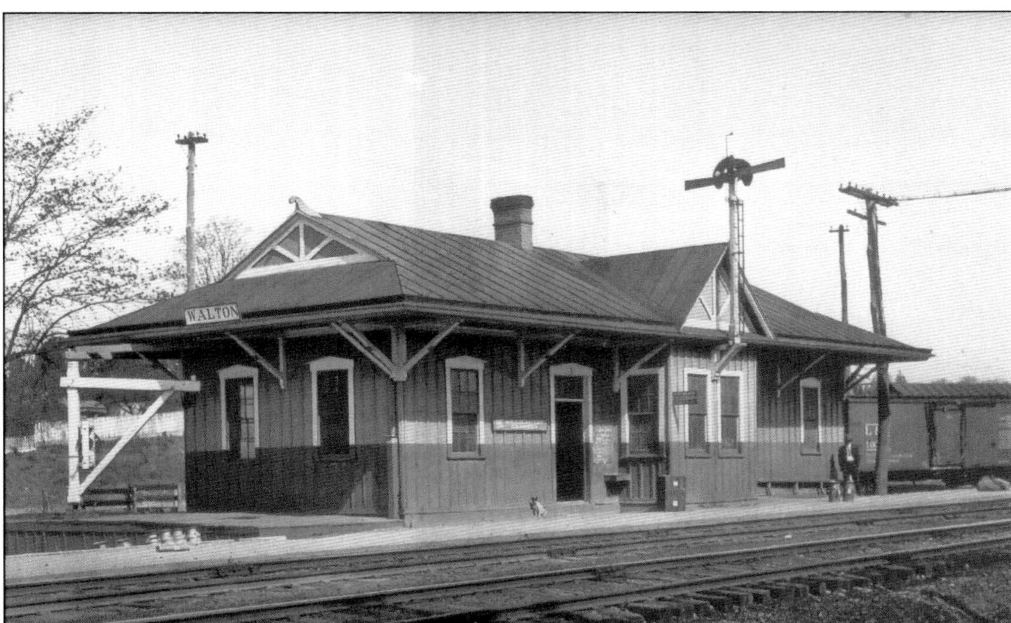

Southern Depot. The Cincinnati Southern Railroad, also known as the Queen and Crescent, passed through Walton several times a day. The depot was located on Locust Street, just off North Main Street, and was a busy hub of activity for students riding the train to the high school nearby, workers going into Cincinnati, and for goods for delivery and pickup by local residents. (Courtesy of the Boone County Historic Preservation Review Board.)

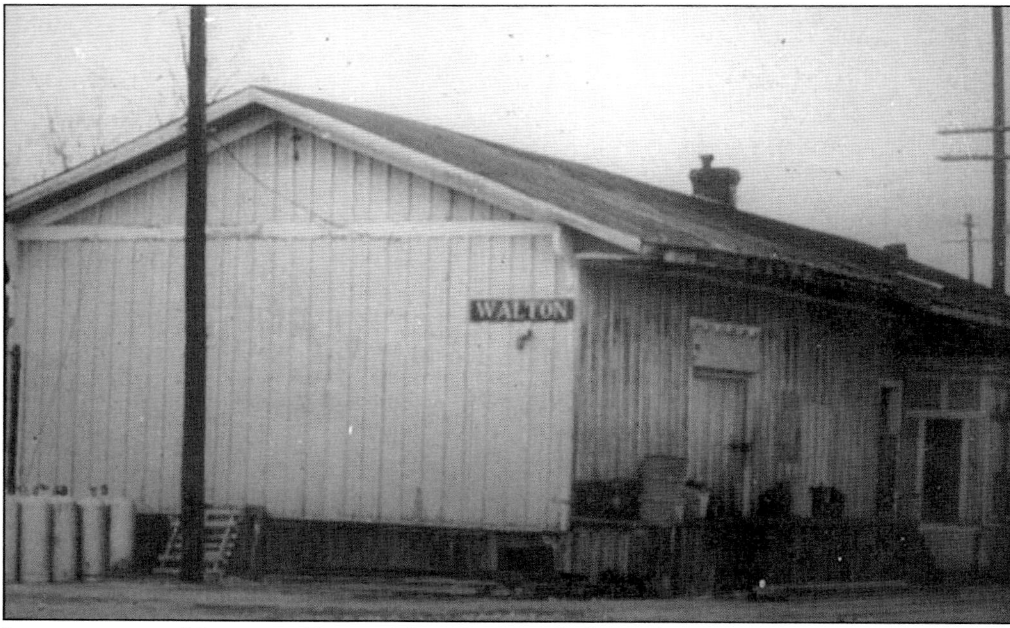

LOUISVILLE AND NASHVILLE DEPOT. This photograph shows the Louisville and Nashville Depot during the 1900s. Located just off Depot Street behind the current U.S. Bank, the depot provided a close drop-off point to the hotels in town and stock pens for the hog trade. Like the Cincinnati Southern Depot, it was torn down after falling into disuse when cars became the popular mode of transportation. (Courtesy of Bernie Spencer, www.nkyviews.com.)

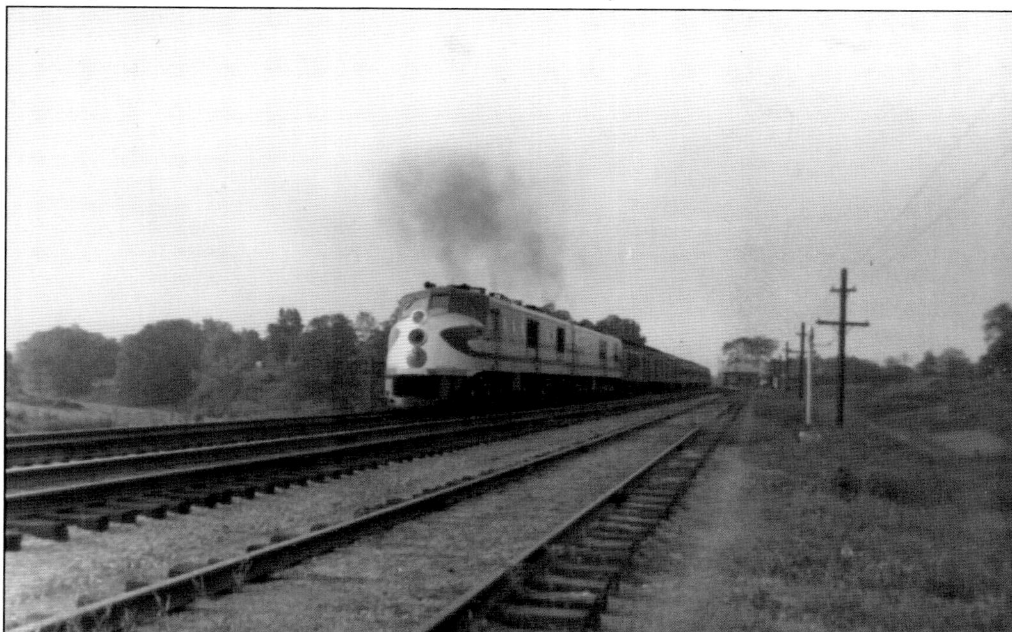

THE L&N. This photograph of the Louisville and Nashville train is typical of the daily runs the train made through the winding farmland of southern Boone County on the way into Walton. The double tracks no longer exist. (Courtesy of Charlie Holder.)

Heading Towards Walton. The Cincinnati Southern train approaches Walton on an array of tracks. The Southern and the Louisville and Nashville tracks crossed each other just north of town. Note the old bridge in the distance that connected Walton-Nicholson Road to the old turnpike near the Gaines house. (Courtesy of Russell Groger.)

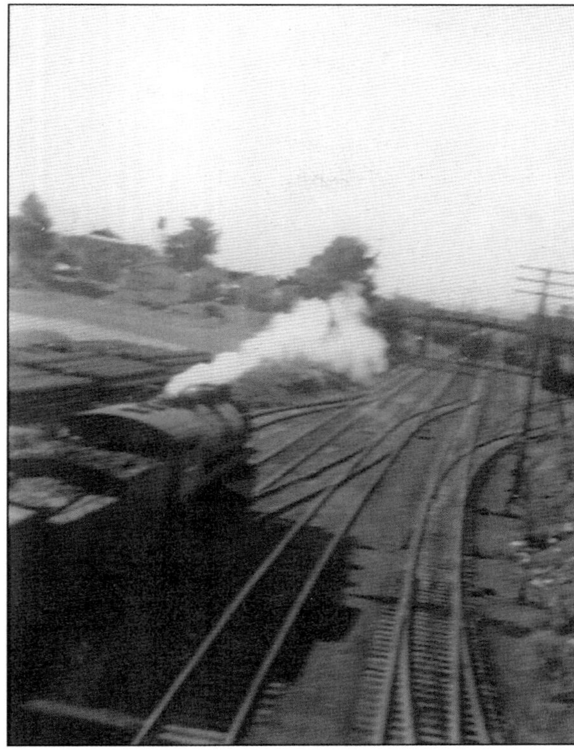

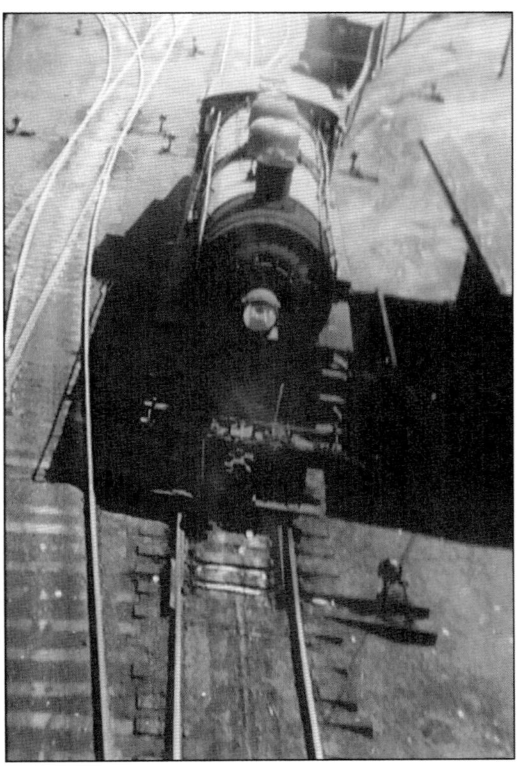

Coming Around the Bend. This photograph shows the Cincinnati Southern coming around the bend, past the section house, before heading into Walton. The railroad played a vital role in the economy and growth of Walton and Verona. (Courtesy of Russell Groger.)

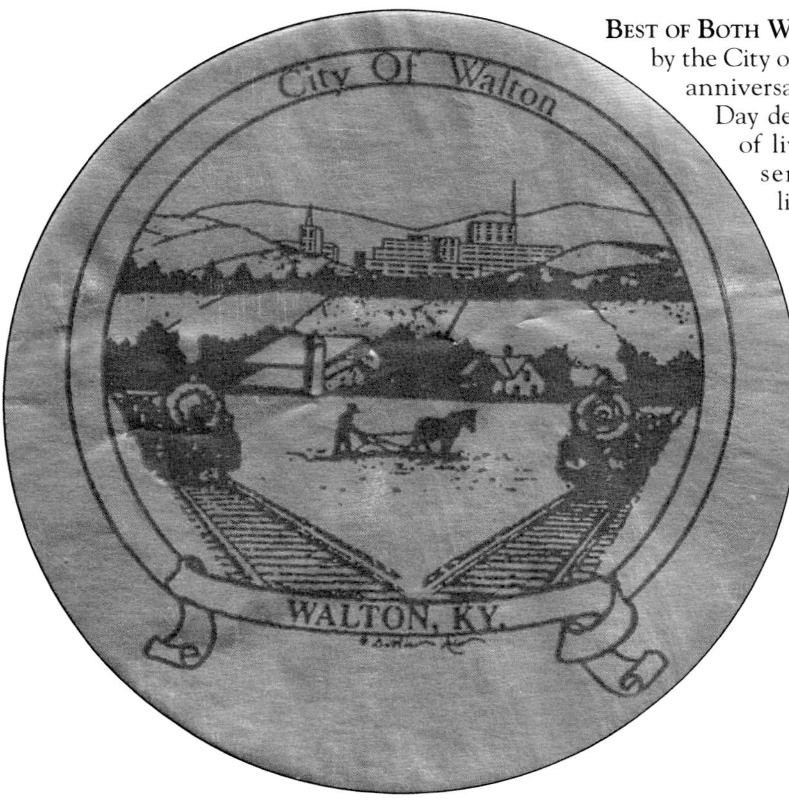

Best of Both Worlds. This seal used by the City of Walton for the silver anniversary of Old-Fashioned Day depicts the advantages of living in Walton: the serenity of country living with a backdrop of the city lights of Cincinnati, Ohio. (Courtesy of the City of Walton.)

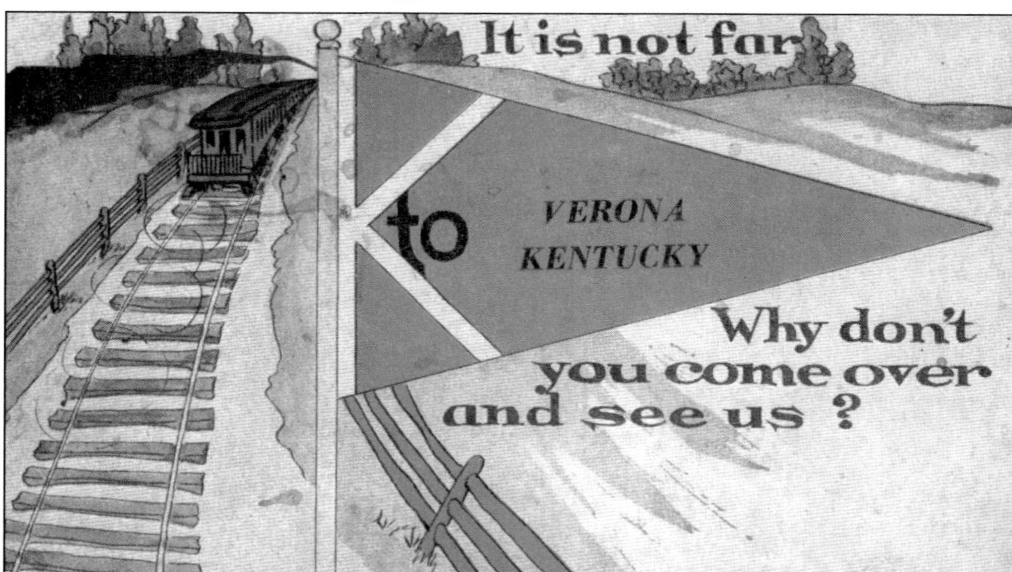

Greetings from Verona. Postcards were a prime source of communication in the early 1900s, often with scenic views of the communities from which they originated. This postcard shows Verona's identity as a farming community with rolling hills but connected to the city by the railroad. (Courtesy of Paul Webster.)

VERONA DEPOT. Carroll and Nora Webster stand beside the Louisville and Nashville Depot in this rare photograph c. 1920. The depot was located on Route 491 just past the crossroads of Verona-Mudlick and Walton-Verona Roads. Like the other depots, it fell into disuse and was torn down. It is now an empty lot on the corner of town. (Courtesy of Paul Webster.)

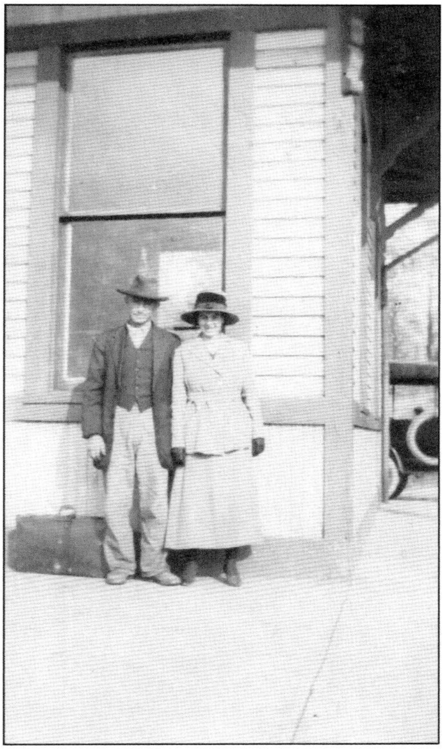

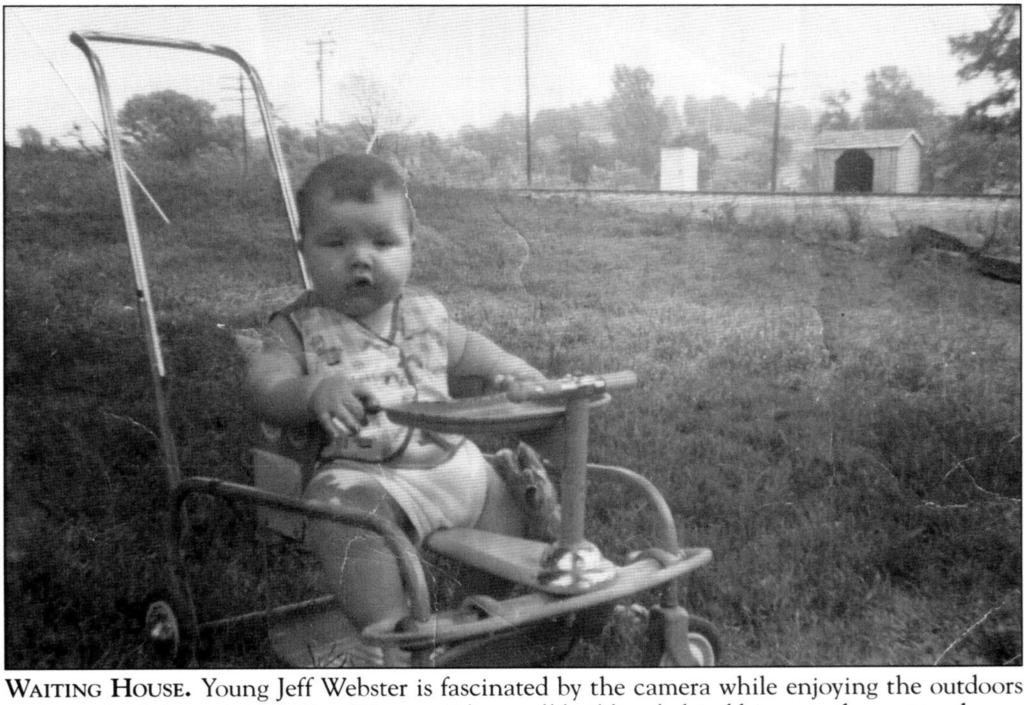

WAITING HOUSE. Young Jeff Webster is fascinated by the camera while enjoying the outdoors against a backdrop of the hills of Verona. The small building behind him was the waiting house for the Louisville and Nashville Railroad. (Courtesy of Paul Webster.)

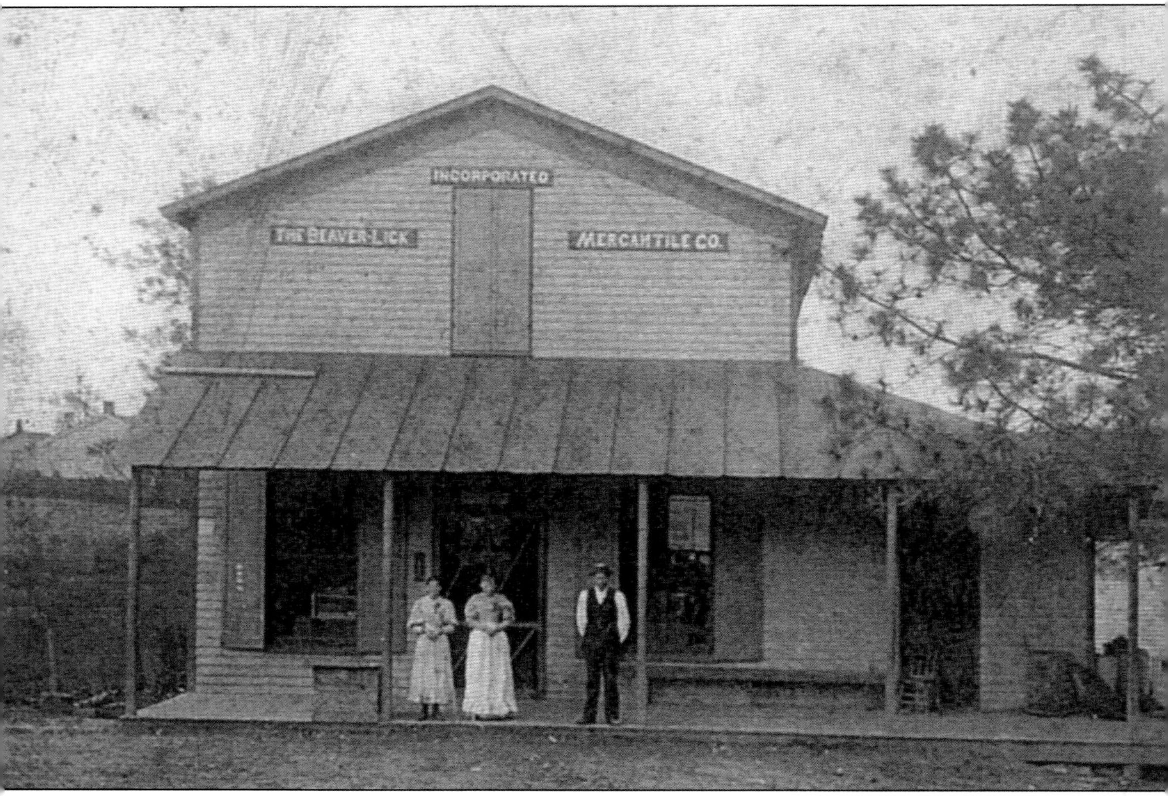

Beaver Lick Mercantile Company. Beaver Lick is a small community just west of Walton with close ties to the Walton-Verona area. As an up-and-coming area in the latter part of the 1800s, it boasted a saloon, post office, millinery shop, and general store. This *c.* 1900 photograph shows the old general store run by J. Merit Jack. Beaver Road kept the two communities close, running from Main Street in Walton through Beaver Lick, before being cut in half and rerouted when Interstate 75 was built in 1963. (Courtesy of Bernie Spencer, www.nkyviews.com.)

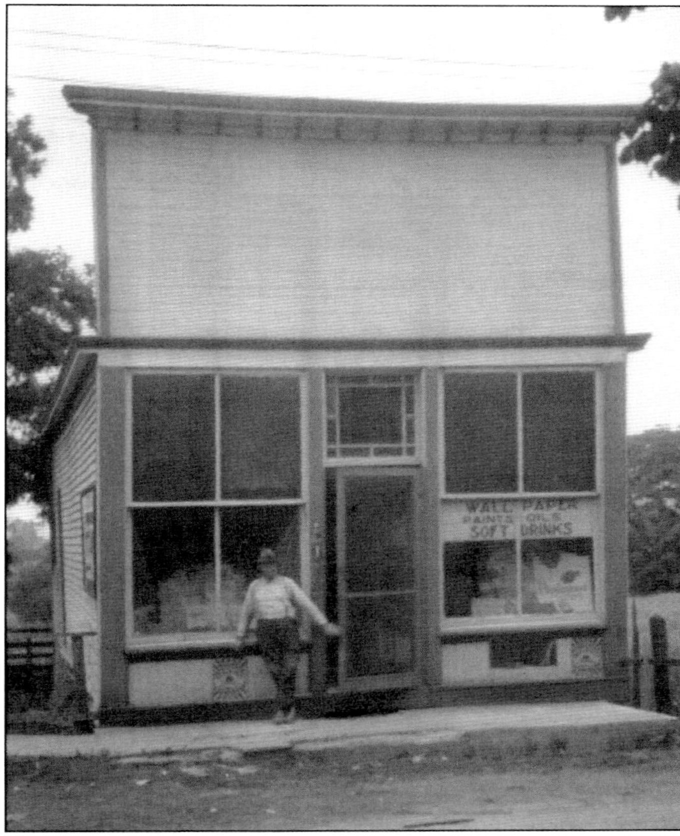

VERONA STORE. This early-1900s photograph shows the old hardware store that was located next to the Verona Bank. Stores such as this one in a small town made every effort to provide goods for town residents and usually offered everything from paint to soft drinks. (Courtesy of Bernie Spencer, www.nkyviews.com.)

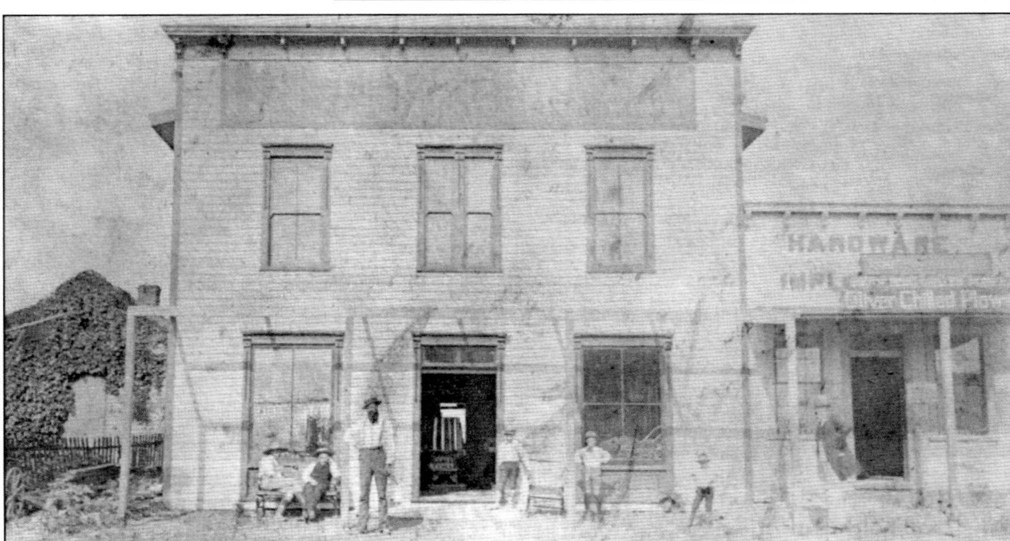

HARDWARE STORE. This faded image shows the hardware store owned by S. L. Edwards in Walton. Edwards, who was the postmaster at the time, also used it as a post office and a building and loan association. It was located on Main Street at the site currently occupied by AQW, Inc. Edwards had the first elevator and telephone in town. (Courtesy of the City of Walton.)

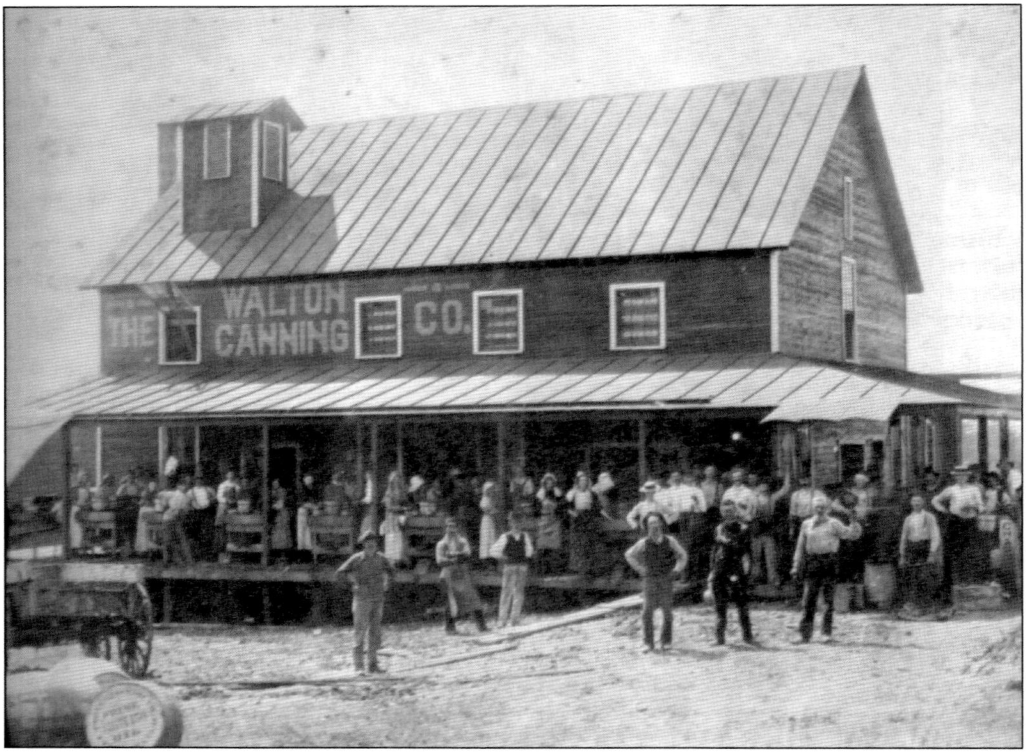

THE WALTON CANNING COMPANY. In this *c.* 1904 photograph, workers take a break for the camera. The canning company, owned by Columbus C. Metcalf, was located on Nicholson Avenue. By the beginning of the 20th century, canning companies were experiencing tremendous growth with advancements in processing technology, and they provided jobs for men and women in the community. (Courtesy of the City of Walton.)

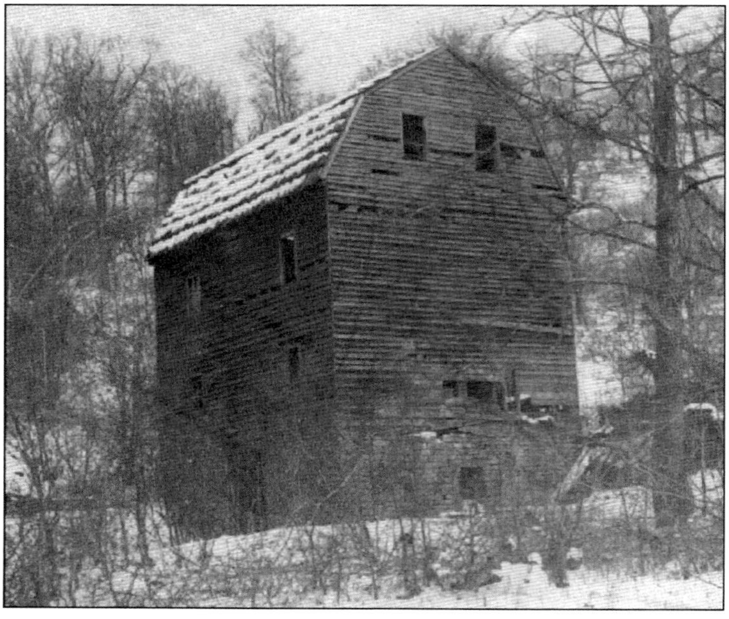

STEPHENSON MILL. The Stephenson family owned a large tract of land that ran from the northern end of present-day Old Stephenson Mill Road south to the intersection of McCoy's Fork near Verona. The family owned a grain mill and a sawmill, powering them from the waters that flowed through the fork that split off from Mud Lick Creek. This undated photograph shows the remains of one of the mills. (Courtesy of the Boone County Historic Preservation Review Board.)

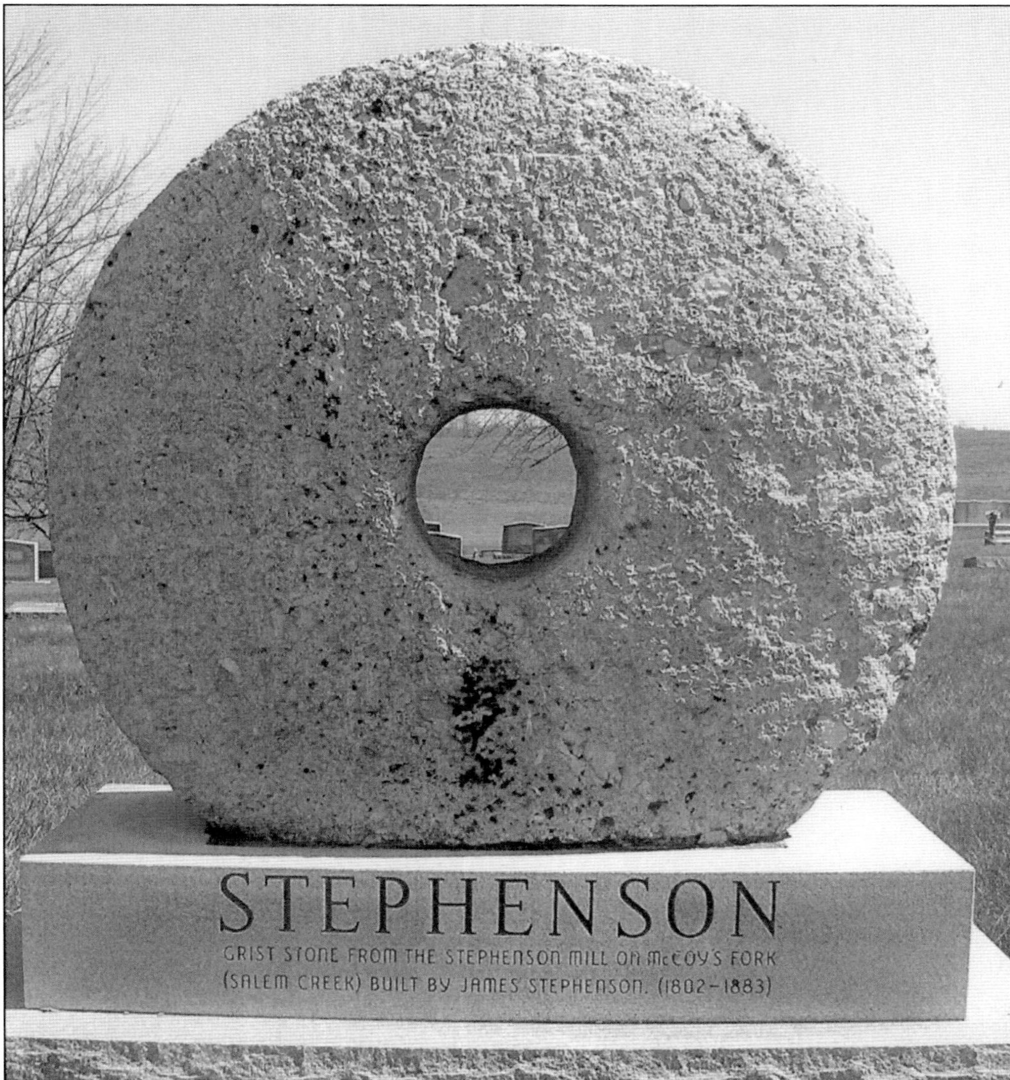

GRIST STONE. The remains of the old Stephenson Mill were removed when Interstate 71 was constructed directly through the location of the mill. The grist stone was turned into a monument, resting beside the burial site of James Stephenson, builder of the old mill. The stone is located in New Bethel Cemetery in Verona. (Photograph by Melinda Sartwell.)

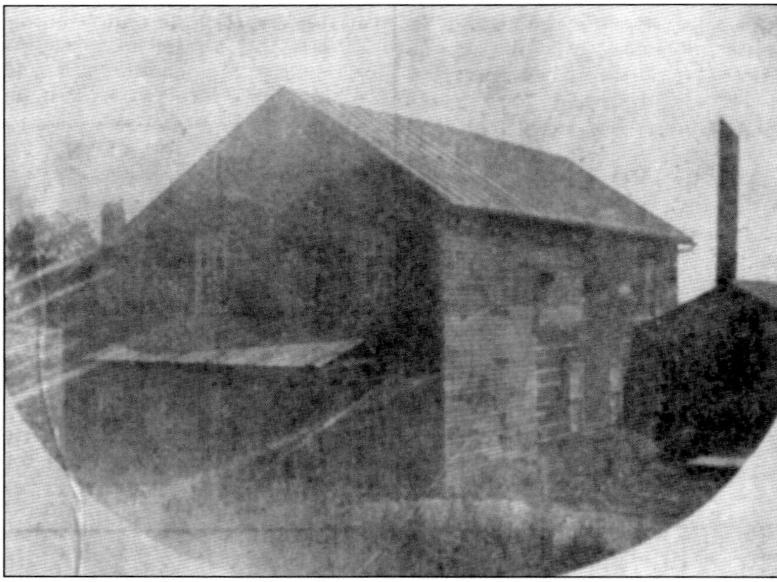

ROUSE BROTHERS' MILL. Built in 1879, the Rouse Brothers' Mill featured two wheat mills and one corn mill. It was located on South Main Street near current-day Loreco Street and the intersection with old Verona Road (Needmore Street). The mill burned in 1916. (Courtesy of Bernie Spencer, www.nkyviews.com.)

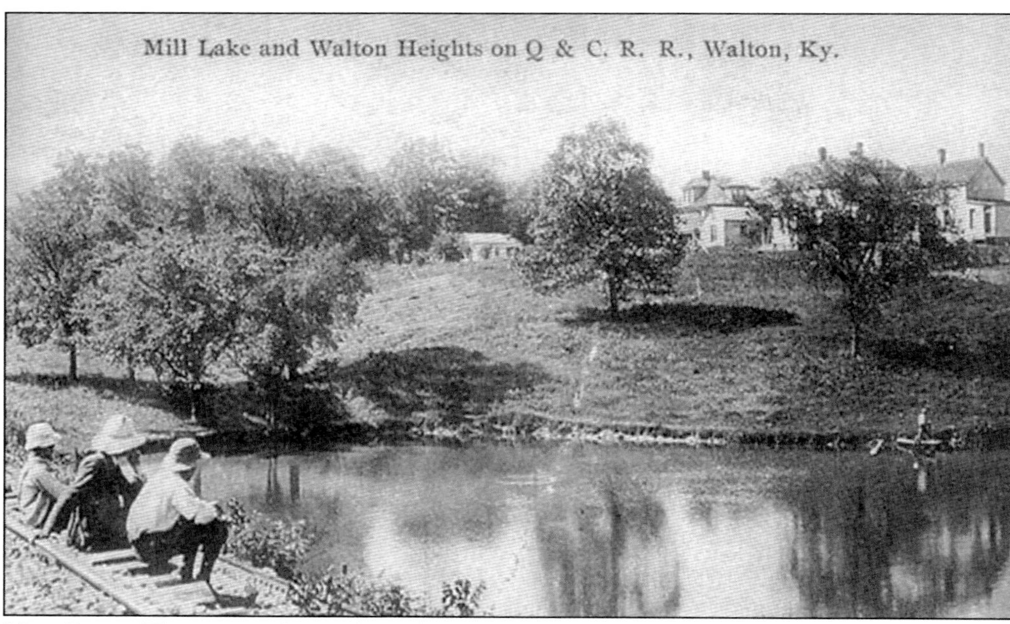

MILL POND. This postcard view from the Queen and Crescent Railroad (Cincinnati Southern) shows the pond that serviced the Rouse Brothers' Mill. The pond no longer exists, but it was located behind the mill just south of the end of Loreco Street. (Courtesy of Bernie Spencer, www.nkyviews.com.)

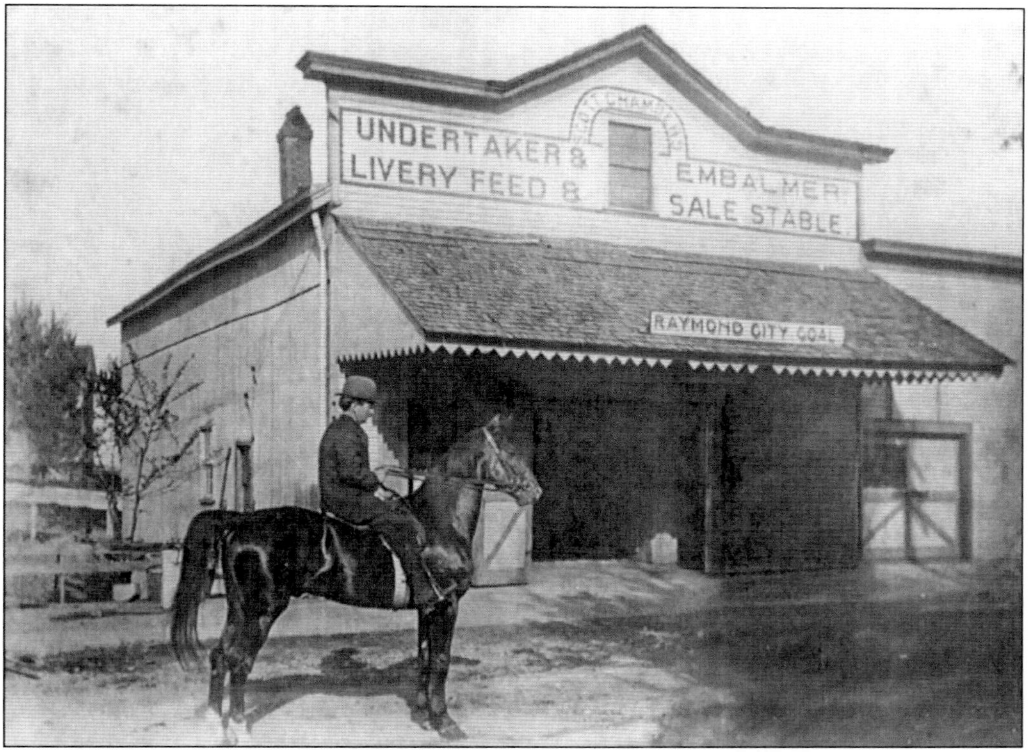

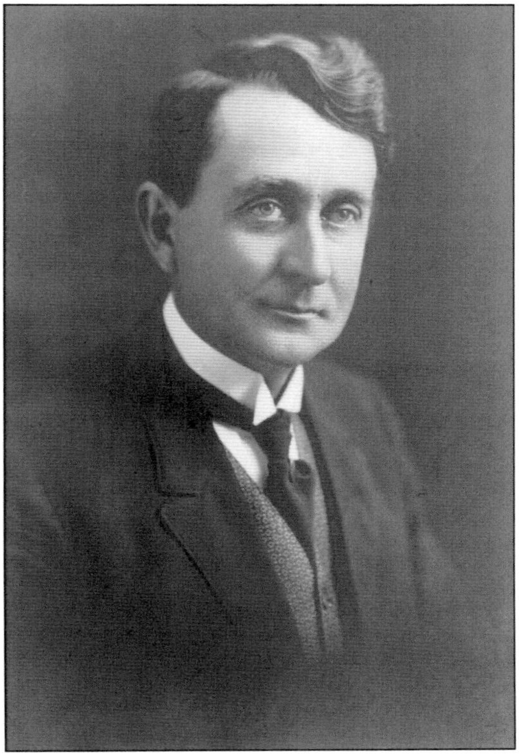

Beginning of a Dynasty. Cleveland Scott Chambers, pictured at right, moved his family to Walton from Petersburg, Kentucky, in about 1900. By 1906, he operated a combination livery stable, feed shop, and undertaking business. Undertakers in that time period generally went to the home of the deceased to perform their duties, as funeral homes as they are known today did not exist. Chambers found great success in the undertaking business, the beginning of a family-run business for over 100 years. The photograph above shows Chambers in front of his old shop located on the corner of Locust and Main Streets, a prime location near the old Cincinnati Southern Depot. (Both, courtesy of Janice Grubbs.)

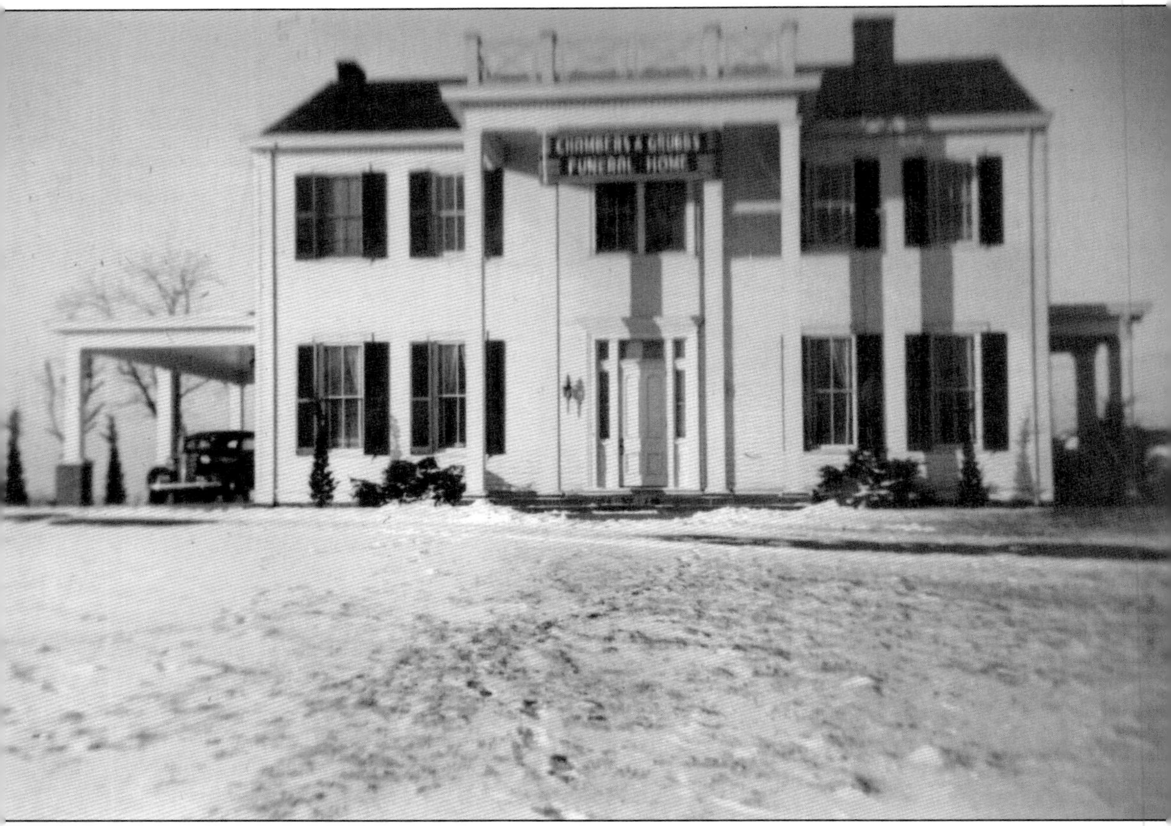

The Dynasty Continues. This 1940s view of the Chambers and Grubbs Funeral Home portrays the success and elegance of the family business. The joint venture between C. Scott Chambers's daughter Mary and her husband, Wallace Grubbs, kept pace with societal changes, establishing the first funeral home in Boone County in 1936. Chambers and Grubbs celebrated its 100th anniversary in 2006, still a family business operated by the third and fourth generations of the family. (Courtesy of Russell Groger.)

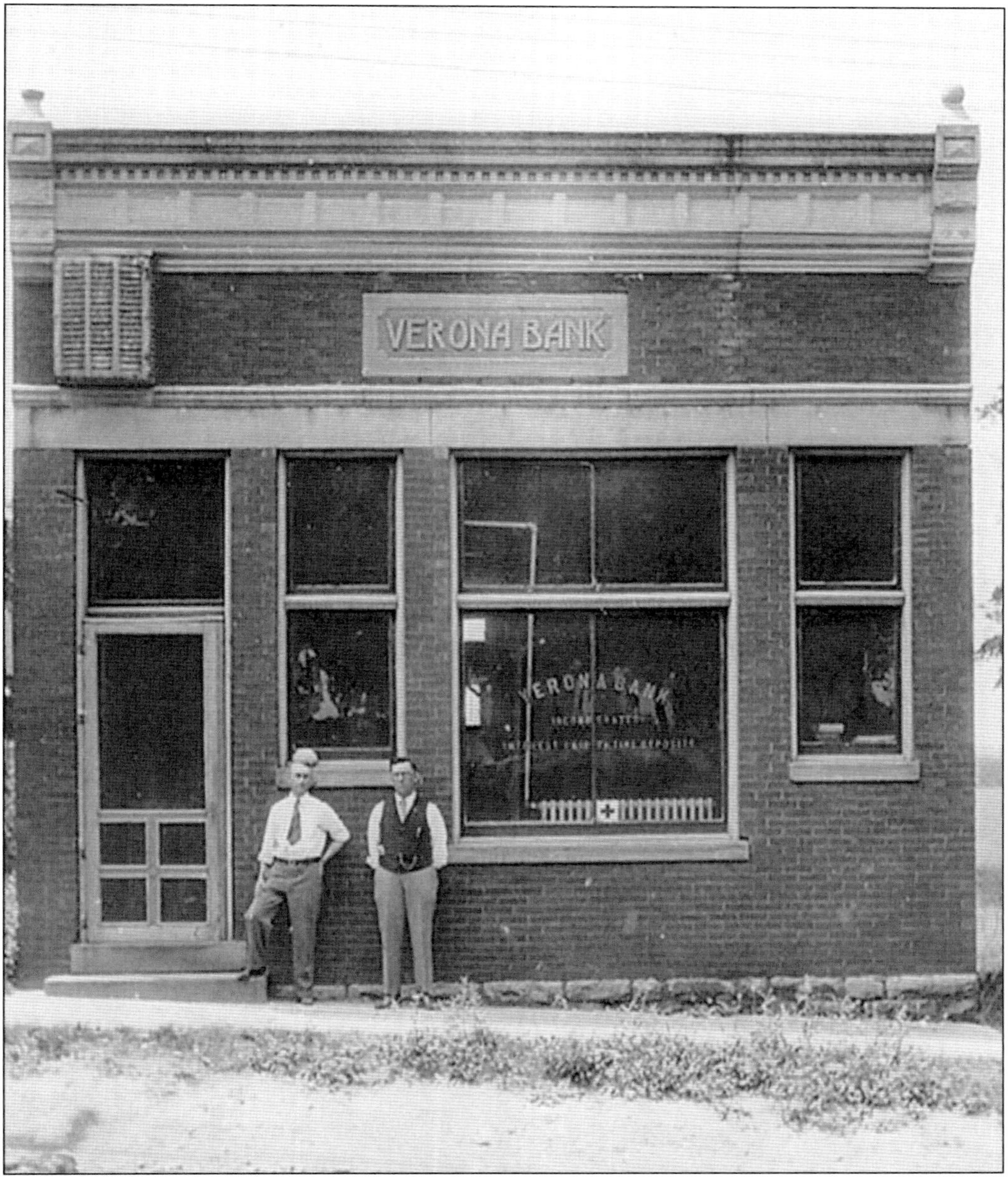

VERONA BANK. Two men stand in front of the Verona Bank, established in 1903. As a small town bank, it found a niche in the community, serving the residents of the Verona area for almost 80 years before it merged with Star Bank in 1981. (Courtesy of Bernie Spencer, www.nkyviews.com.)

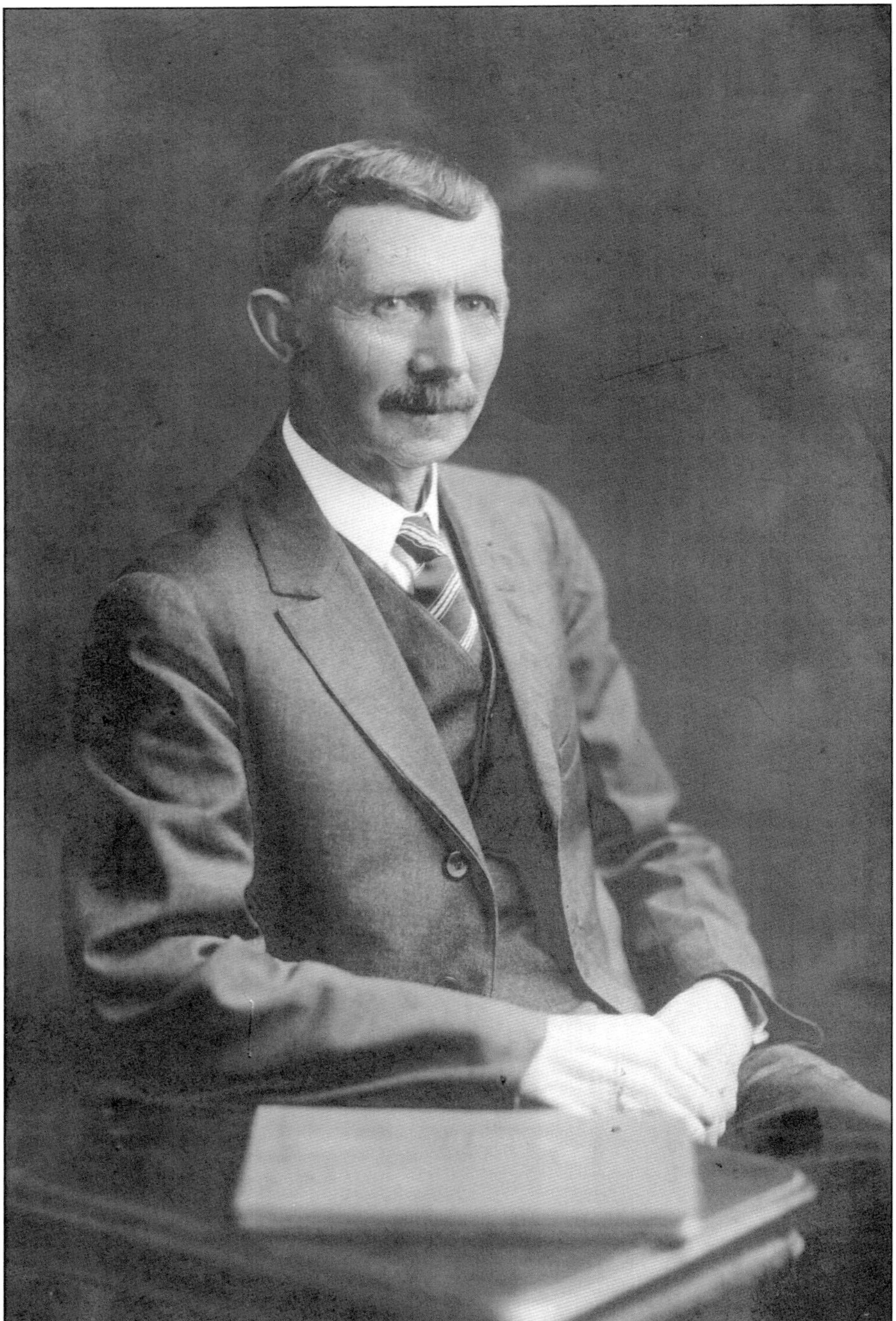

Bank President. William Marshall Whitson was the president of the Verona Bank from its origin in 1903 until his retirement after serving for 30 years. Born on a farm in Verona, Whitson devoted his life to community, not only as the bank president but also as a member of the local school board and deacon at the New Bethel Baptist Church. His daughter Mary Rose married Jess Hamilton, owner of Hamilton and Sons Funeral Home (now Hamilton-Stanley Funeral Home). (Courtesy of Richard Robinson.)

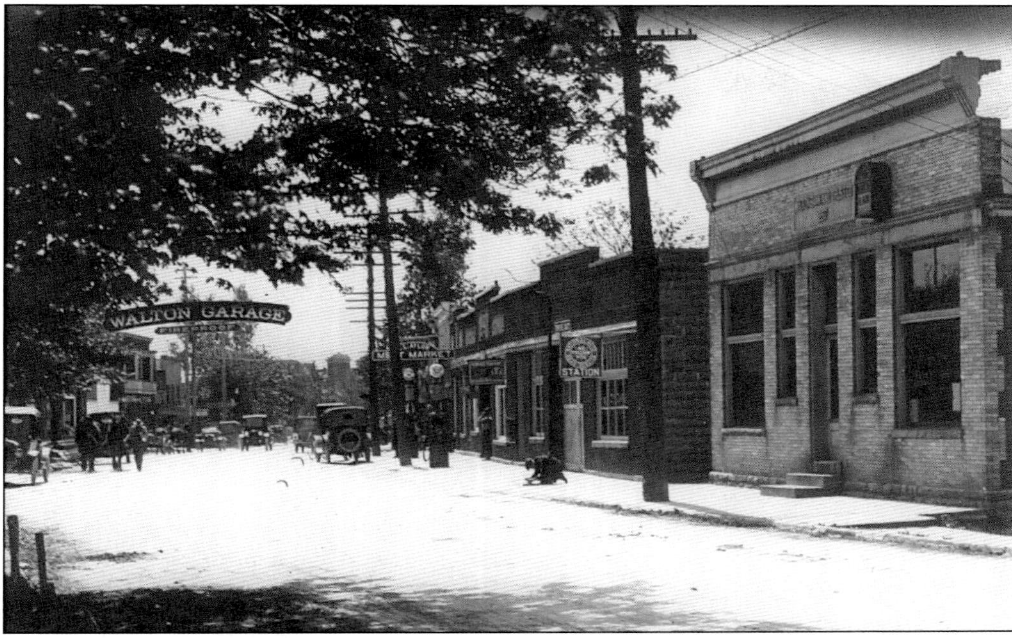

WALTON BANK AND TRUST COMPANY. Founded in 1890 as the Walton Deposit Bank, it was the only bank in the early years on the turnpike between Williamstown and Covington. In 1907, the name changed to the Walton Bank and Trust Company, located just south of the current U.S. Bank on Main Street. (Courtesy of Bernie Spencer, www.nkyviews.com.)

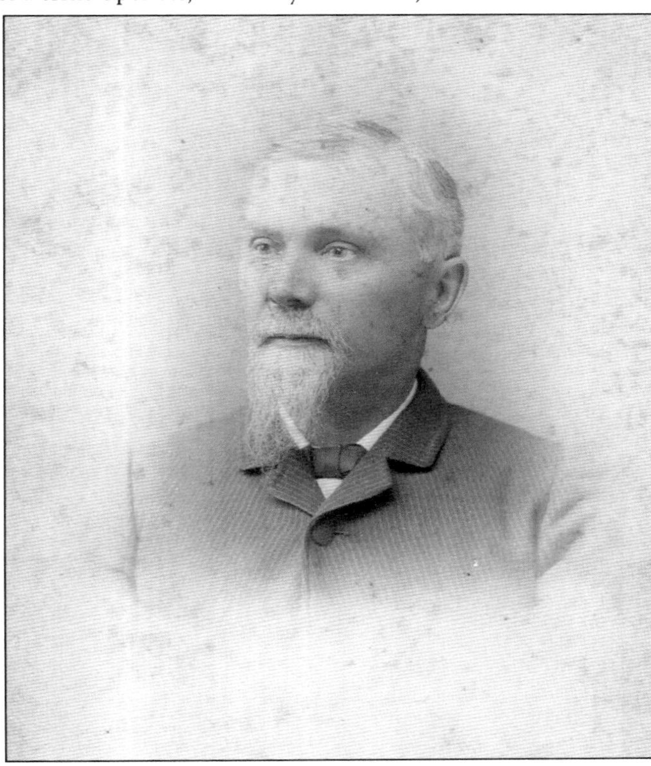

EARLY BANK EXECUTIVE. Orrin Percival Jr. was vice president of the Walton Deposit Bank (later the Walton Bank and Trust) during the 1890s. He was also a tobacco farmer and owned a large amount of land near Cruise's Creek Road (current-day Percival Road). Percival's great-grandfather was a Revolutionary War captain from Connecticut who settled in Boone County in the early 1800s. (Courtesy of Margaret Percival Armstrong.)

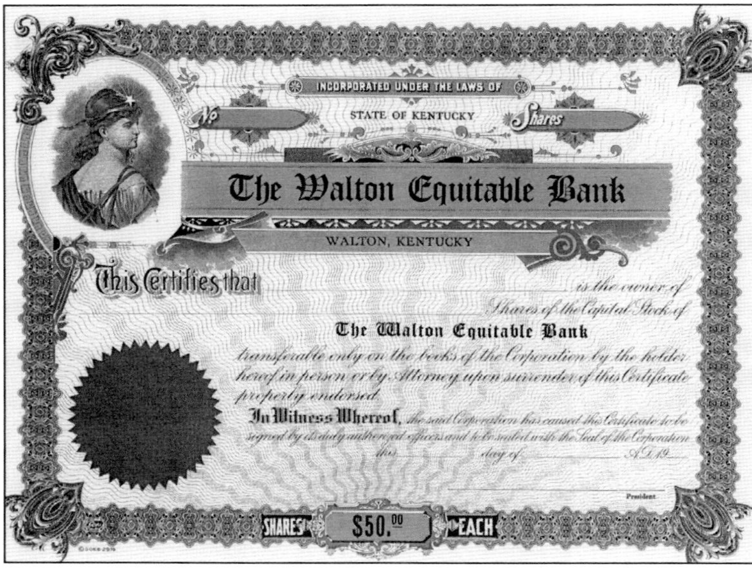
INCORPORATED UNDER THE LAWS OF

STATE OF KENTUCKY

No

Shares

The Walton Equitable Bank

WALTON, KENTUCKY

This Certifies that ... is the owner of ... Shares of the Capital Stock of

The Walton Equitable Bank

transferable only on the books of the Corporation by the holder hereof in person or by Attorney upon surrender of this Certificate properly endorsed.

In Witness Whereof, the said Corporation has caused this Certificate to be signed by its duly authorized officers and to be sealed with the Seal of the Corporation this ... day of ... A.D. 19

President

SHARES $50.00 EACH

STOCK CERTIFICATE. After its merger with the Walton Bank and Trust in 1927, the Walton Equitable Bank offered stock to the public for $50 a share. Companies often did this to help offset expenses and losses they might incur. The Equitable did not survive the Great Depression, and was absorbed by neighboring Dixie State Bank. (Courtesy of Richard Robinson.)

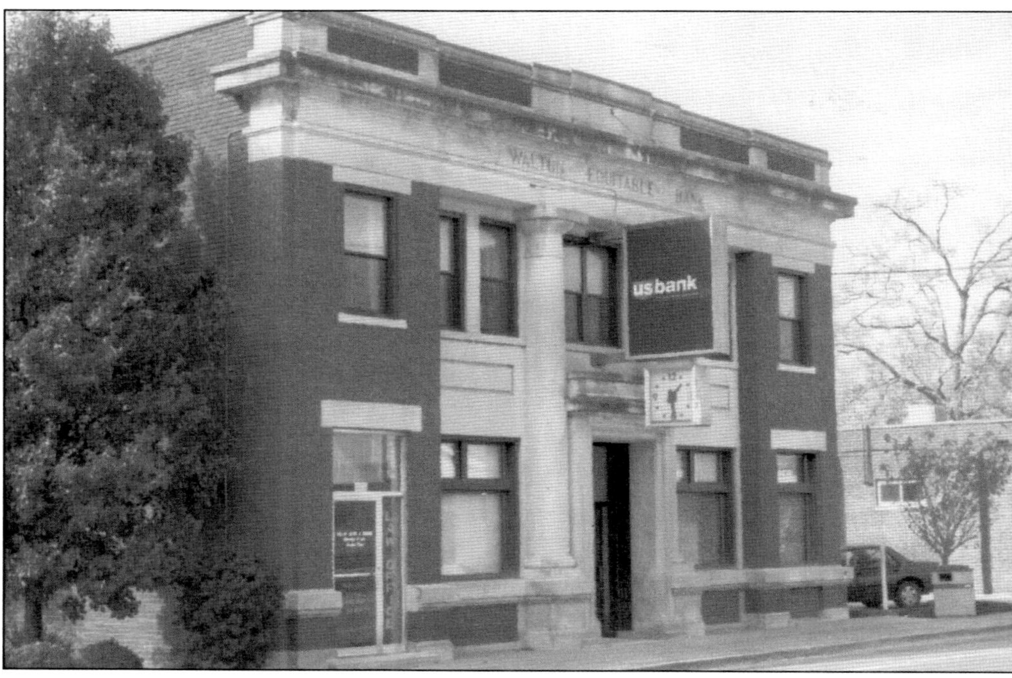

WALTON EQUITABLE BANK. Currently the U.S. Bank, this building was erected after the merger in 1927 of the Walton Bank and Trust Company and the Equitable Bank and Trust Company. The bank struggled during the years of the Great Depression and was taken over by the other town bank, Dixie State, in 1936. (Courtesy of Richard Robinson.)

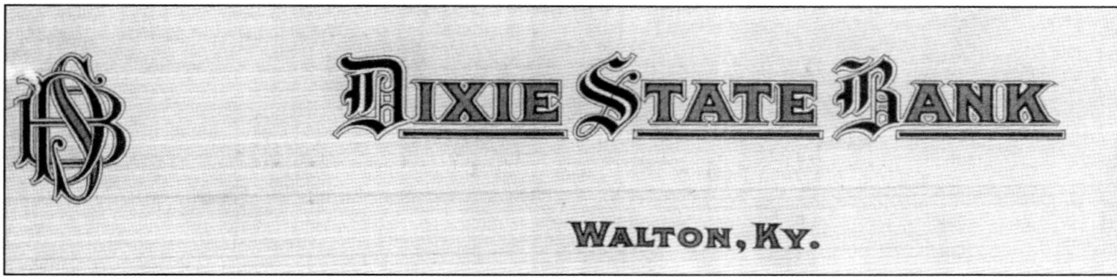

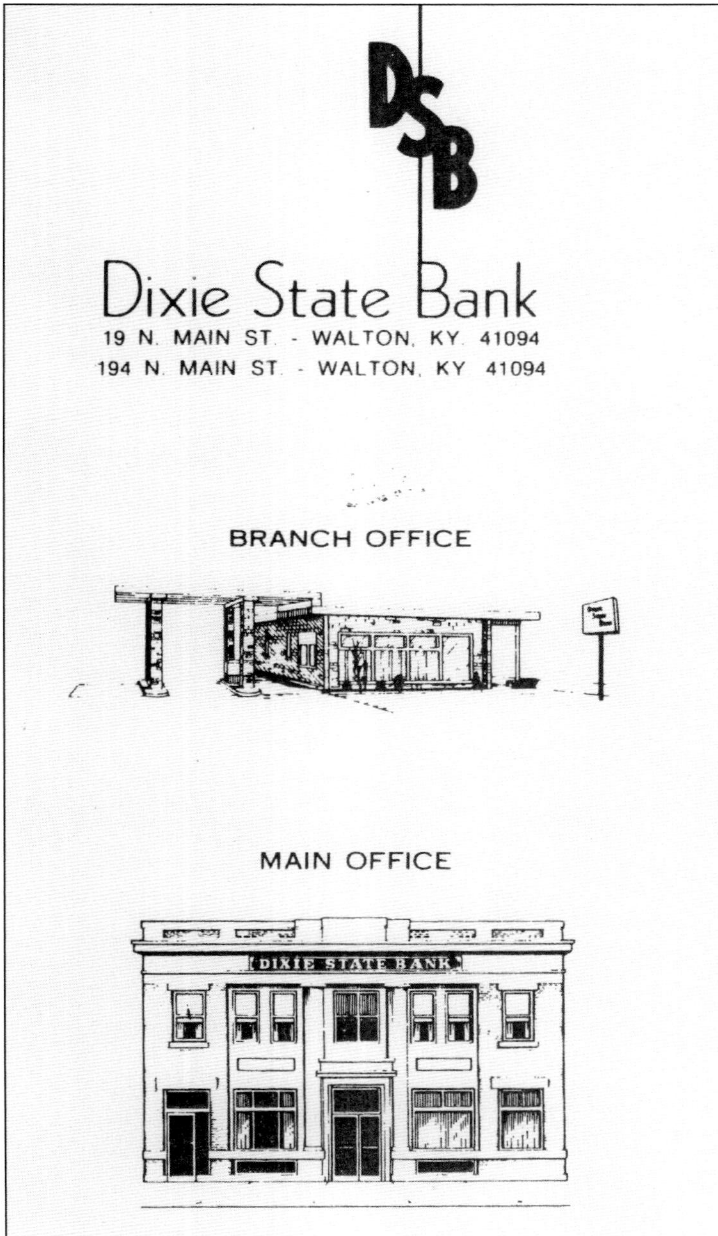

New Bank in Town. Dixie State Bank was founded in about 1927, named after the new U.S. 25 (Dixie) highway system that was routed along Main Street. The bank was originally located on Main Street next to the Odd Fellows Hall (currently Simple Times General Store) and later moved across the street to the Walton Equitable Bank building after merging with that bank in 1936. Dixie State became Kentucky National Bank, then Star Bank, Firstar Bank, and finally current-day U.S. Bank. (Both, courtesy of Richard Robinson.)

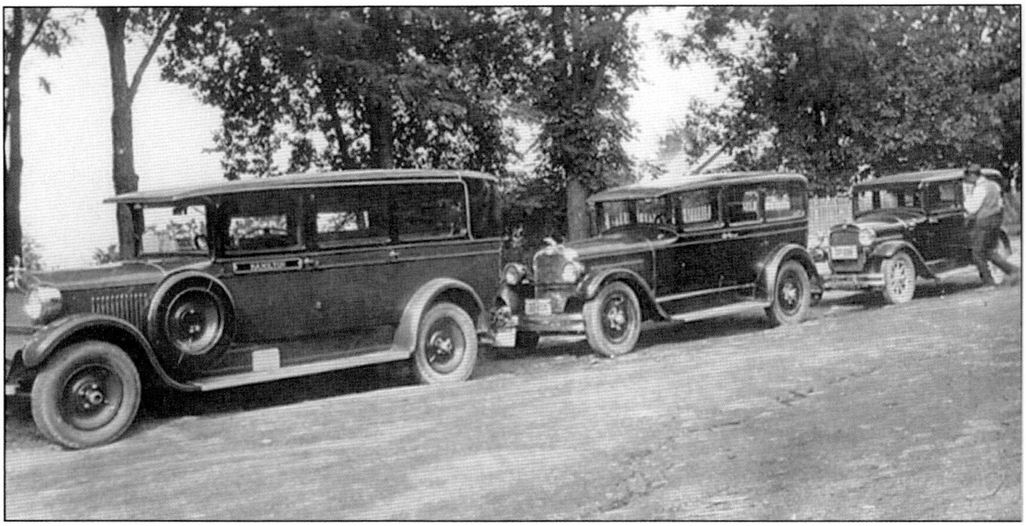

Verona Dynasty. In 1912, Jess Hamilton opened Hamilton and Sons Funeral Home, located at the crossroads in Verona. After one son moved away, Hamilton and his other son Fred H. operated the funeral home for many years, serving residents of Verona and the surrounding area. Fred continued in the funeral business until his retirement, then merging the business with Stanley Funeral Home based in nearby Williamstown. The above photograph shows the 1930s-era vehicles used by the funeral home, and the photograph below is the 150-year-old building on Route 491, just past the crossroads, when it burned in 1979. The current location is north of Verona on Walton-Verona Road. (Above, courtesy of Bernie Spencer, www.nkyviews.com; below, courtesy of Paul Webster.)

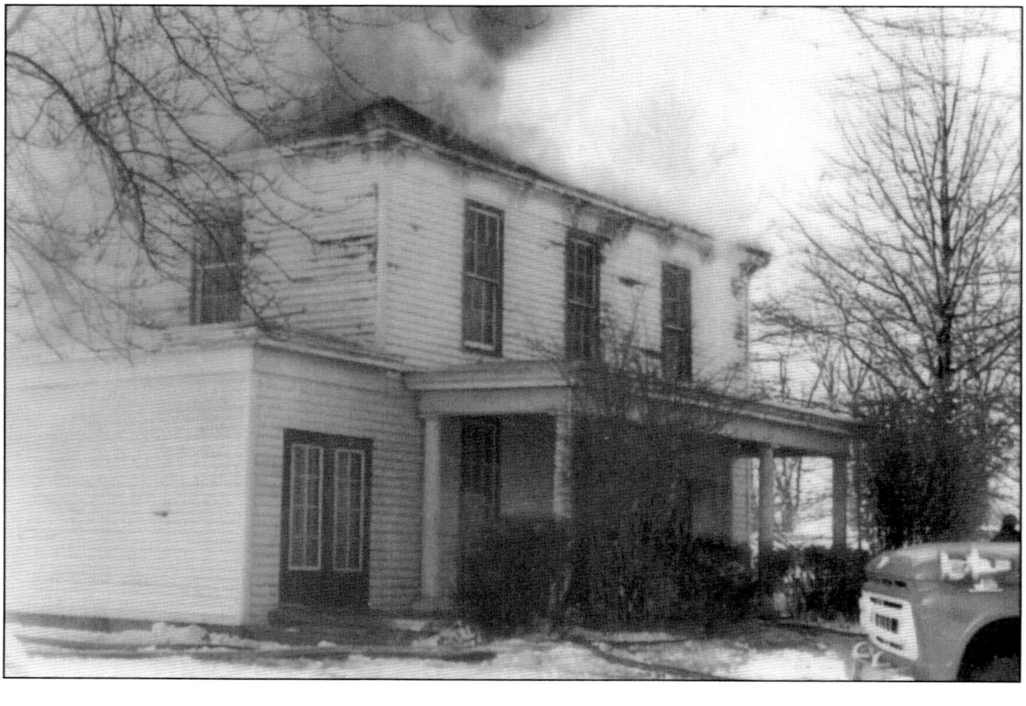

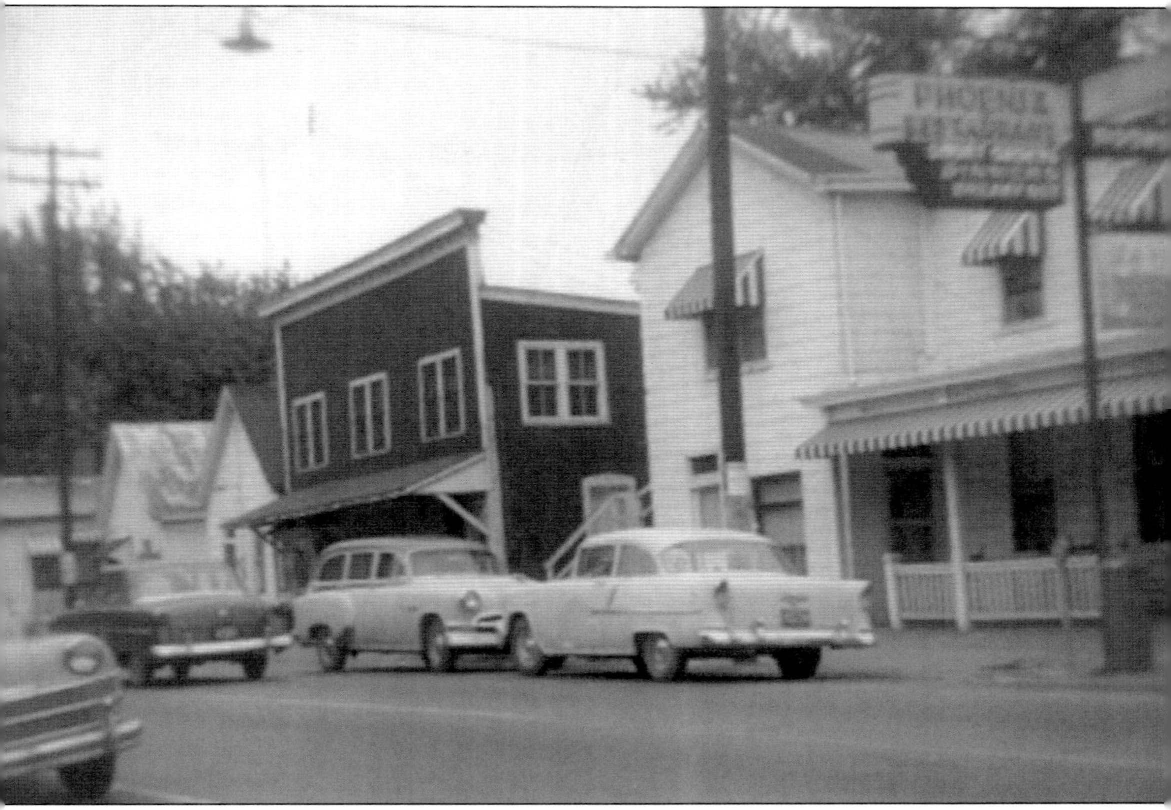

PHOENIX HOTEL. As the largest building in downtown Walton, the Phoenix Hotel and Restaurant was the center of activity for many years. At the time of its demolition in 1971, the hotel was over 100 years old, coming into prominence when the railroad depot was located just across the street in the early 1870s. During the 1880s, it was known as the George Stamler Hotel, and by the beginning of the 20th century, it became known as the Phoenix Hotel. It survived two fires, one of them a particularly devastating blaze in 1950 that was set intentionally, almost destroying it completely. (Courtesy of Bernie Spencer, www.nkyviews.com.)

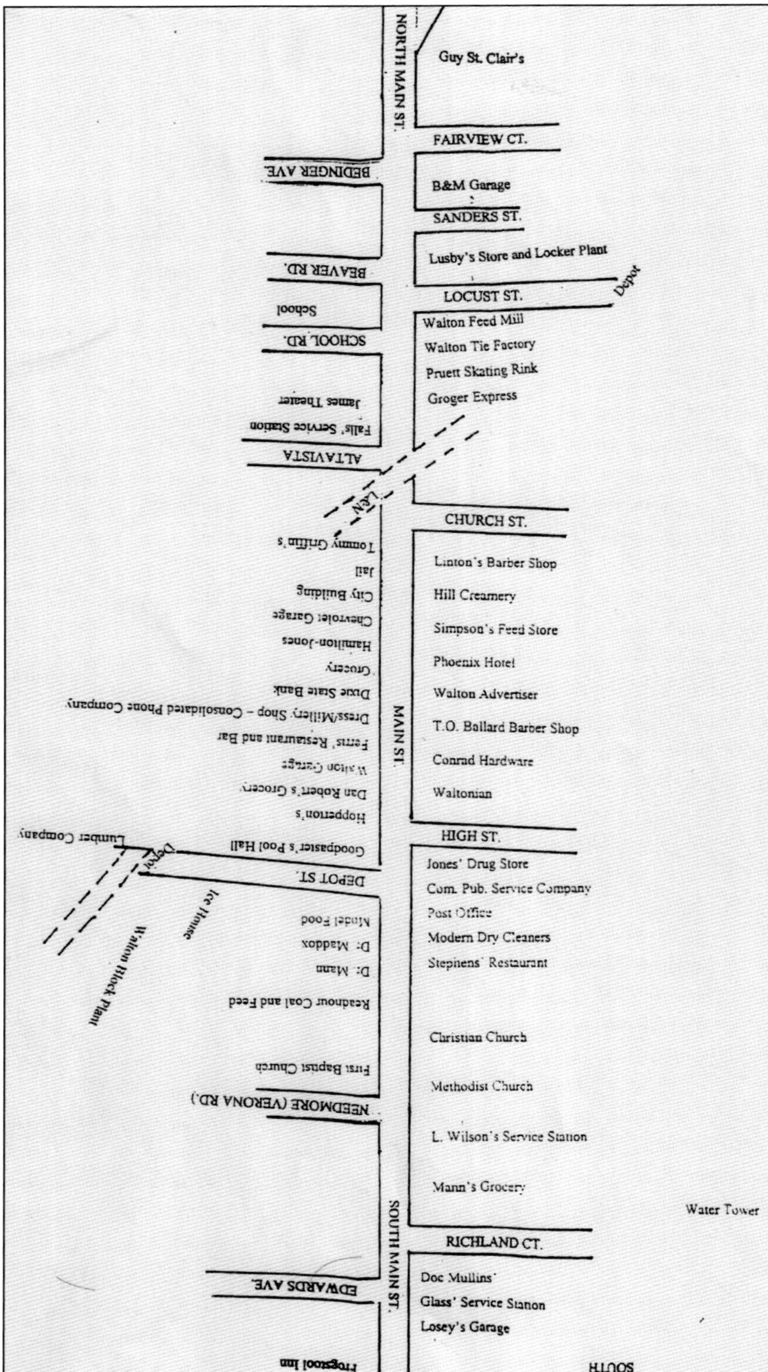

Business Map. This map, made by Dr. J. M. Huey in 1950, shows the diverse business interests spread throughout town from the north end of Main Street to the south side in Walton. Residents had everything they needed close by, including grocery stores, restaurants, churches, service stations, a drugstore, and even a tavern. (Courtesy of Richard Robinson.)

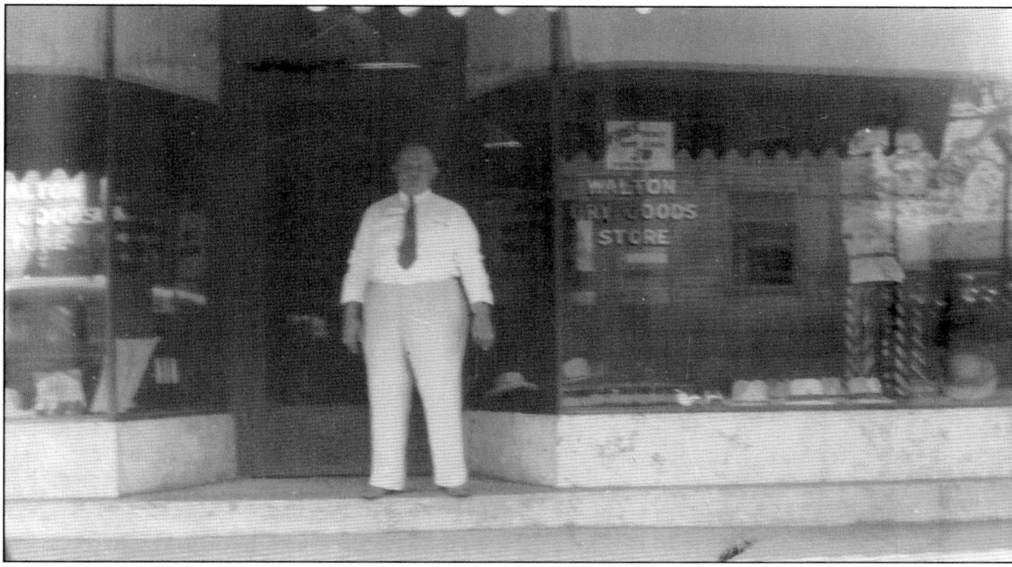

Walton Dry Goods. Tom Percival stands in front of his shop in this 1940s photograph. A son of prominent businessman Ira Percival, he was a deputy sheriff in the 1920s, a cattle broker, and owned the dry goods store until 1945. The shop was located on Main Street next to the Walton Garage (present-day Daugherty Realtors). (Courtesy of Margaret Percival Armstrong.)

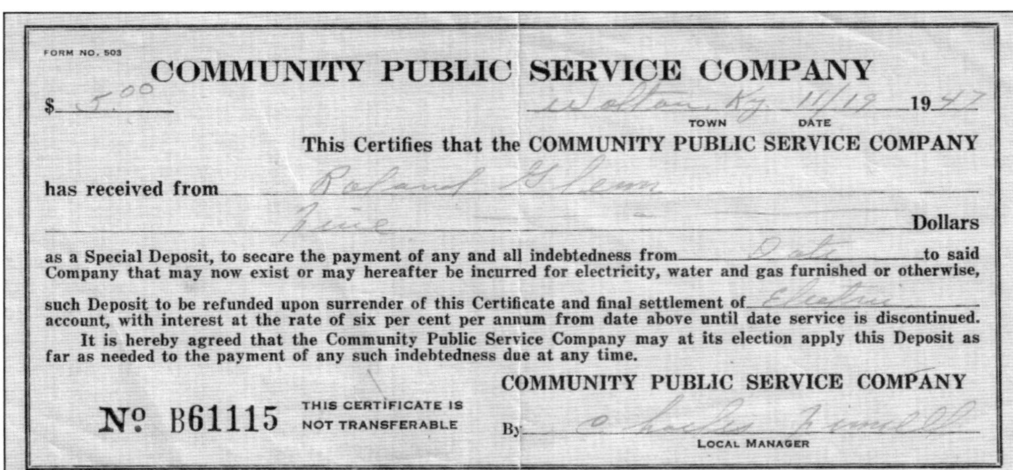

FORM NO. 503

COMMUNITY PUBLIC SERVICE COMPANY

$ 5.00 Walton, Ky. 11/19 1947

TOWN DATE

This Certifies that the COMMUNITY PUBLIC SERVICE COMPANY

has received from Roland Glenn

Five Dollars

as a Special Deposit, to secure the payment of any and all indebtedness from Date to said Company that may now exist or may hereafter be incurred for electricity, water and gas furnished or otherwise, such Deposit to be refunded upon surrender of this Certificate and final settlement of Electric account, with interest at the rate of six per cent per annum from date above until date service is discontinued.

It is hereby agreed that the Community Public Service Company may at its election apply this Deposit as far as needed to the payment of any such indebtedness due at any time.

COMMUNITY PUBLIC SERVICE COMPANY

No. B61115 THIS CERTIFICATE IS NOT TRANSFERABLE By

LOCAL MANAGER

Power Company. The Community Public Service Company, based out of Fort Worth, Texas, provided electricity to parts of Kentucky in the 1920s. By the 1940s, its Kentucky headquarters moved to Walton, providing jobs for local residents as linemen, office workers, and service repairmen. The company sold in 1950 to Cincinnati Gas and Electric, and then became known as Union Light, Heat, and Power Company. (Courtesy of Ruth Meadows.)

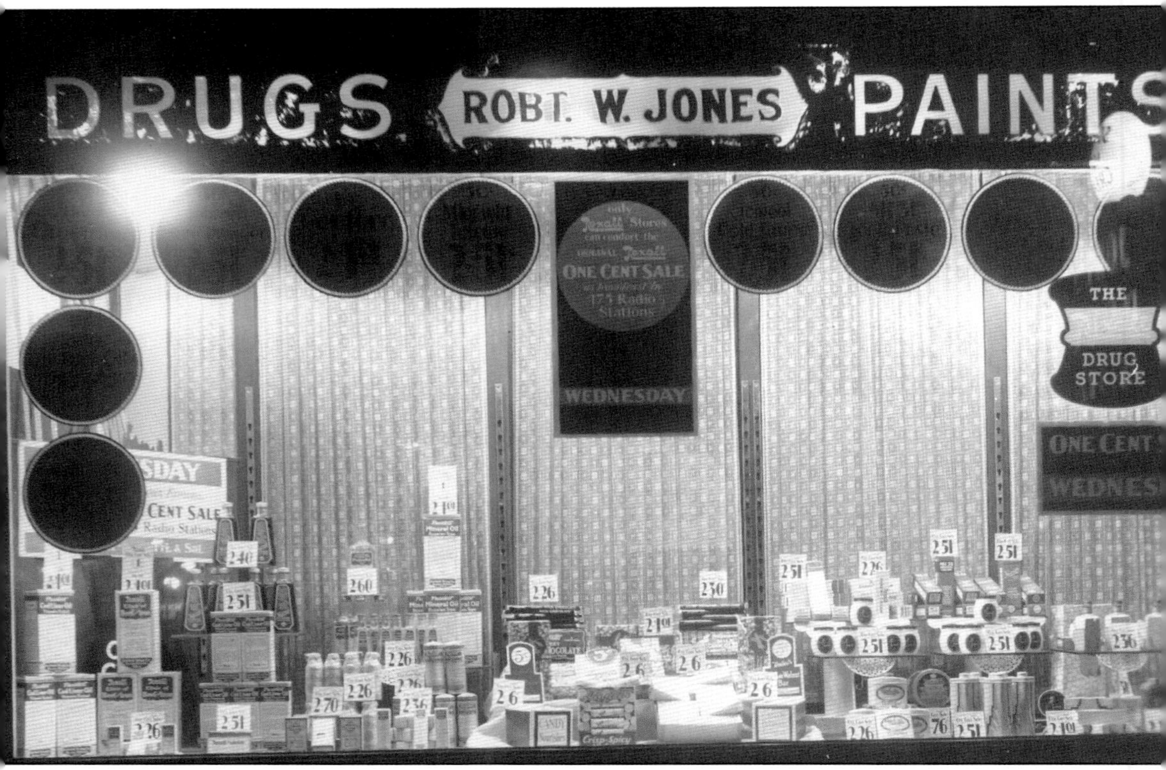

Jones Drugstore. This striking window display for the Robert Jones Drugstore takes a step back in time to the days of 1¢ sales and the Rexall brand. Jones ran the drugstore, located in the Odd Fellows building on the corner of High and Main Streets, for many years before it became Brakefield Drugs. It is currently in use as an office for the attorneys Rouse and Rouse. (Courtesy of Bernie Spencer, www.nkyviews.com.)

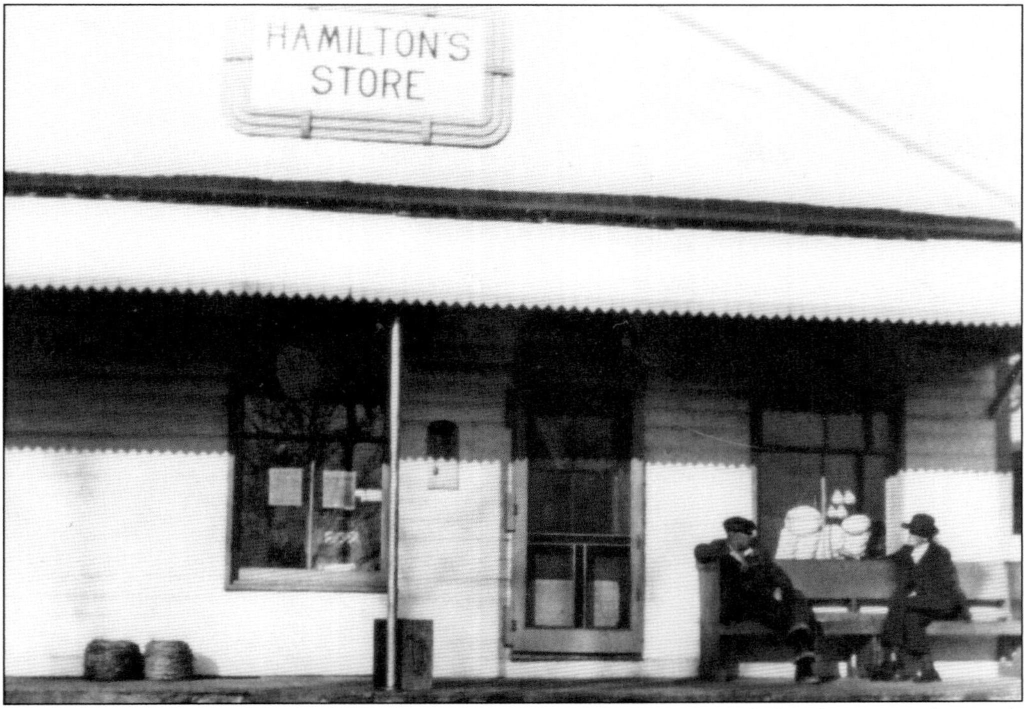

VARIETY STORE. Charlie Richards and Mr. Roberts catch up on stories while relaxing on the porch of the Hamilton's Store in 1947. The store was located on Verona-Mudlick Road, across from Verona Garage. Later it became Chandler's Variety Store (1979 photograph below) before being bought by the New Bethel Church next door and torn down for a parking lot. The small white building next to it still stands and serves as a meeting place for local residents. The old house on the opposite side belonged to Lucy Cook. (Both, courtesy of Paul Webster.)

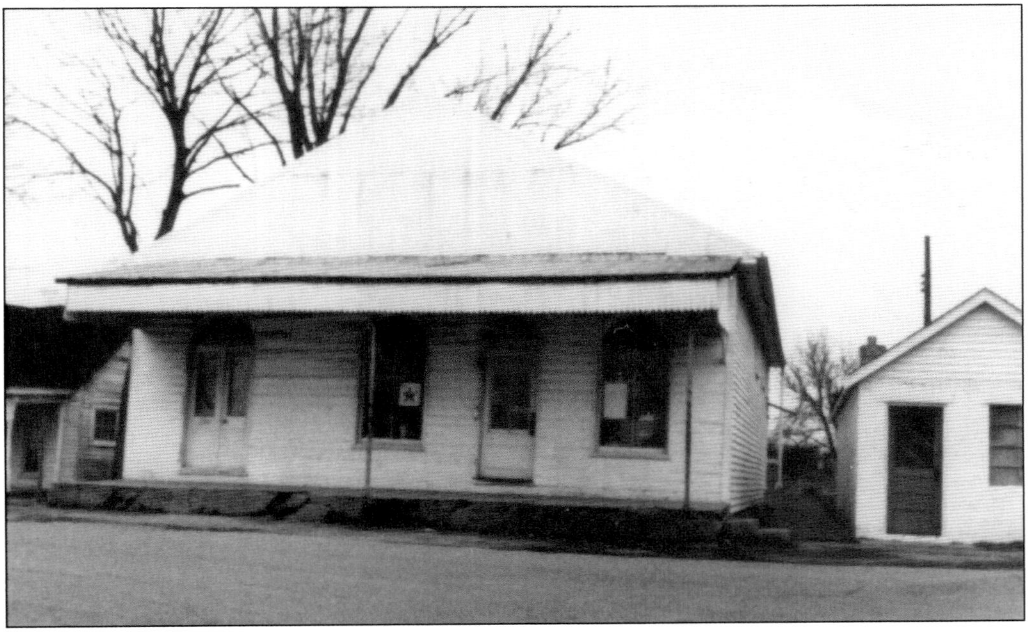

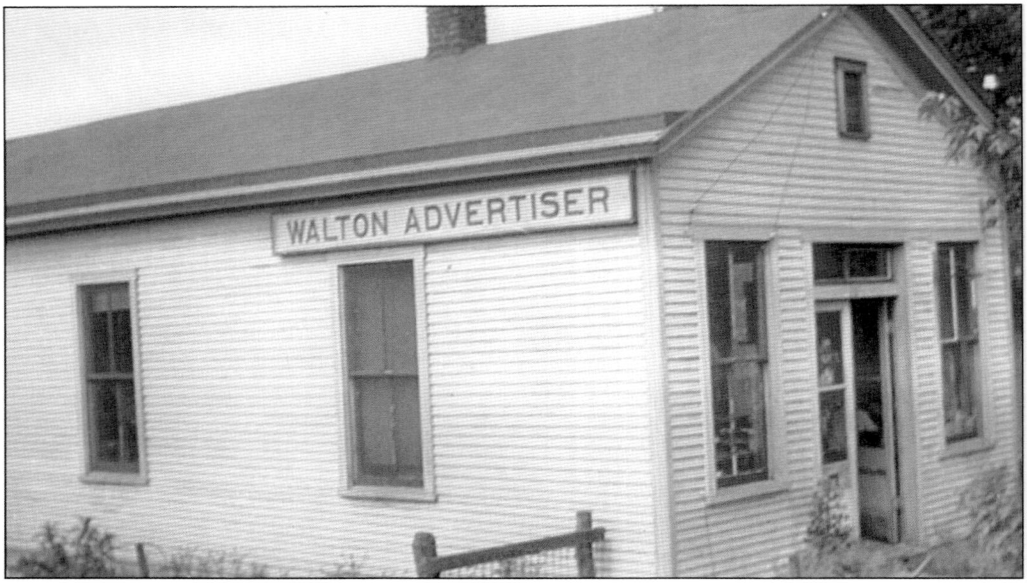

WALTON ADVERTISER. The *Walton Advertiser* was founded in 1914 by G. B. Powers and Roy Stamler (joined by James R. Wallace in 1915) as a way to report local news. It quickly gained popularity and was soon being published on a regular basis, supported by strong sales and advertisements by local businesses. The original building was located just across the High Street Bridge, was moved to Main Street in 1943, and then to its final location at 186 North Main Street (currently Colonial Press Printers), where it was run by the Meadows family until 1977. (Courtesy of Ruth Meadows.)

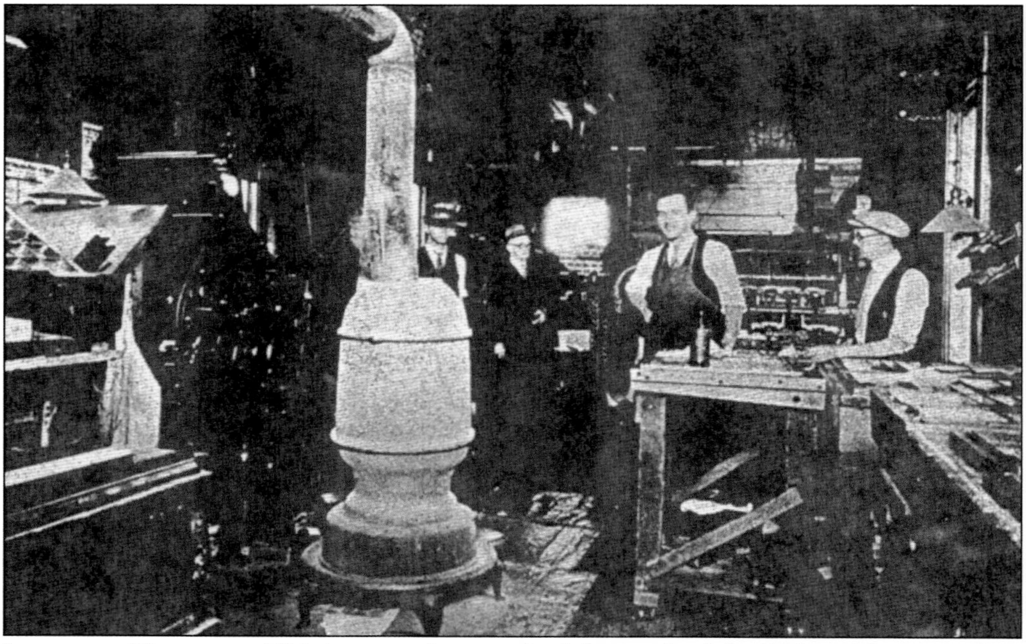

INSIDE THE NEWSROOM. This is a rare photograph of the inside of the *Walton Advertiser* office. Gathered around the potbellied stove from left to right are John Engle, associate editor J. R. Wallace, Malcolm Simpson (Simpson bought the paper in 1962), and associate editor Roy Stamler. (Courtesy of Ruth Meadows.)

E. K. STEVENS, Fancy Groceries **WALTON, KY.**

THE FARMERS' NURSERY CO.

Branch Office, Walton, Ky.

Capital $250,000.00 — 1400 Acres in Cultivation

ALL TREES BUDDED ON WHOLE STOCK

We furnish Model Orchards to good parties. Write and ask about them

Refer you to any Bank as Reference

H. C. DIERS, State Mgr., Phone 72, Walton, Ky.

We can use a few good sober and industrious salesmen.

C. SCOTT CHAMBERS

Embalmer and Funeral Director

LIVERY and COAL

PHONE 35 WALTON, KY.

S. L. Edwards and Son

HARDWARE & FARMING IMPLEMENTS

WALTON, - KY.

WHEN IN WALTON

Hotel Phoenix

H. R. DIXON, Proprietor

A. M. EDWARDS

Livery, Funeral Director

Coal, Buggies, Real Estate

WALTON, KY.

The Northcutt Mercantile Co.

FOR EVERYTHING

Walton, - Kentucky

T. F. CURLEY, General Merchandise **WALTON, KY.**

EARLY ADVERTISEMENTS. These advertisements appeared on the back page of the first issue of the *Walton Advertiser* on August 14, 1914. Walton enjoyed the benefits of having several grocers and general merchandise establishments from which to choose, as well as the convenience of the specialized services of both Chambers and Edwards as local funeral directors and livery owners. (Courtesy of Ruth Meadows.)

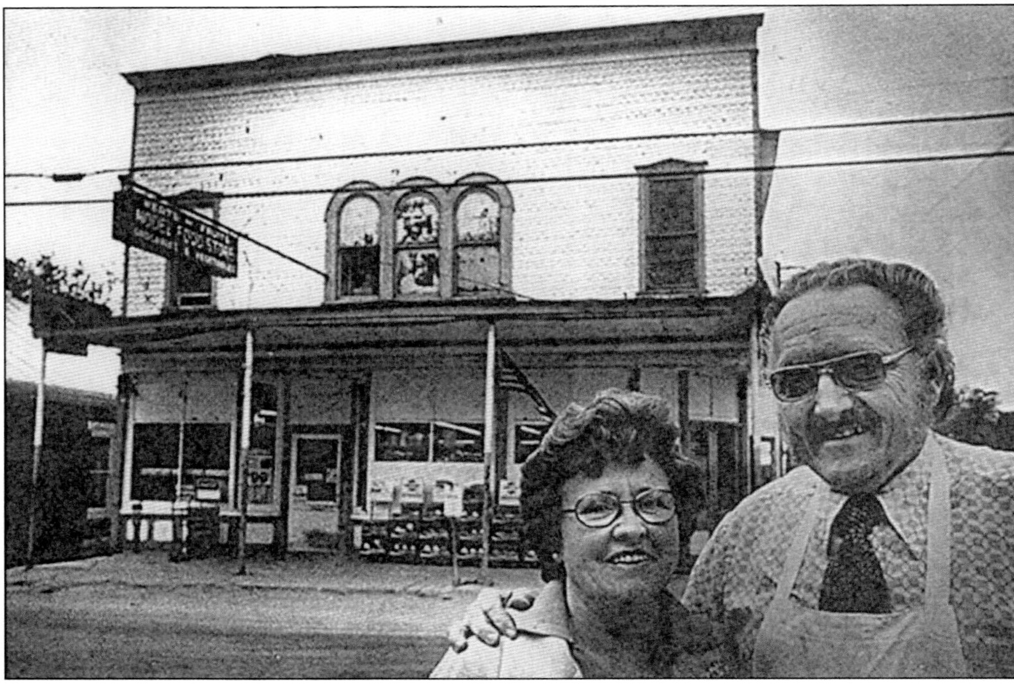

Model Food Store. The Model Food Store, run by Charlie and Violet Praither, served the residents of Walton for many years. It was located in the old opera house building (now the site of Boone County Public Library) at the corner of Main and Depot Streets. The building was torn down in 1976. The Model survived a few more years in another building nearby, eventually becoming a Pic Pac grocery store, and is currently the site of the First Baptist Center. (Courtesy of the Kenton County Public Library, Covington, Kentucky.)

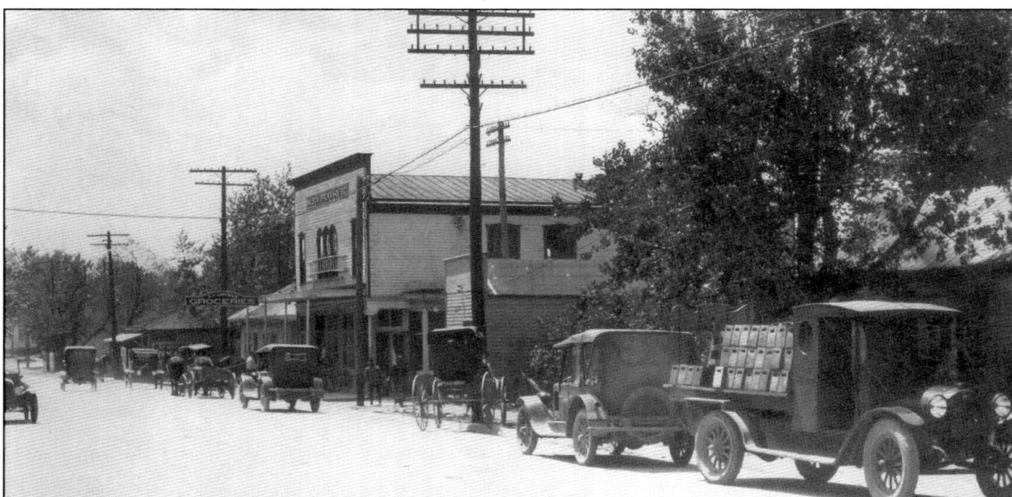

Walton Opera House. Like most small towns of that era, a focal point in town was the opera house, hosting traveling shows and political speakers for local residents to enjoy. This c. 1920s photograph shows the opera house after it was already converted to a Coffman's Grocery Store, following its heyday of entertainment. Later it was the Model Food Store for many years. (Courtesy of the Boone County Historic Preservation Review Board.)

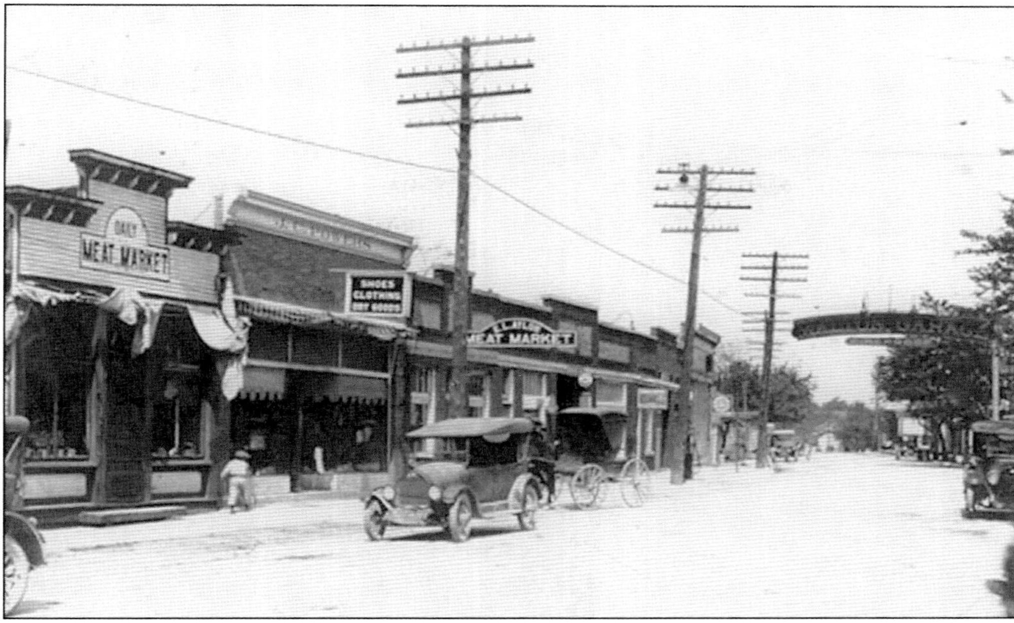

Business District. This *c.* 1920s photograph of Main Street, looking north, is a mix of meat shops, general stores, and a car garage. Notice the early vehicles alongside the buggy in front of the meat store. The Walton Garage is on the left, directly in front of the hanging sign, and just north of it, the old Walton Bank and Trust Company, currently the site of U.S. Bank and parking lot. (Courtesy of Bernie Spencer, www.nkyviews.com.)

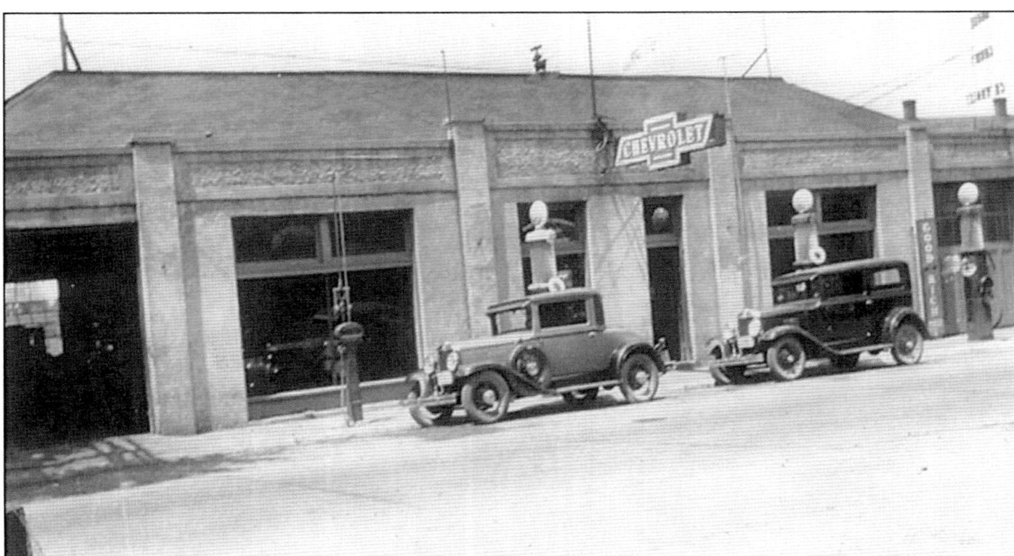

Chevrolet Dealership. Walton was early to jump on the bandwagon when motor vehicles became popular, with Hess Vest opening the first dealership in town. The shop was located where the current-day city garage is, across from the city building on Main Street. (Courtesy of the Boone County Historic Preservation Review Board.)

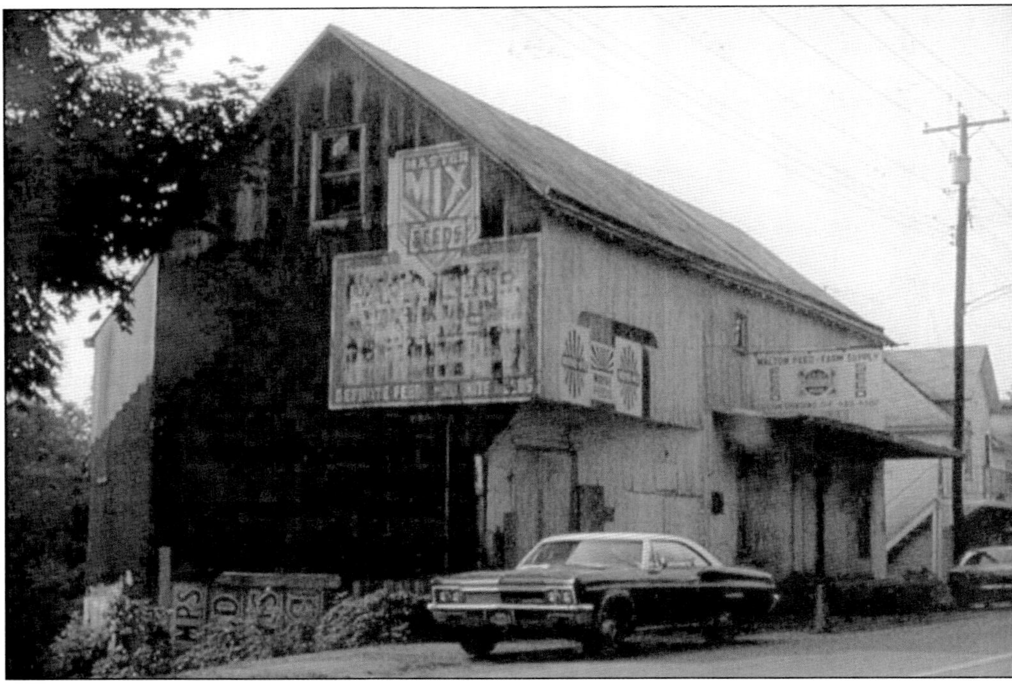

Walton Feed Mill. Located on North Main Street at the south corner of Locust Street, the Walton Feed Mill was opened by Leonard Cook in 1924 and served the Walton area for many years. Just south of the mill was the old tie factory, and next to it was the roller rink. (Courtesy of Bernie Spencer, www.nkyviews.com.)

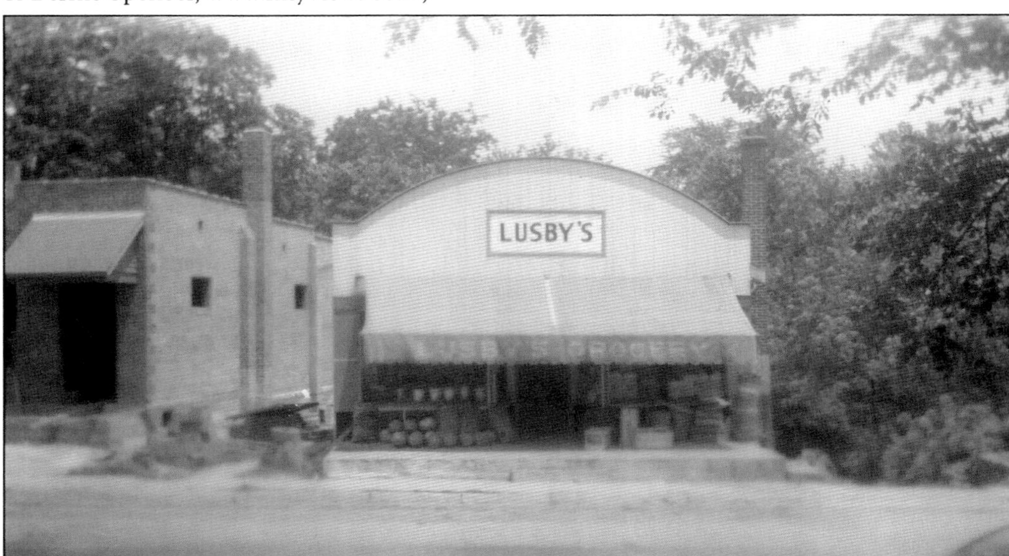

Lusby's Grocery. Walton boasted several grocery stores, most located in the center of town. Lusby's, which catered to the folks that lived on the north end of town, was located on the corner of Locust and Main Streets (currently Brooks Meats and Restaurant), in front of the old Southern Depot and across from the Walton Feed Mill. Lusby's also maintained the locker plant next door. The grocery was destroyed by fire in 1941. (Courtesy of Johnny Gault.)

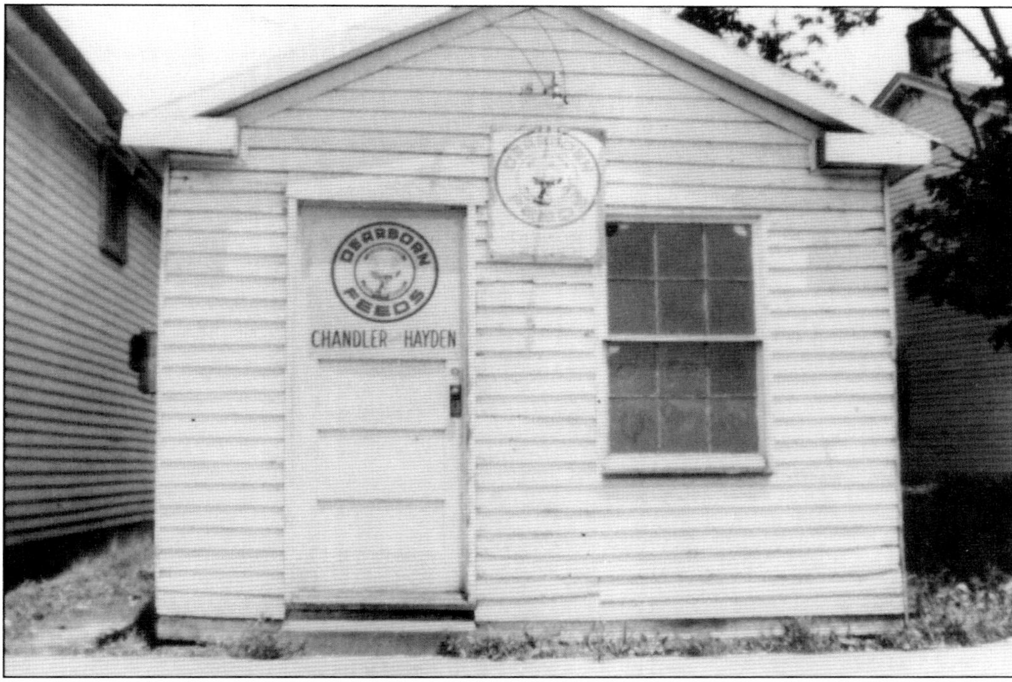

Feed Store. This tiny white building at the crossroads in Verona was a Chandler and Hayden Feed Store. At other times in its existence, it was Dr. Finnell's office, a joint called the Blue Goose, and in its present incarnation, the town hall. (Courtesy of Paul Webster.)

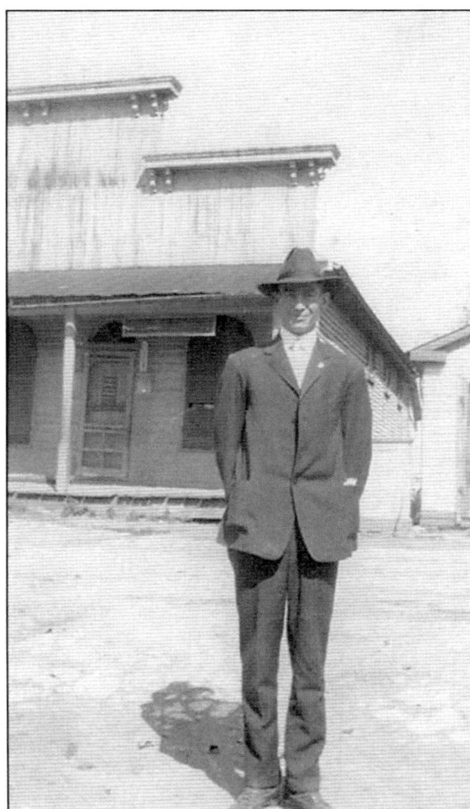

Verona Store. An early-1900s view of Verona shows Perry Mann standing in the street near a boarded-up storefront (later Hamilton's, still later Chandler's) and the tiny building that served as Dr. Finnell's office. (Courtesy of Bernie Spencer, www.nkyviews.com.)

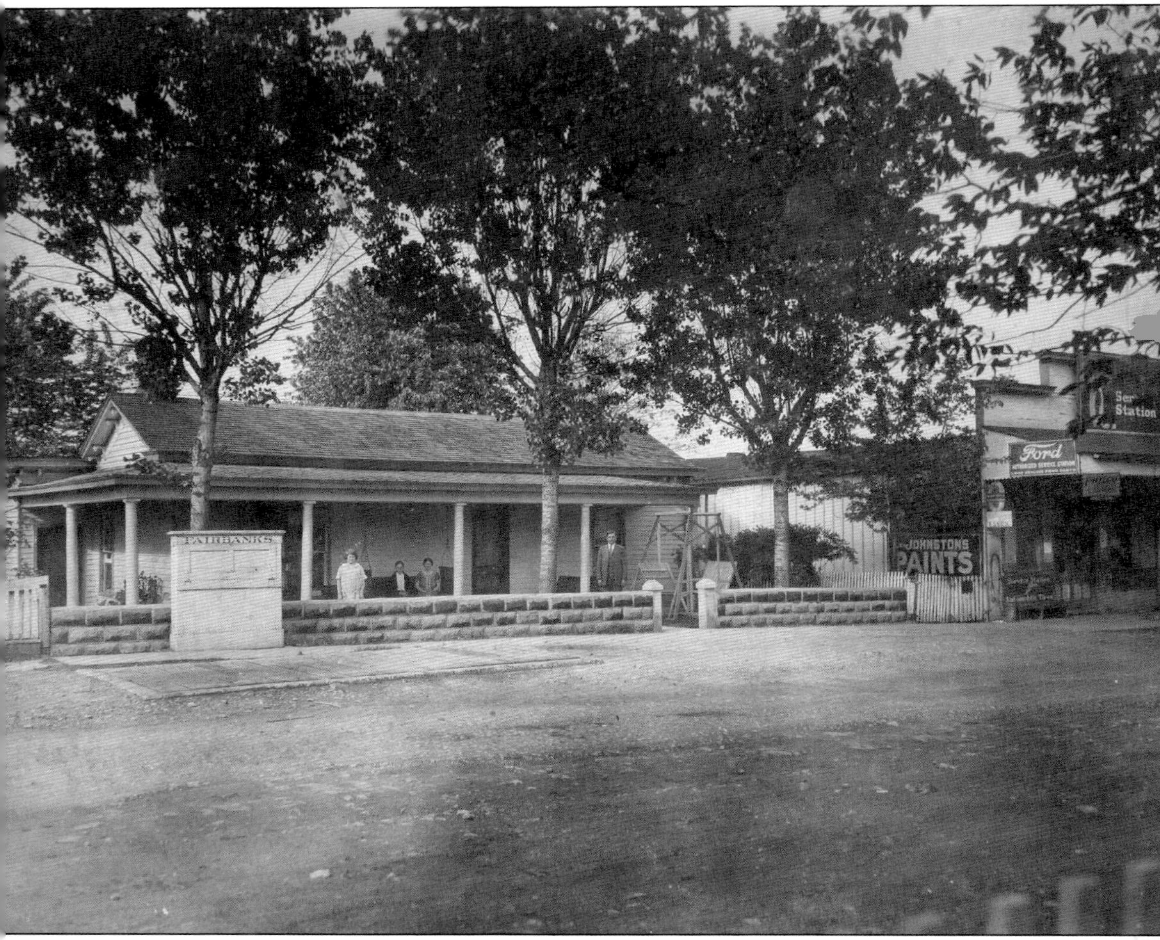

Renaker Family. This 1923 photograph shows the Renaker family posing on the front porch of their home on Verona-Mudlick Road in the center of town. From left to right are daughter Mildred, son Clayton, Grace Cotton Renaker, and W. T. Renaker. Next door is Verona Garage, operated by the Renaker family until it burned in 2003. (Courtesy of Jeff Renaker.)

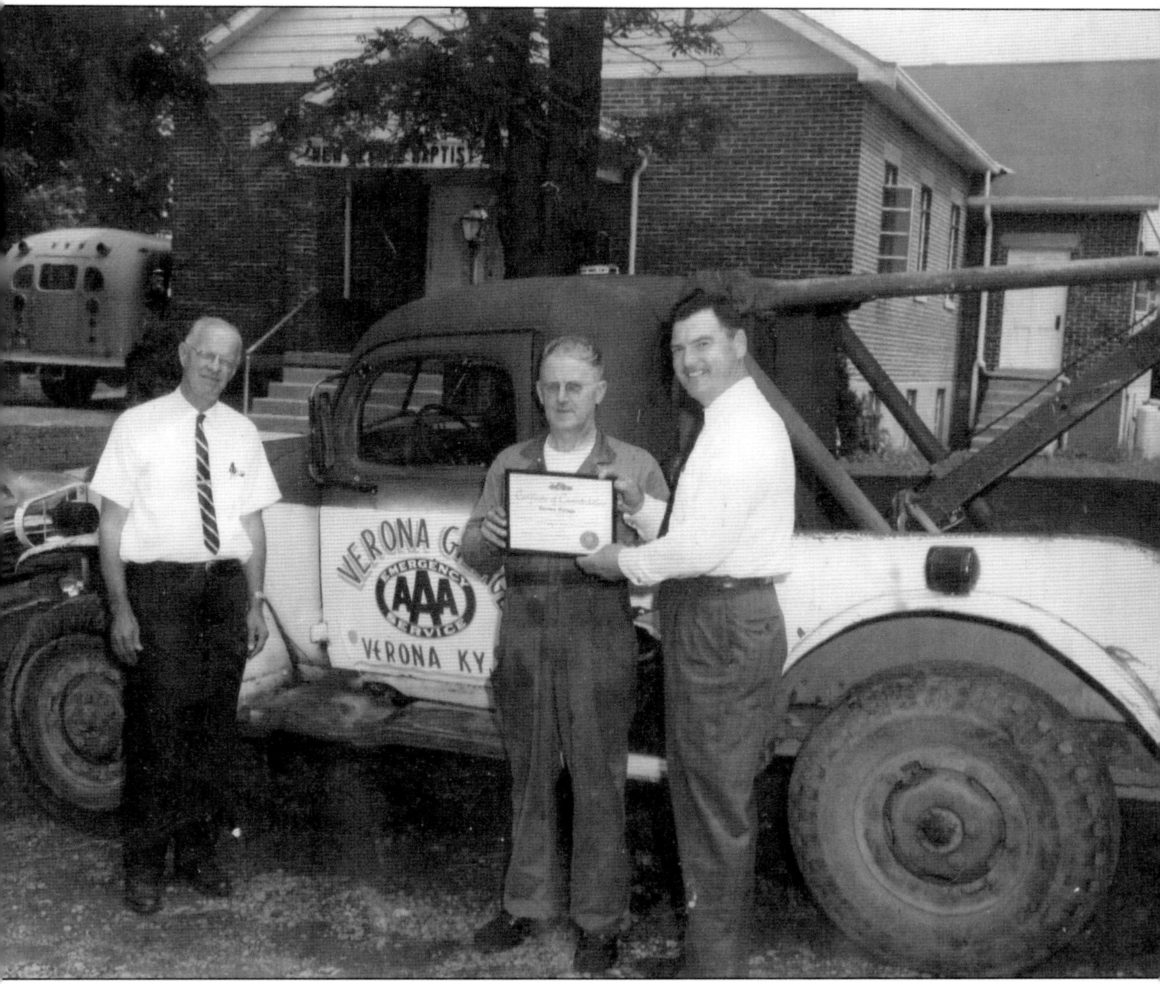

Award-Winning Business. Standing in front of New Bethel Baptist Church, Clayton Renaker receives recognition for a job well done from insurance representatives. The Verona Garage was a landmark in this town throughout the 20th century, with Clayton taking over the family business and then passing it on to his son Jeff. (Courtesy of Jeff Renaker.)

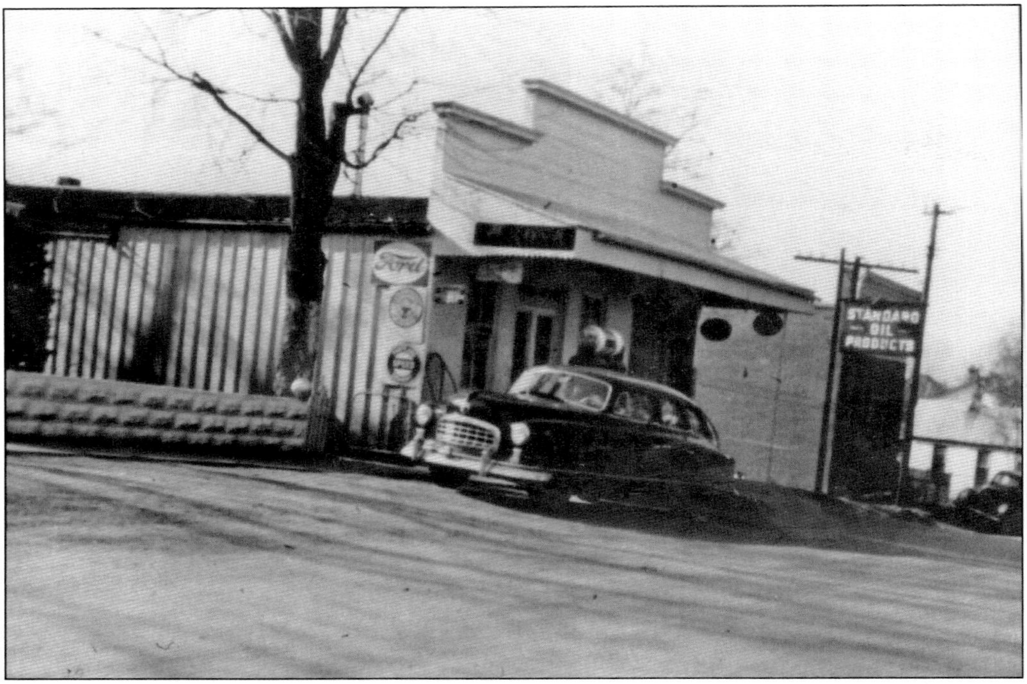

VERONA GARAGE. This 1949 photograph shows Herbert Stamper's car sitting in front of the garage. The wall next to it is in front of the Renaker house, and the building just south is the Verona Bank. The garage served as the town hall for many years. (Courtesy of Paul Webster.)

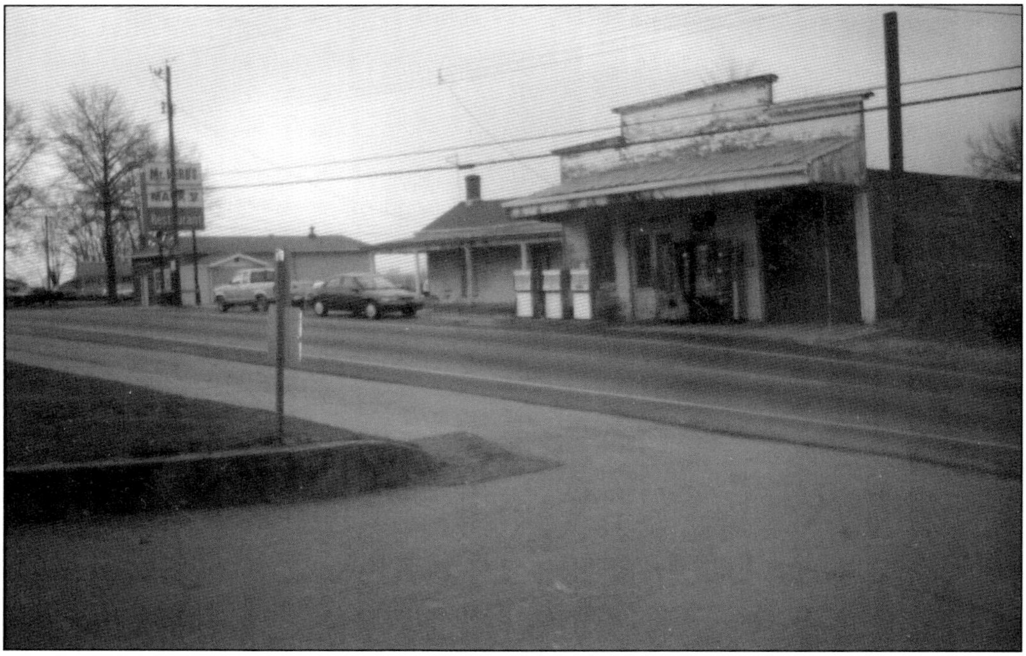

LOOKING EAST. A more modern view of the garage, looking east from the driveway of the New Bethel Baptist Church, shows the old garage and house, and Mr. Herb's Restaurant is next door, famous all over Northern Kentucky for its fried fish. (Courtesy of Paul Webster.)

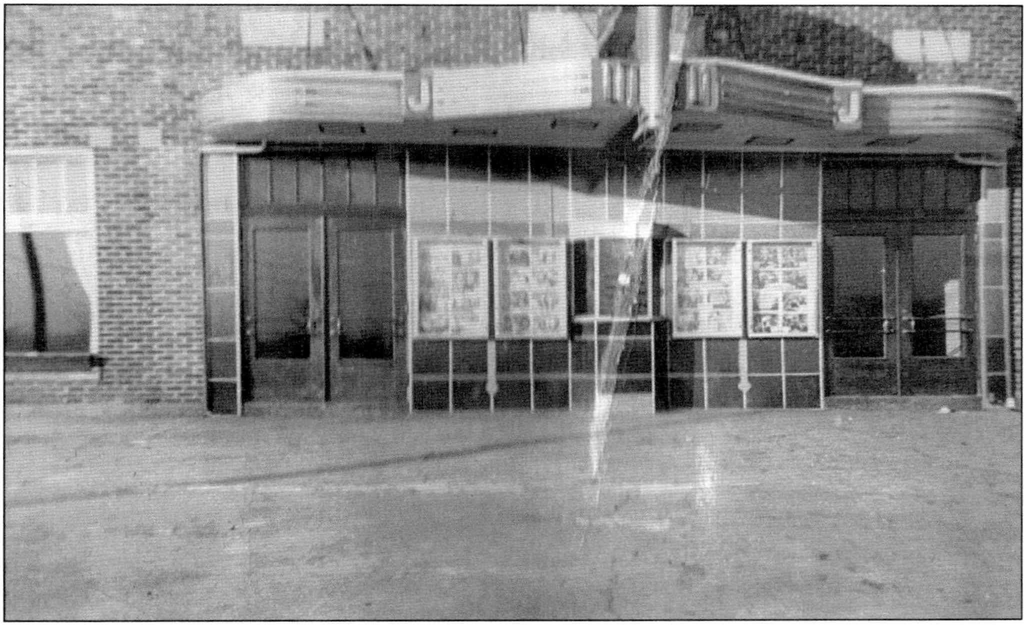

JAMES THEATER. Walton not only had plenty of shopping for its residents, but also boasted a roller rink and movie theater to provide entertainment. This 1940s photograph of the James Theater, run by Jimmy Falls, was located on Main Street just by the Louisville and Nashville Railroad crossing (present-day Ameristop). (Courtesy of Russell Groger.)

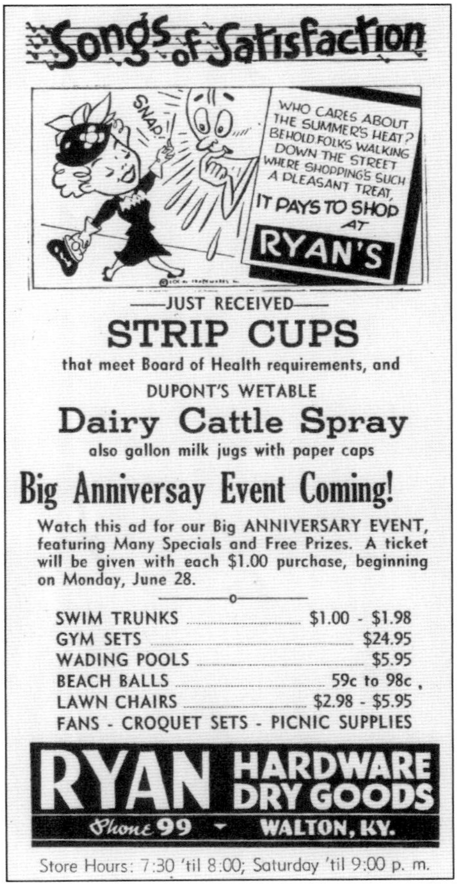

DEPARTMENT STORE. This announcement from the 1954 *Walton Advertiser* for Ryan's Hardware and Dry Goods Store shows the variety of merchandise available for sale, as Ryan's carried everything from beach balls to cattle spray. It was located on Main Street near the Chevrolet Garage. (Courtesy of Boone County Public Library.)

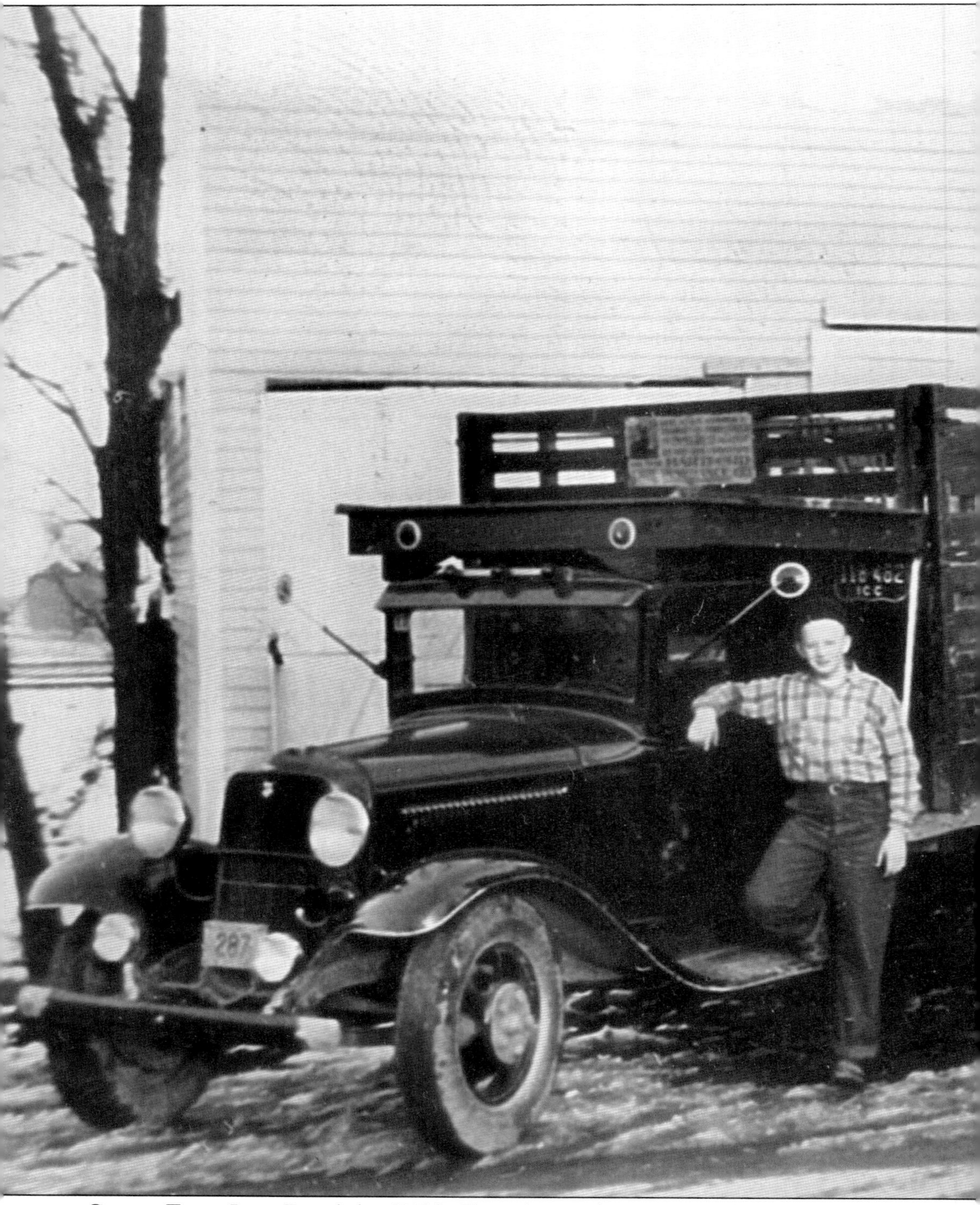

GROGER TRUCK LINE. Founded in 1922 by Elmer Groger, the Groger Truck Line spent the next 70 years serving Walton and the surrounding areas. The early days were spent running a milk route from local farms, transporting milk and produce across the river into Cincinnati. The truck line

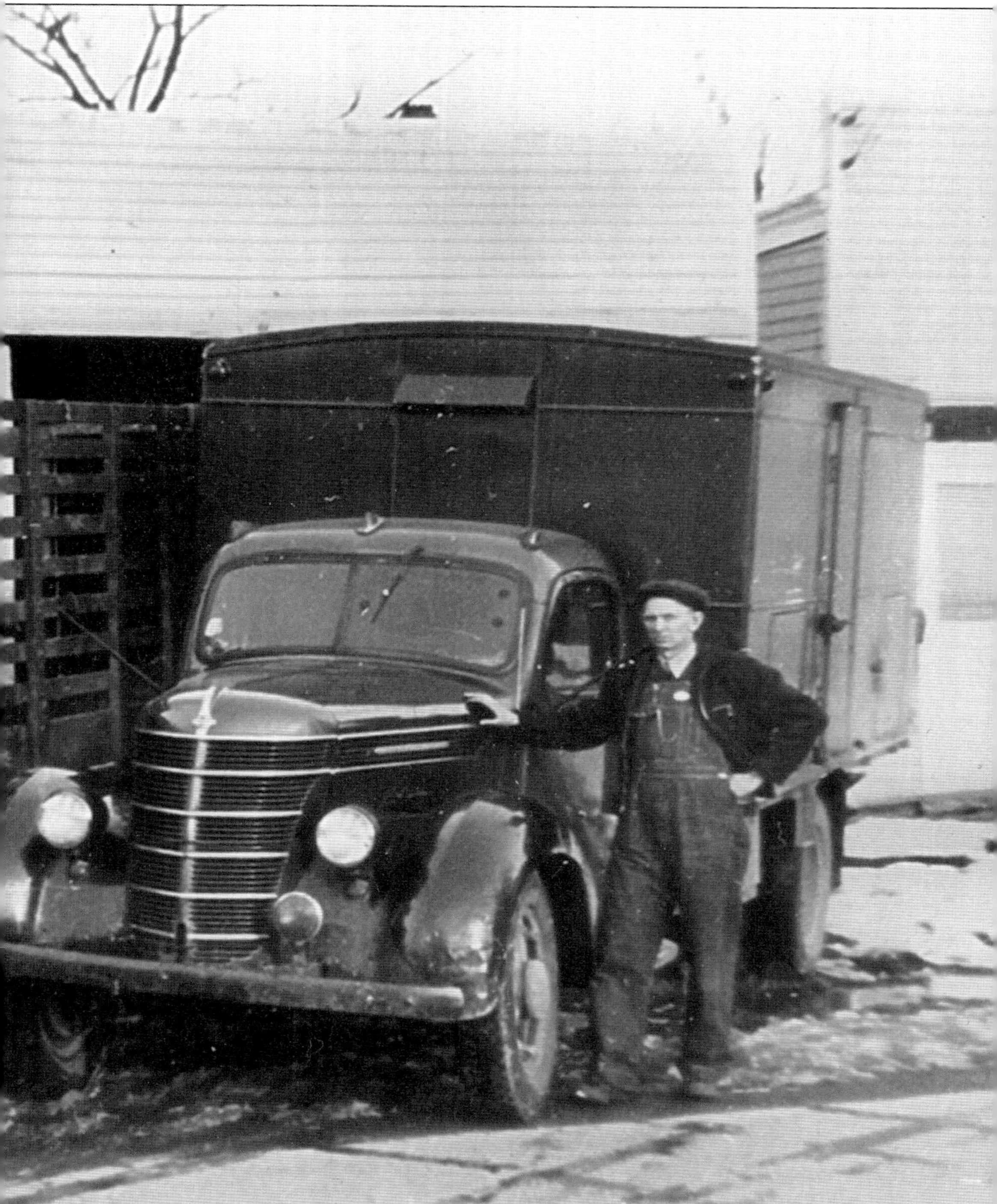

played a vital role in the local economy, providing not only an outlet for farmers' goods, but also a way to bring merchandise into town to stock local stores. (Courtesy of Russell Groger.)

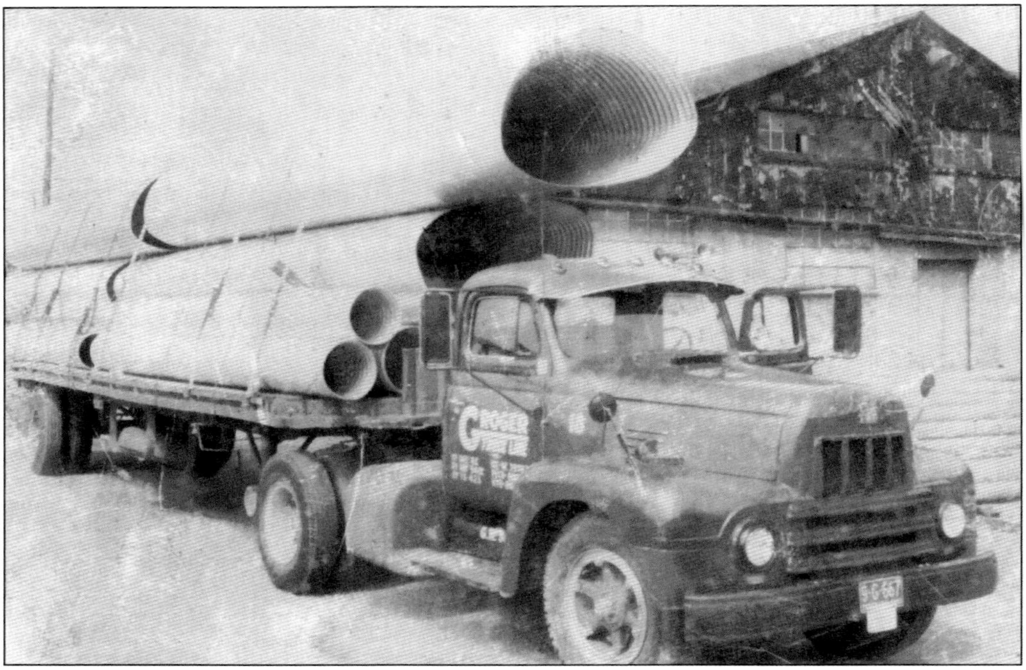

GROGER TRUCKING GROWS. After Gilbert Groger joined the family business, the company kept up with a growing demand for the transport of goods, eventually expanding to a fleet of 15 trucks with a terminal located in Cincinnati to facilitate timely deliveries. Keeping the company a family affair, Gilbert's sons Russell and Elmer also joined the business, and daughter Carol worked the office. The photograph below shows the loading dock for the company that was located on Main Street across from High School Court, next to the Mayhugh Manufacturing Company. (Both, courtesy of Russell Groger.)

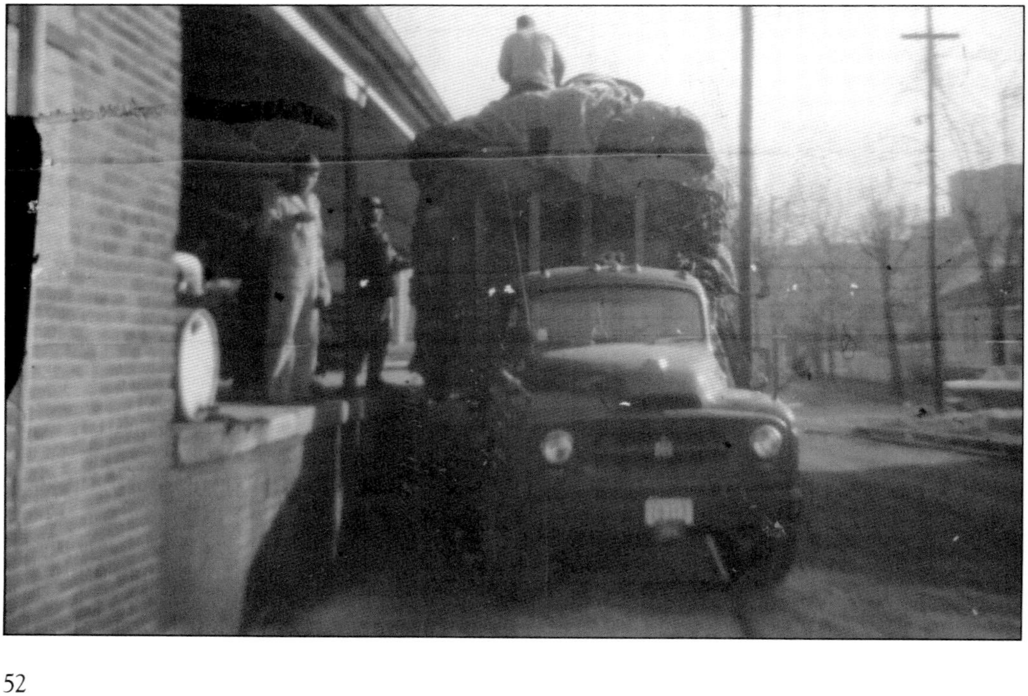

THE OLD HAUNTED HOUSE ANTIQUE SHOP

This house was built in 1791 by Col. Abner Gaines, one of the pioneers of this section, whose son was the first Governor of Oregon.

John Gault **WALTON, KENTUCKY** **Phone 607**

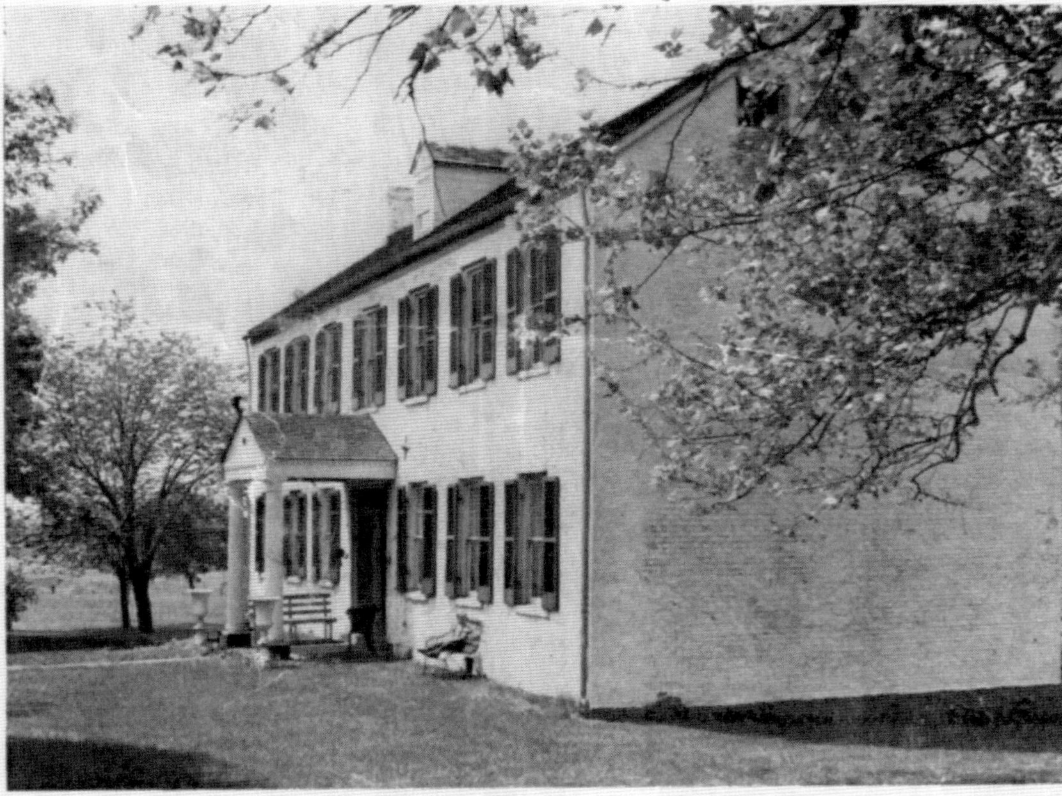

This historic old mansion is still standing and in good repair.

ANTIQUE SHOP. Col. John Gault bought the old Gaines house in the 1930s, renting a house in town while the property was restored. Gault operated the Old Haunted House Antique Shop for many years, drawing customers from different areas to shop his vast collection of antiques. The family sold the property in 1991, and it was converted back into a private residence. (Courtesy of Johnny Gault.)

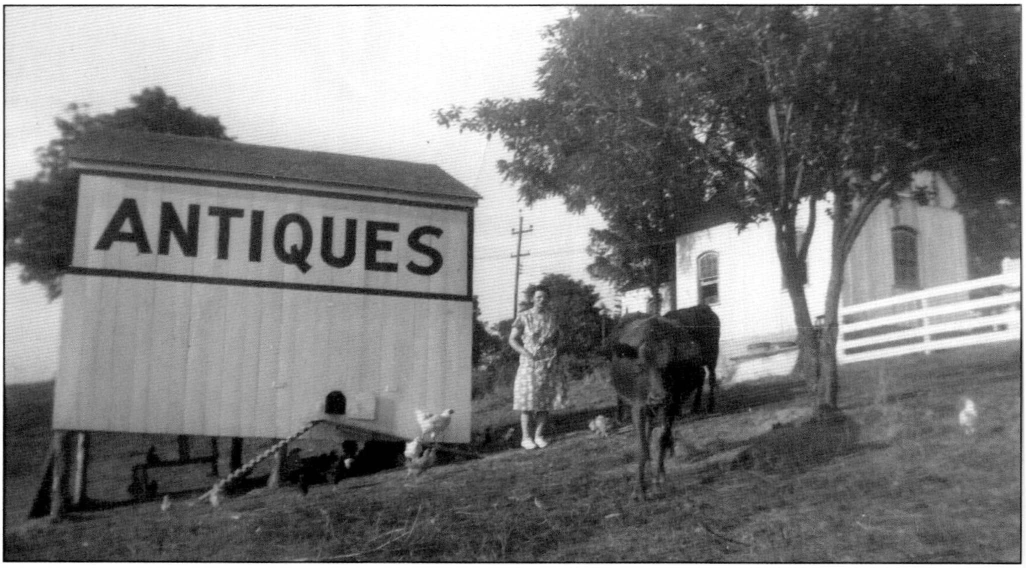

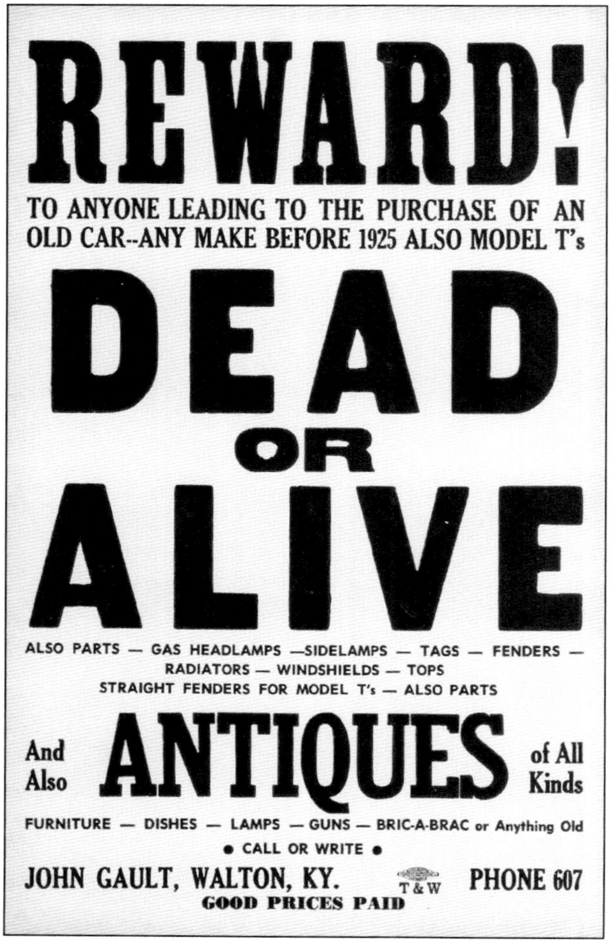

ANTIQUES AND CHICKENS. Colonel Gault's wife, Madeline, feeds the chickens in the pen behind the house. The chicken coop faced Dixie Highway, which made it useful for free advertising to passersby. The photograph at left shows another of Colonel Gault's advertisements. He had a great love for and collected antique cars, storing them in the big outbuilding behind the house. (Both, courtesy of Johnny Gault.)

Three

Religious Foundations

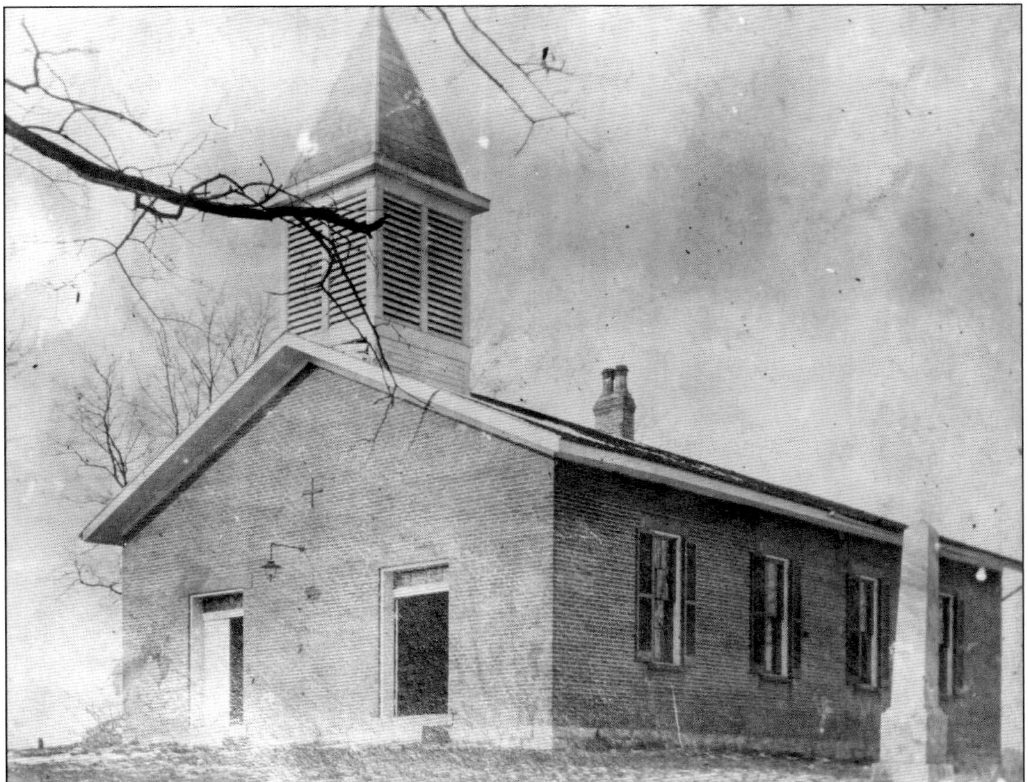

Old Baptist Church. Founded in 1866, the First Baptist Church of Walton occupied a tract of land on Cruise's Creek Road (Church Street), sitting on a small hill in what is now the Walton Cemetery. The first burial in the church grounds took place in 1876, according to church records, even though no marker has been found. The headstone shown in the photograph is dated in the 1880s. The church eventually moved to South Main Street, maintaining the cemetery until turning it over the city in the 1960s. (Courtesy of Ann Leake.)

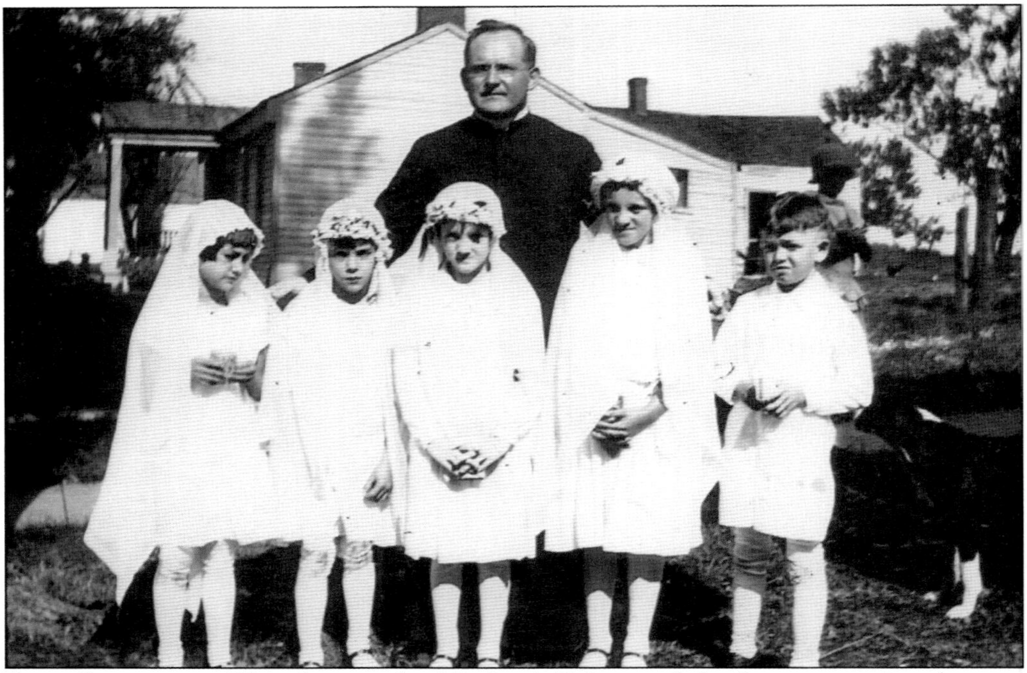

First Communion. This photograph of Fr. Louis DeJaco and the first communion class was probably taken in the yard of the new All Saints Parish in Walton. Father DeJaco was parish priest in 1930, three years after the parish was established. (Courtesy of Mary Berkemeier.)

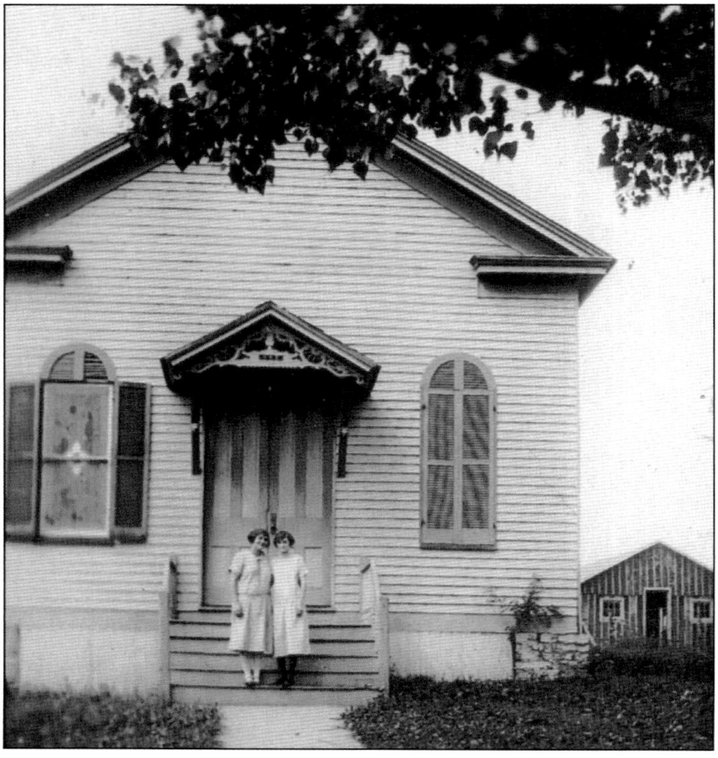

St. Patrick's. The first Catholic mission to serve the Walton and Verona area was located on Verona-Mudlick Road. Established as a parish in the 1870s, it continued to grow, eventually moving the parish to a larger building in Walton, keeping St. Patrick's as a mission where it continued to hold mass until the 1960s. The parish building burned in 2001, leaving only the St. Patrick's Cemetery as proof the church existed. (Courtesy of Mary Berkemeier.)

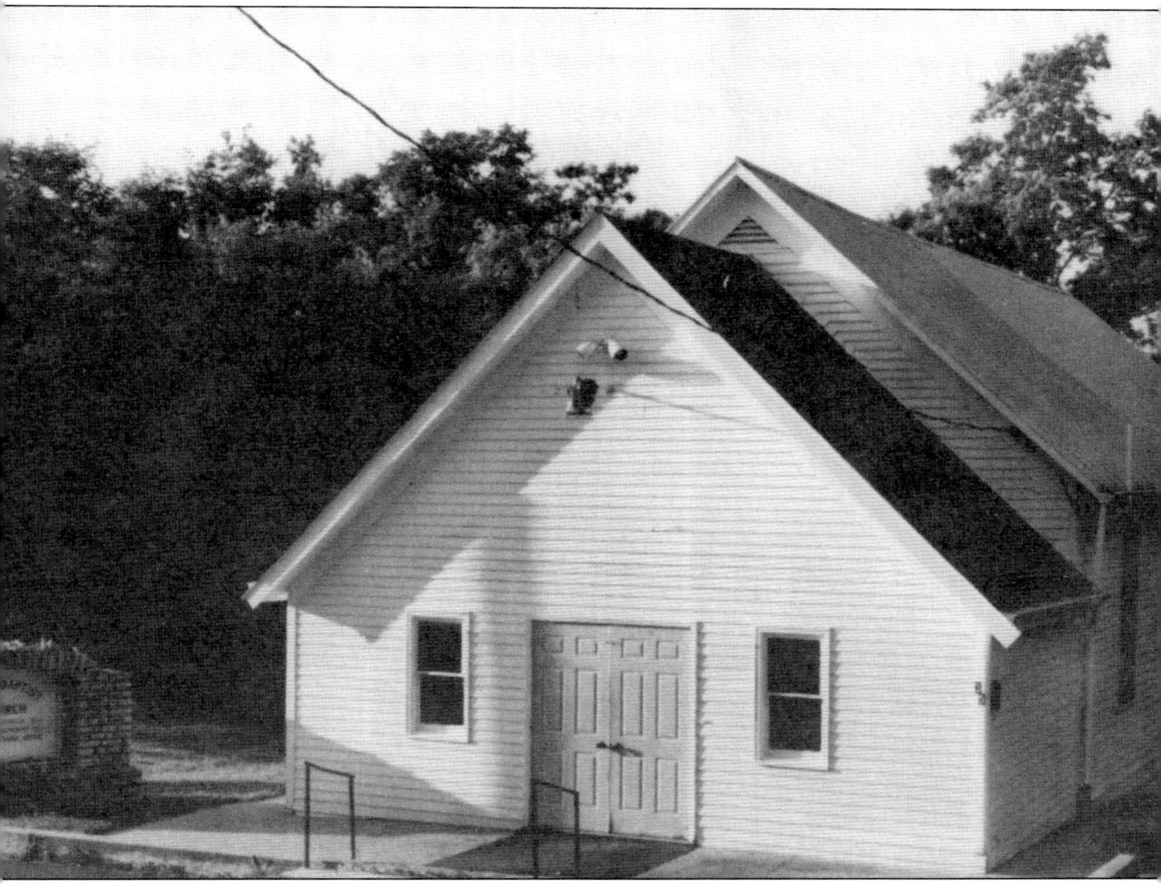

Zion Baptist Church. When the Civil War ended, a small community of former slaves began to thrive along Cruise's Creek Road (Church Street). This community was anchored by the Zion Baptist Church, founded in 1872. The first church was on the hill directly behind the current location, which is across the street from the Walton Cemetery. Zion has been in its current building since 1922 and is still a vital part of the community. (Courtesy of the City of Walton.)

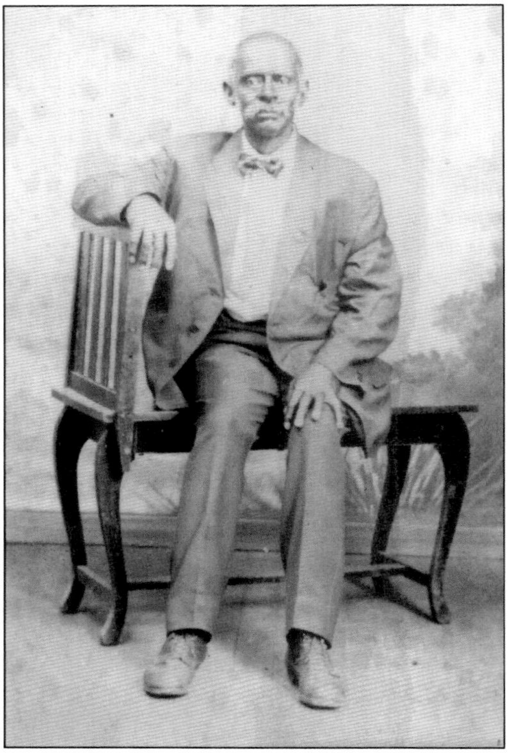

Early Church Member. The Steele family was a backbone of the Zion Baptist community. Laton Steele, son of a freed slave, was a deacon for the first church on the hill and was an integral part of the group of church members that helped erect the church in 1884. (Courtesy of Zion Baptist Church.)

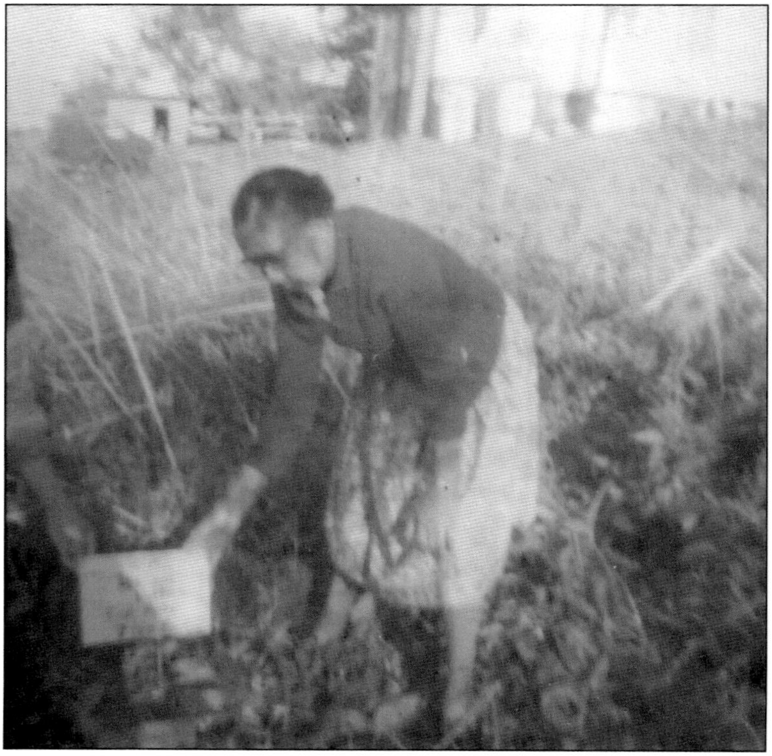

Burial Site. This photograph shows the marker for the burial site of Zion Baptist's first minister, Solomon Watkins. Watkins was buried on the hill at the site of the old church building, and a small fence surrounded the spot for some time to mark it. Unfortunately, over the years, the spot has been lost, but Pastor Watkins still holds an important place in the history of Zion Baptist. (Courtesy of Zion Baptist Church.)

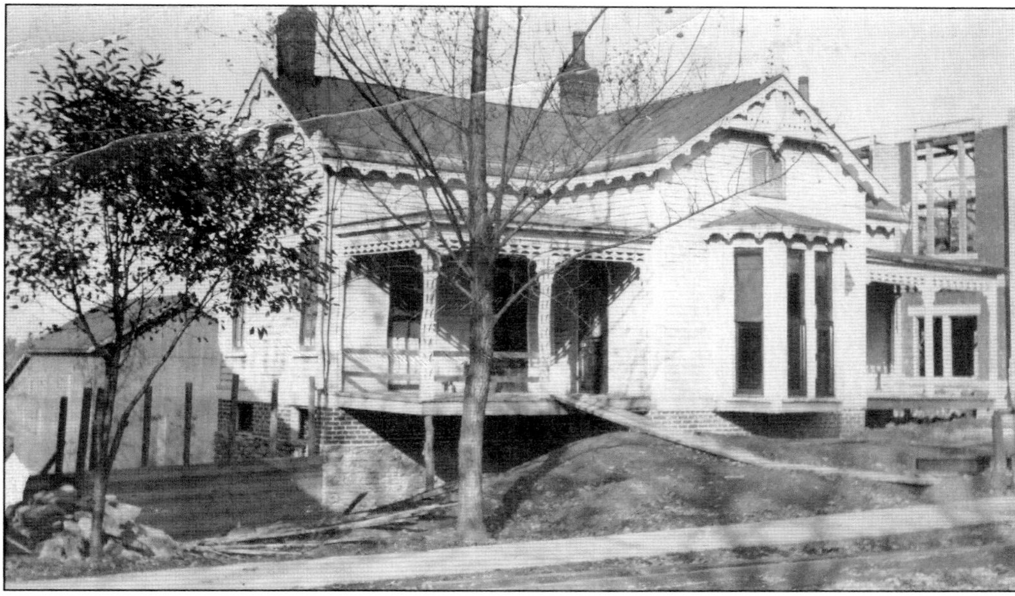

Baptist Church Parsonage. This house served as the parsonage for the First Baptist Church after the church moved from its location on Church Street to a lot on South Main Street. The house was located on the actual site of the new church location and was moved by the builder to make room for the church structure. Notice the church construction next door and the new foundation for the house. (Courtesy of Ann Leake.)

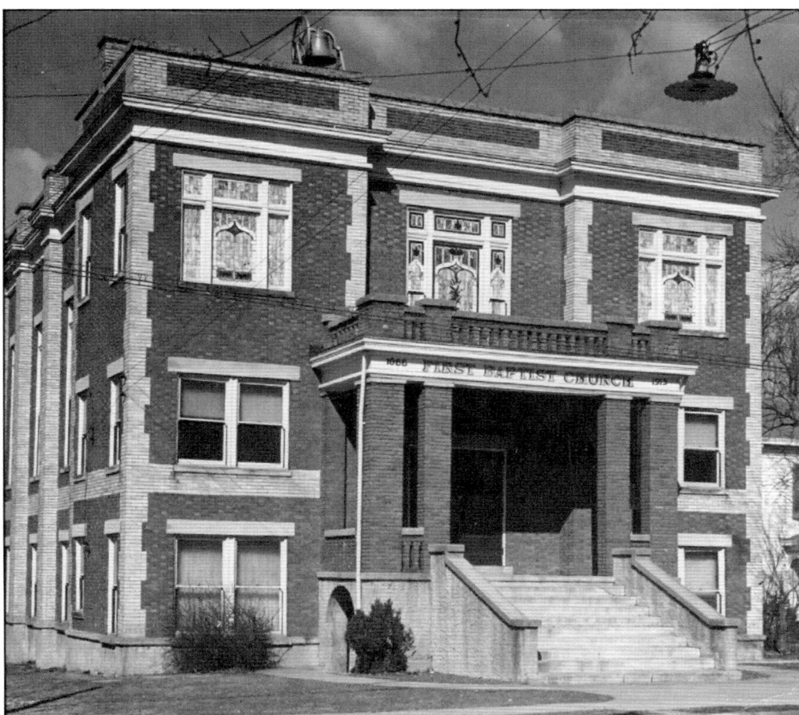

First Baptist Church. Built in 1913 by local architect George P. Nicholson, the First Baptist Church grew throughout the 20th century, adding a library in 1941 and an educational center in 1952. A new sanctuary was built in 1968 and the old one torn down in 1976. (Courtesy of Ann Leake.)

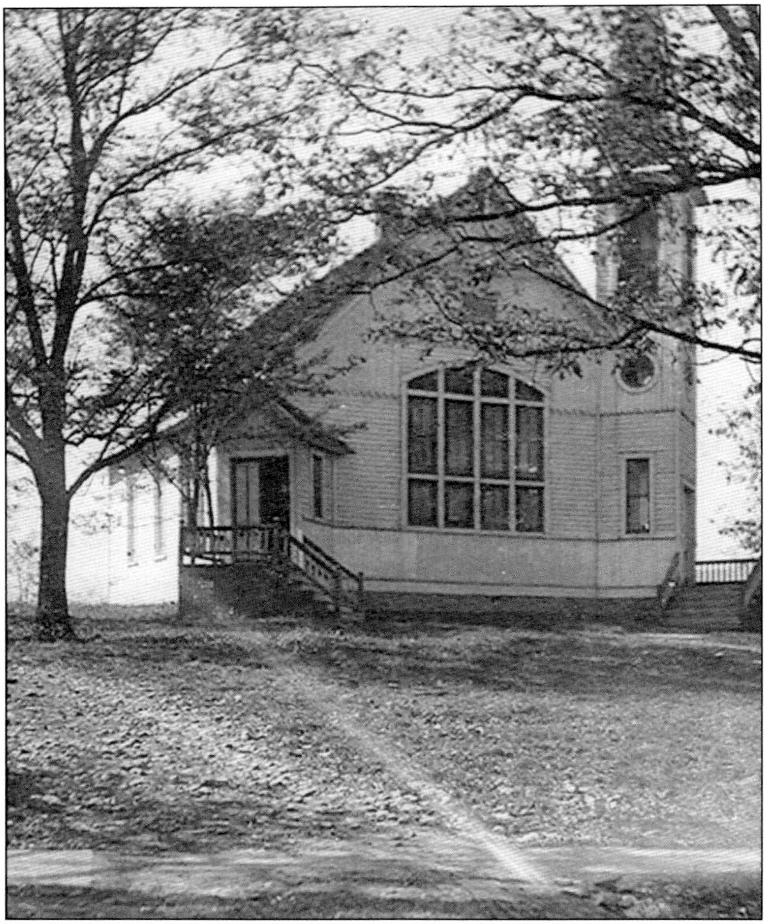

WALTON METHODIST CHURCH. The Walton Methodist Church was organized in 1879, holding its early services in the old Baptist and Christian churches until a church of its own was built in 1886 on land donated by John Walls Murphy just north of the public school on Main Street. The second photograph shows another view of the church next door to the Hance house. The present location on South Main Street was built in the 1920s. (Left, courtesy of Bernie Spencer, www.nkyviews.com; below, courtesy of Ann Leake.)

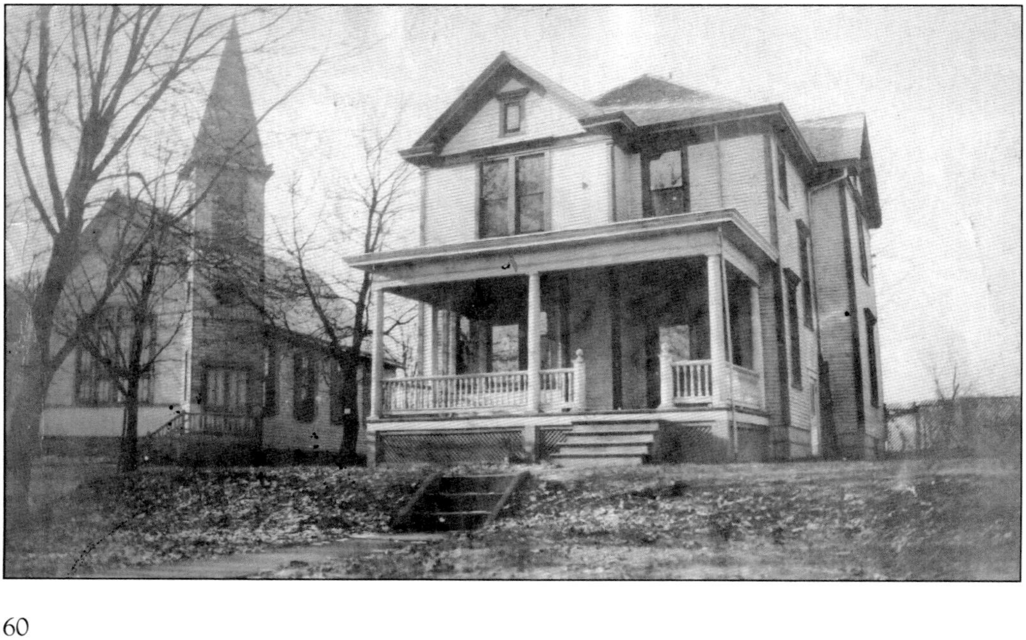

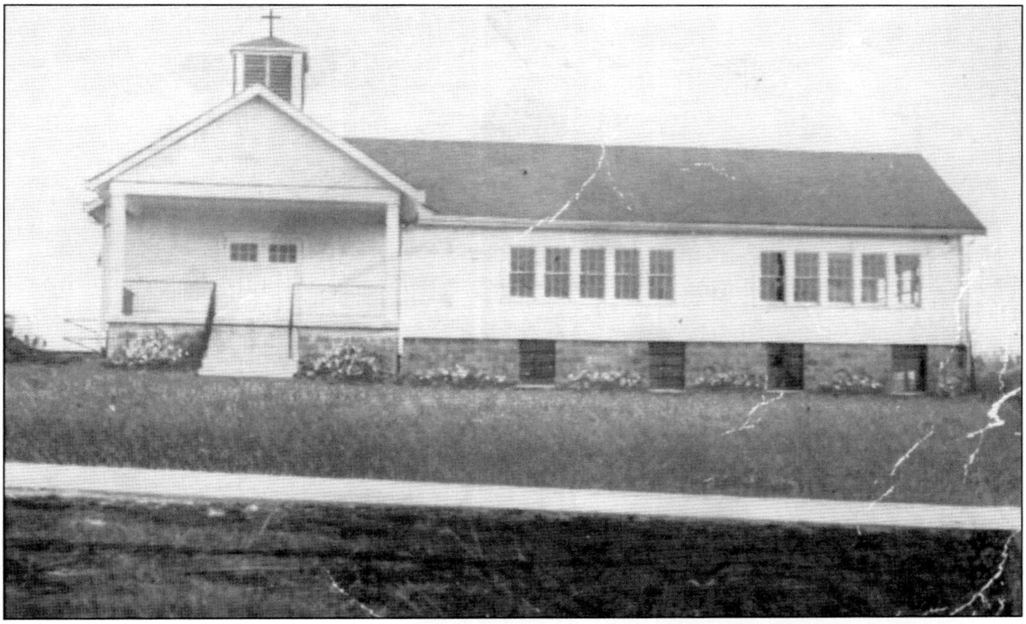

All Saints Parish. The first parish for the Walton and Verona area was established at St. Patrick's in Verona, but by the mid-1900s, it was determined that the parish center should be in the larger city of Walton. A mission church had been built in 1927 in Walton, and after expansion to this building, it was dedicated as All Saints Parish in 1951. (Courtesy of Mary Berkemeier.)

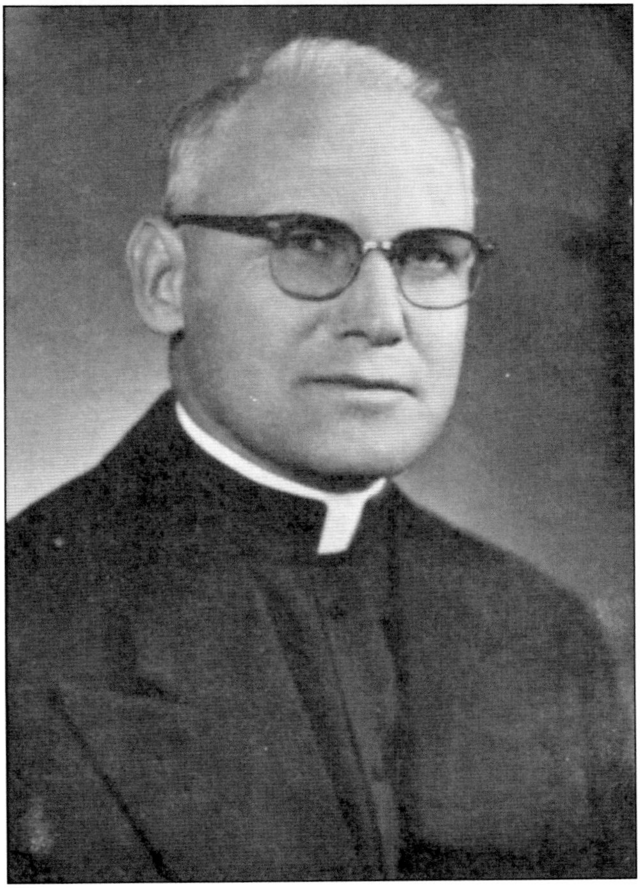

Fr. Henry Busmeyer. Father Busmeyer came to the Walton mission in 1949 and was instrumental in the expansion to the building and in adding classrooms and living quarters for the sisters. After this expansion was completed, the parish was moved from Verona to Walton. (Courtesy of Mary Berkemeier.)

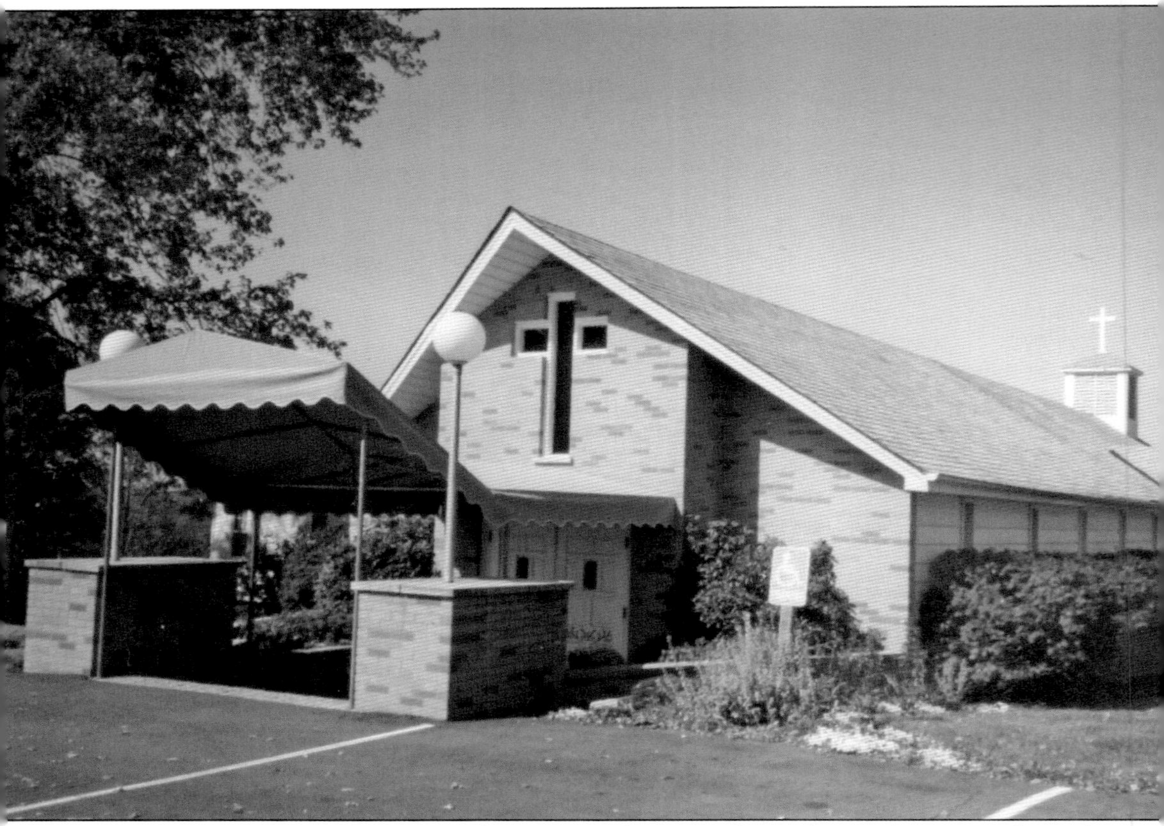

Parish Expansion. All Saints Parish experienced continued growth over the years as the Walton area grew. After closing St. Patrick's mission in 1964, the need for more room became imperative. This photograph shows the parish after its next expansion in 1973; this building was torn down and replaced with a large, new structure in 2000. The parish is located on the corner of Needmore Street (old Verona Road) and School Road. (Courtesy of Mary Berkemeier.)

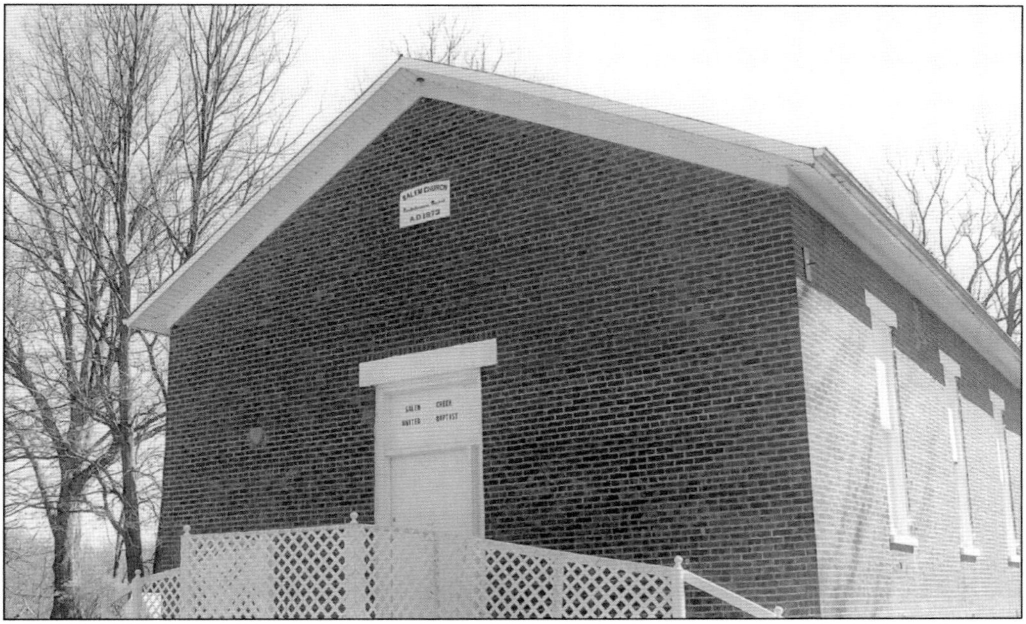

OLD SALEM BAPTIST. Perched on the hilltop above Salem Creek between Walton and Verona, the Salem Predestination Baptist Church was founded in 1873. The small church also maintains the old cemetery located on the premises. The church is just past the Oak Creek Campground off of Walton-Verona Road. (Photograph by Melinda Sartwell.)

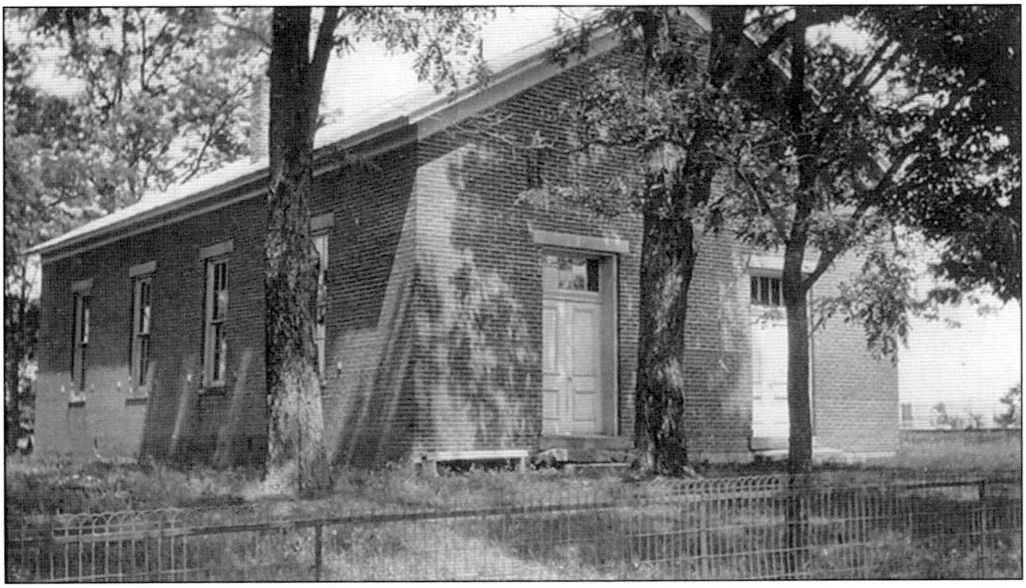

VERONA BAPTIST CHURCH. The Verona Baptist Church was founded in the early 1800s, one of the earliest records of settlement in Verona. Called the New Bethel Church, it was located on Route 491 and was a center of activity for the surrounding farmers. A cemetery was established around the church, but the church was torn down after a new building was erected in town. Note the separate entrances for male and female worshipers. (Courtesy of Bernie Spencer, www.nkyviews.com.)

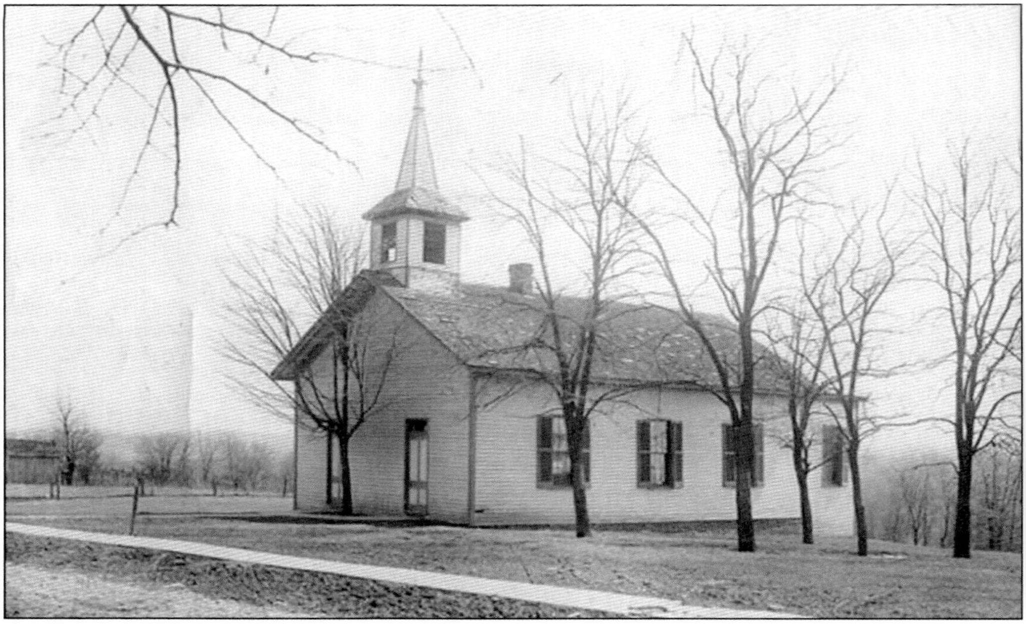

WALTON CHRISTIAN CHURCH. In 1873, a small group of worshipers began holding meetings, out of which the First Christian Church was founded in 1876. A small lot of land was purchased on High Street, and the first church building was erected, using donations and the remains of an old church by Banklick Creek. The church stayed in this location until it moved to the present site in 1918. The new building was located across from the First Baptist Church on South Main Street. It burned in 1947, and the present building was erected in its place in 1949. (Above, courtesy of Bernie Spencer, www.nkyviews.com; below, courtesy of the Boone County Historic Preservation Review Board.)

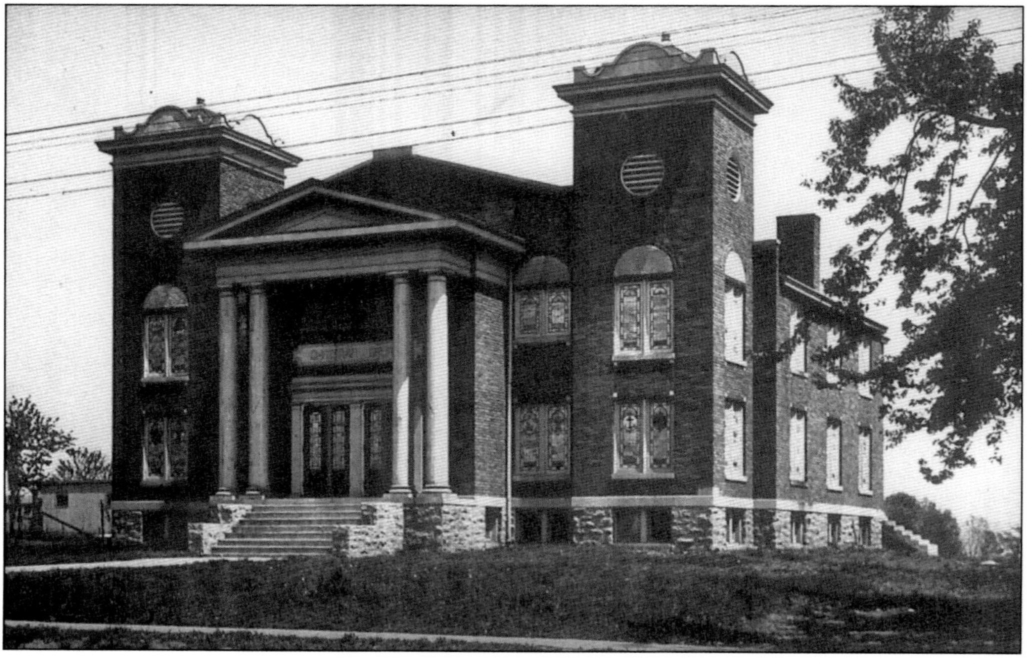

Four

EDUCATION

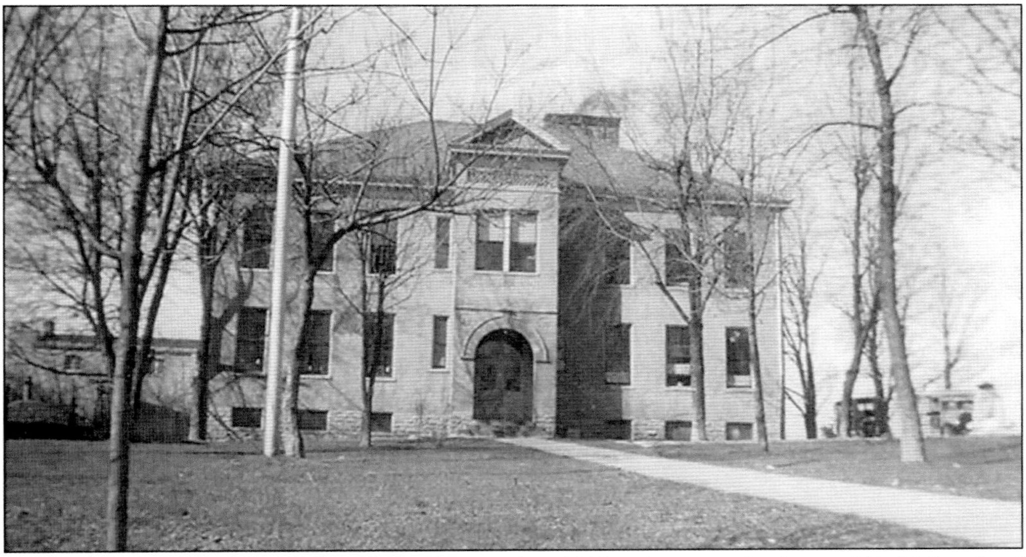

WALTON SCHOOL. When Walton School opened in 1901, it became the first public high school in Boone County. Students would commute by train to attend the school, aided by the school's location on Main Street near the depot. Walton quickly established itself as one of the premier districts in the county, choosing to remain an independent district throughout its existence, consolidating with the Verona schools in 1935. Today the school building is used for apartments. (Courtesy of Bernie Spencer, www.nkyviews.com.)

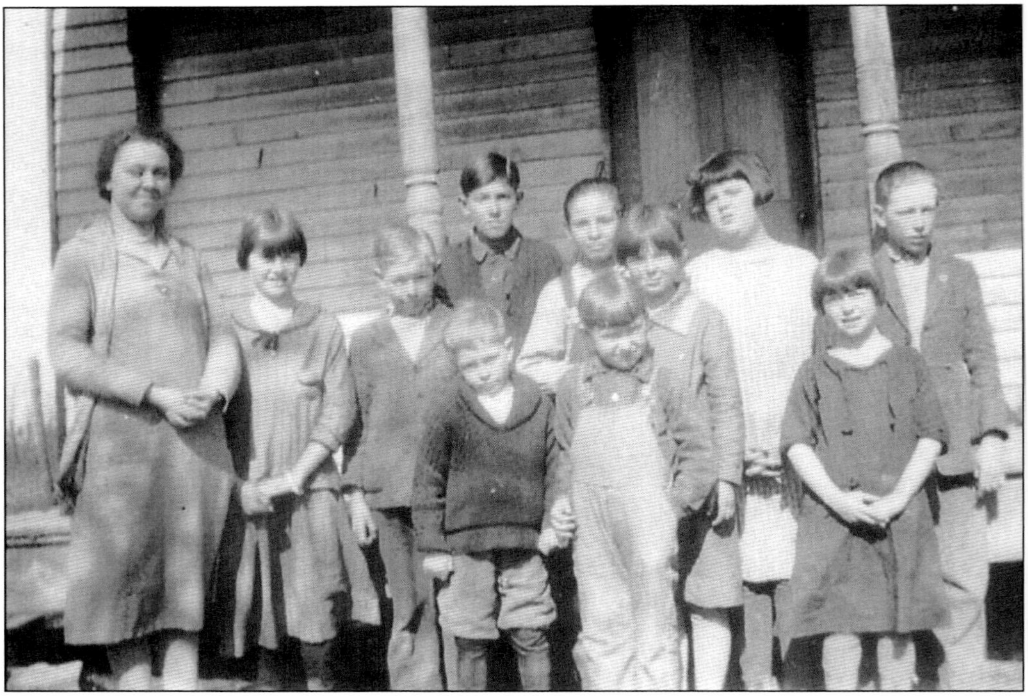

One-Room Schoolhouse. These *c.* 1925 photographs show the old one-room schoolhouse, located at the fork of Beaver Road and Stephenson Mill Road near Main Street in Walton. The county landscape was dotted with similar schoolhouses, disappearing after the emergence of formal school districts. Sarah Sleet was the instructor of this class of young schoolchildren. The building remains standing, currently in use as a private residence. (Both, courtesy of Bernie Spencer, www.nkyviews.com.)

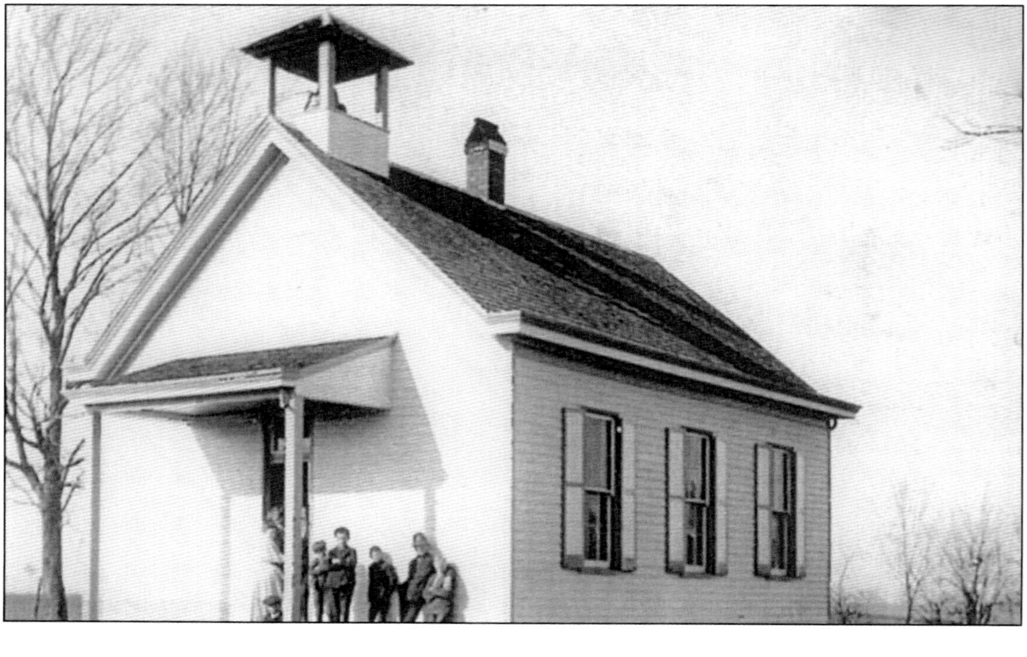

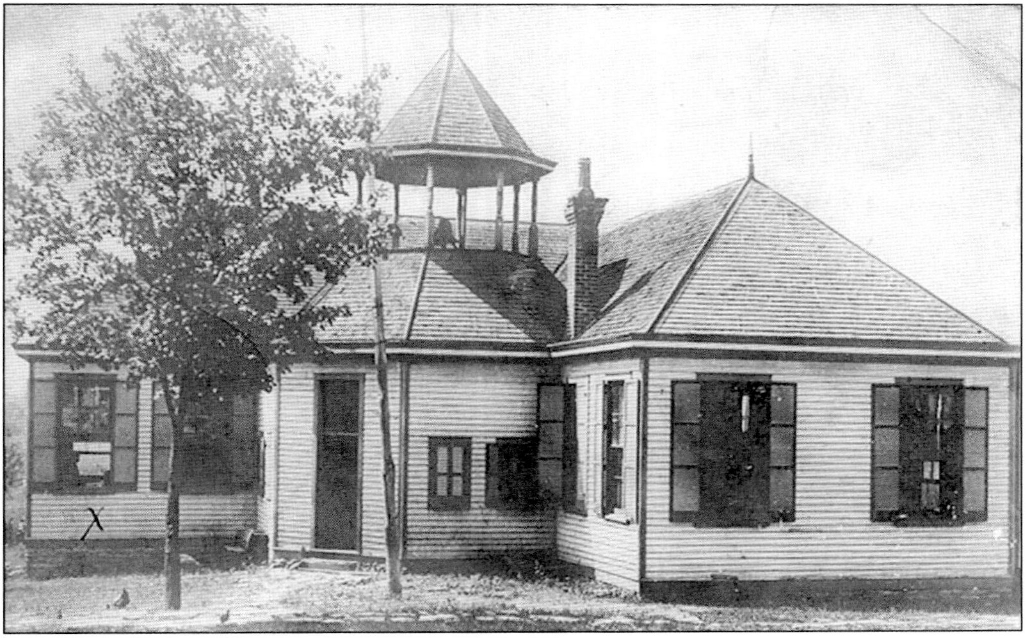

Early Verona School. This 1914 photograph shows a schoolhouse located in Verona. Most small communities had their own schoolhouses before consolidating into larger districts later in the 20th century. (Courtesy of Bernie Spencer, www.nkyviews.com.)

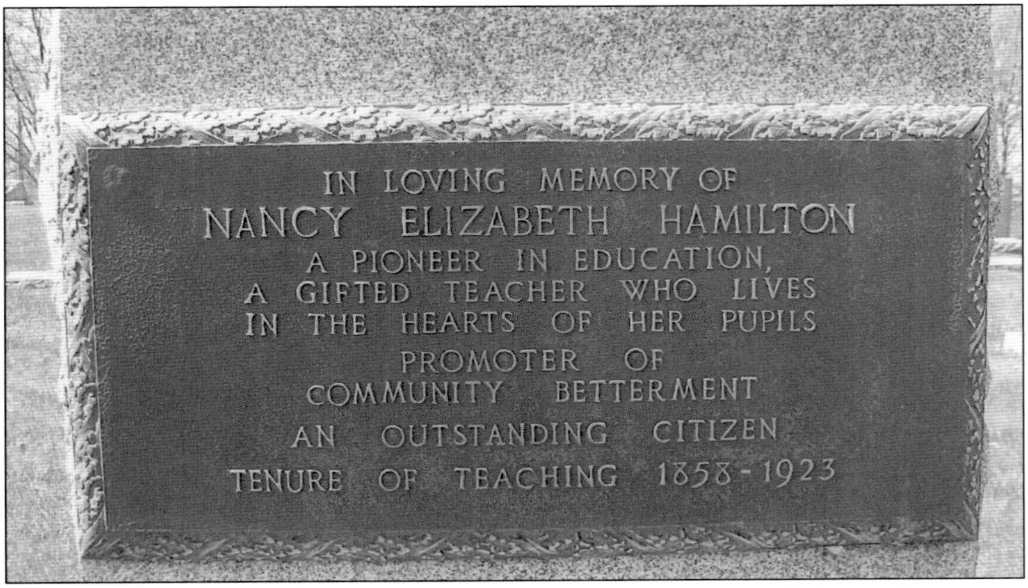

A Special Teacher. Nannie Hamilton ran a private school known as the League Institute in Verona for many years; in a time when schooling in a farming community was not a high priority, Hamilton's school brought in students from all over, as it was one of the few schools in Northern Kentucky to have a four-year high school. This plaque is placed on the back of her headstone in the New Bethel Cemetery, a testament to her importance and respect from the citizens of Verona. (Photograph by Melinda Sartwell.)

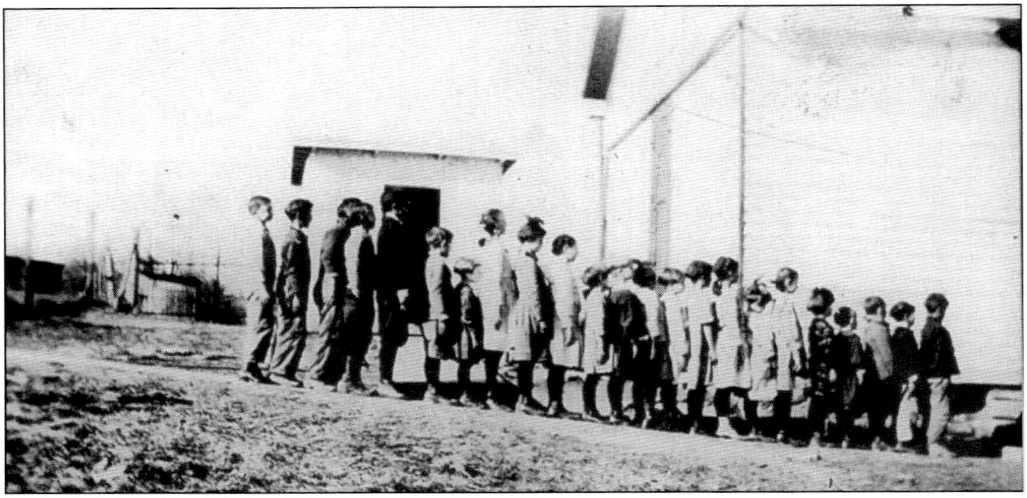

YOUNG STUDENTS. Children line up to start their day at the Beaver Lick School in this *c.* 1920 photograph. Students from the Beaver school normally went on to attend the Walton High School. In addition to their studies, the students also found time to relax and enjoy the outdoors, as shown in this photograph taken behind the old Verona School *c.* 1920. (Above, courtesy of Kathleen Wiley; below, courtesy of the Kathleen Wiley Collection, Northern Kentucky University Special Collections.)

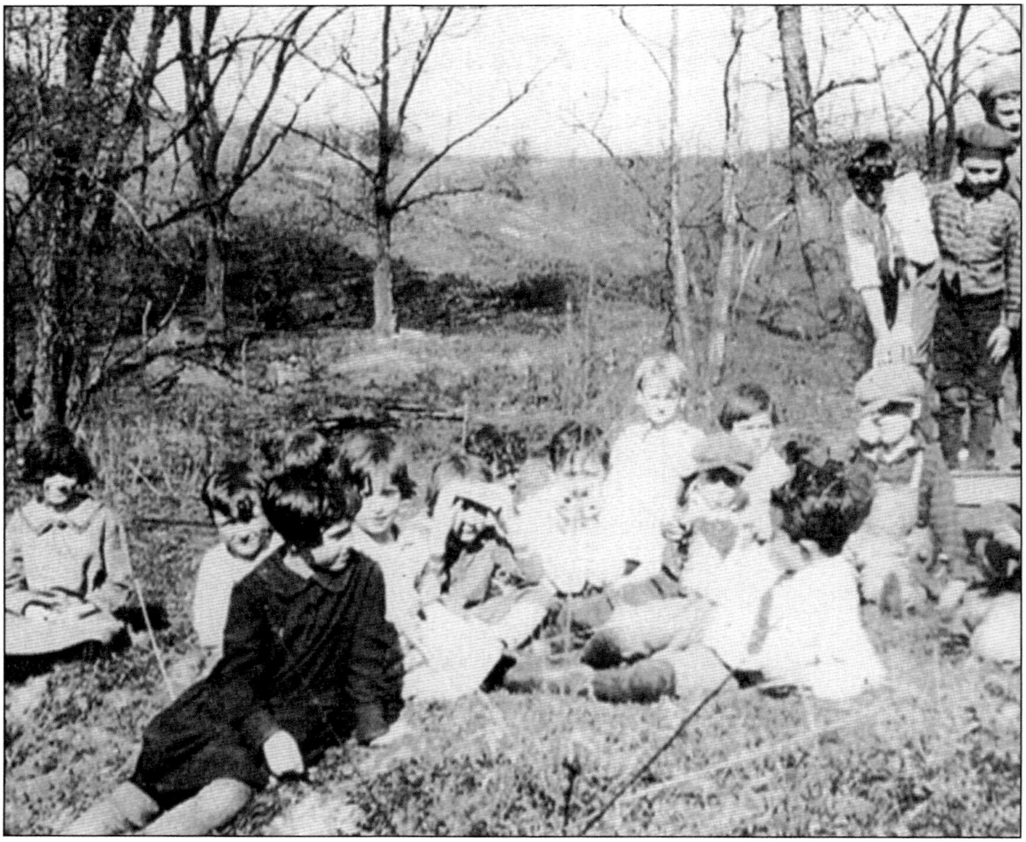

SCHOOL TOURNAMENTS. The early graded schools routinely held tournaments in various categories that would seem archaic by today's standards. This program from the 1916 tournament held in Walton featured such competitions as best housedress and best biscuits. While these seem humorous, in this time period they were extremely important skills to have in order to run a household. In this particular year, Walton won the overall tournament. (Both, courtesy of the Kathleen Wiley Collection, Northern Kentucky University Special Collections.)

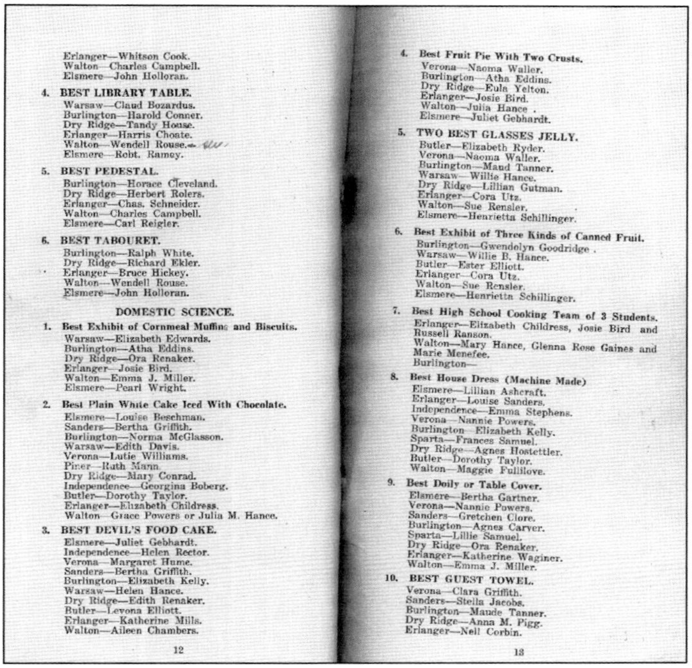

Erlanger—Whitson Cook.
Walton—Charles Campbell.
Elsmere—John Holloran.

4. BEST LIBRARY TABLE.
Warsaw—Claud Bozardus.
Burlington—Harold Conner.
Dry Ridge—Tandy House.
Erlanger—Harris Choate.
Walton—Wendell Rouse.
Elsmere—Robt. Ramey.

5. BEST PEDESTAL.
Burlington—Horace Cleveland.
Dry Ridge—Herbert Rolers.
Erlanger—Chas. Schneider.
Walton—Charles Campbell.
Elsmere—Carl Reigler.

6. BEST TABOURET.
Burlington—Ralph White.
Dry Ridge—Richard Ekler.
Erlanger—Bruce Hickey.
Walton—Wendell Rouse.
Elsmere—John Holloran.

DOMESTIC SCIENCE.

1. Best Exhibit of Cornmeal Muffins and Biscuits.
Warsaw—Elizabeth Edwards.
Burlington—Atha Eddins.
Dry Ridge—Ora Renaker.
Erlanger—Josie Bird.
Walton—Emma J. Miller.
Elsmere—Pearl Wright.

2. Best Plain White Cake Iced With Chocolate.
Elsmere—Louise Beschman.
Sanders—Bertha Griffith.
Burlington—Norma McGlasson.
Warsaw—Edith Davis.
Verona—Lutie Williams.
Piner—Ruth Mann.
Dry Ridge—Mary Conrad.
Independence—Georgina Boberg.
Butler—Dorothy Taylor.
Erlanger—Elizabeth Childress.
Walton—Grace Powers or Julia M. Hance.

3. BEST DEVIL'S FOOD CAKE.
Elsmere—Juliet Gebhardt.
Independence—Helen Rector.
Verona—Margaret Hume.
Sanders—Bertha Griffith.
Burlington—Elizabeth Kelly.
Warsaw—Helen Hance.
Dry Ridge—Edith Renaker.
Butler—Levona Elliott.
Erlanger—Katherine Mills.
Walton—Aileen Chambers.

12

4. Best Fruit Pie With Two Crusts.
Verona—Naoma Waller.
Burlington—Atha Eddins.
Dry Ridge—Eula Yelton.
Erlanger—Josie Bird.
Walton—Julia Hance .
Elsmere—Juliet Gebhardt.

5. TWO BEST GLASSES JELLY.
Butler—Elizabeth Ryder.
Verona—Naoma Waller.
Burlington—Maud Tanner.
Warsaw—Willie Hance.
Dry Ridge—Lillian Gutman.
Erlanger—Cora Utz.
Walton—Sue Rensler.
Elsmere—Henrietta Schillinger.

6. Best Exhibit of Three Kinds of Canned Fruit.
Burlington—Gwendolyn Goodridge .
Warsaw—Willie B. Hance.
Butler—Ester Elliott.
Erlanger—Cora Utz.
Walton—Sue Rensler.
Elsmere—Henrietta Schillinger.

7. Best High School Cooking Team of 3 Students.
Erlanger—Elizabeth Childress, Josie Bird and Russell Ranson.
Walton—Mary Hance, Glenna Rose Gaines and Marie Menefee.
Burlington—

8. Best House Dress (Machine Made)
Elsmere—Lillian Ashcraft.
Erlanger—Louise Sanders.
Independence—Emma Stephens.
Verona—Nannie Powers.
Burlington—Elizabeth Kelly.
Sparta—Frances Samuel.
Dry Ridge—Agnes Hostettler.
Butler—Dorothy Taylor.
Walton—Maggie Fullilove.

9. Best Doily or Table Cover.
Elsmere—Bertha Gartner.
Verona—Nannie Powers.
Sanders—Gretchen Clore.
Burlington—Agnes Carver.
Sparta—Lillie Samuel.
Dry Ridge—Ora Renaker.
Erlanger—Katherine Waginer.
Walton—Emma J. Miller.

10. BEST GUEST TOWEL.
Verona—Clara Griffith.
Sanders—Stella Jacobs.
Burlington—Maude Tanner.
Dry Ridge—Anna M. Pigg.
Erlanger—Nell Corbin.

13

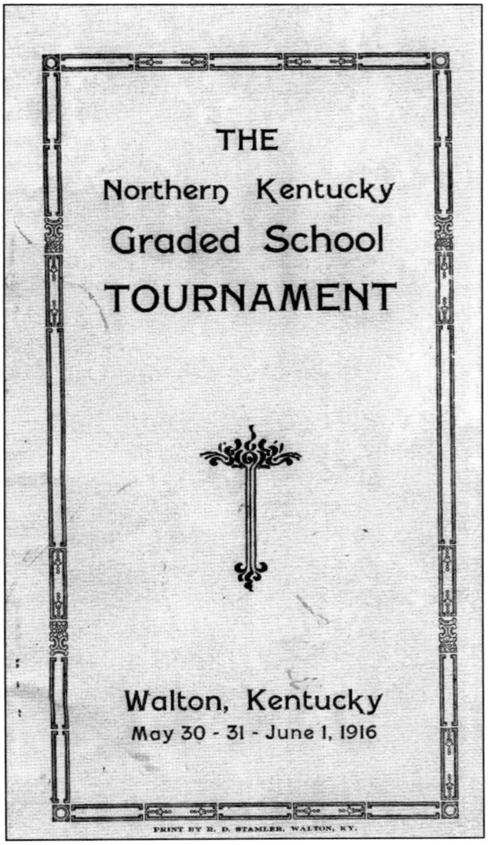

THE
Northern Kentucky
Graded School
TOURNAMENT

Walton, Kentucky
May 30 - 31 - June 1, 1916

PRINT BY R. D. STAMLER, WALTON, KY.

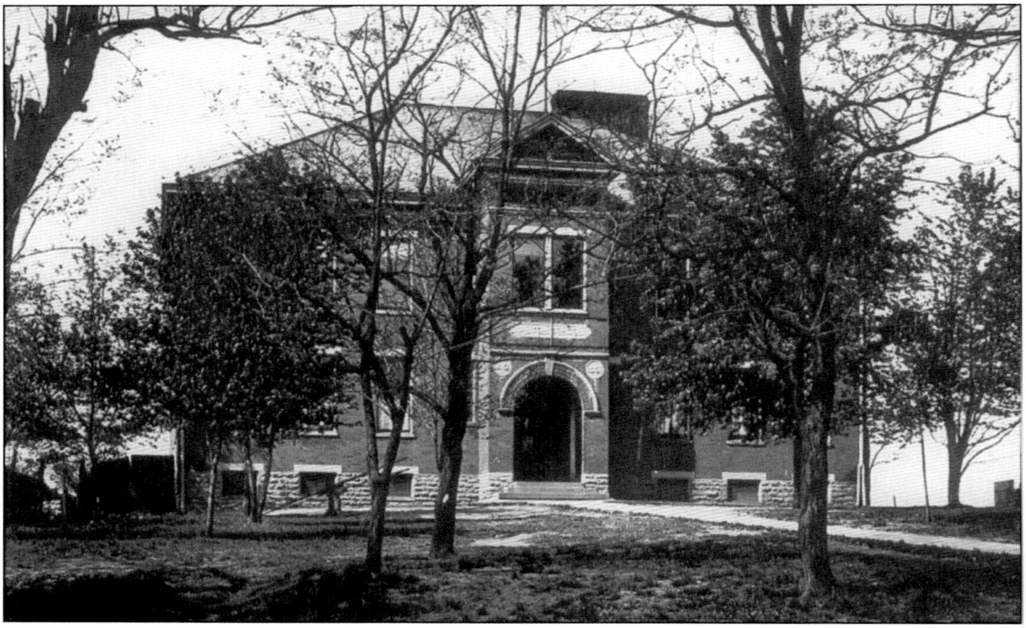

WALTON SCHOOL. An early view of the Walton High School (notice the gym behind the school has not been built yet), an earlier public school existed on this site in the 1880s as a county graded school. The only high school prior to the 1901 opening of the Walton High School was a private school run by Clara Myers. (Courtesy of the Boone County Historic Preservation Review Board.)

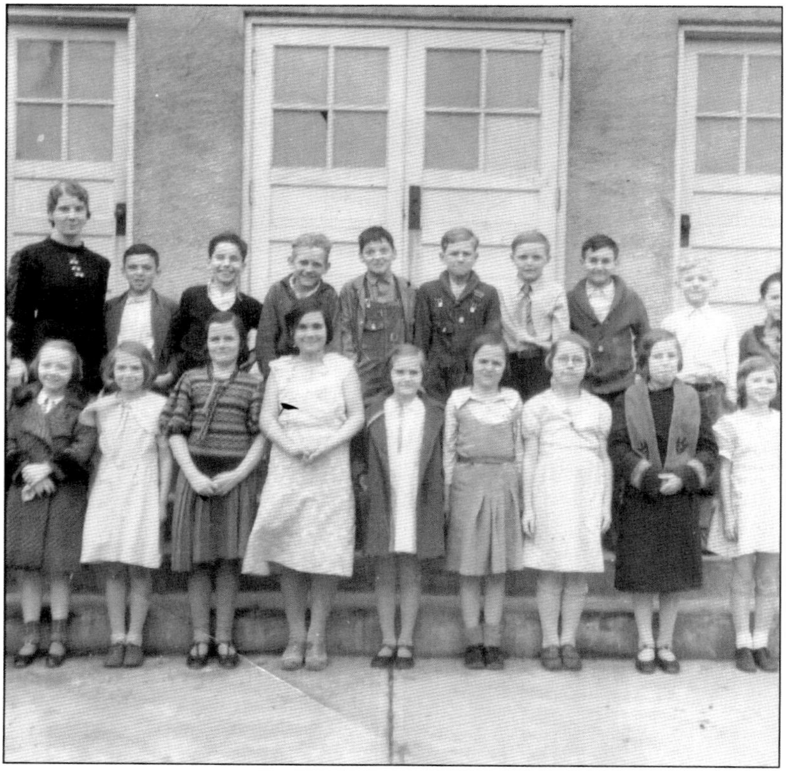

YOUNG STUDENTS. This photograph from around 1935 shows students posing for their class picture, standing on the steps of the Walton gymnasium. Class size varied from year to year; some of the earliest graduating classes only consisted of four or five students. (Courtesy of Russell Groger.)

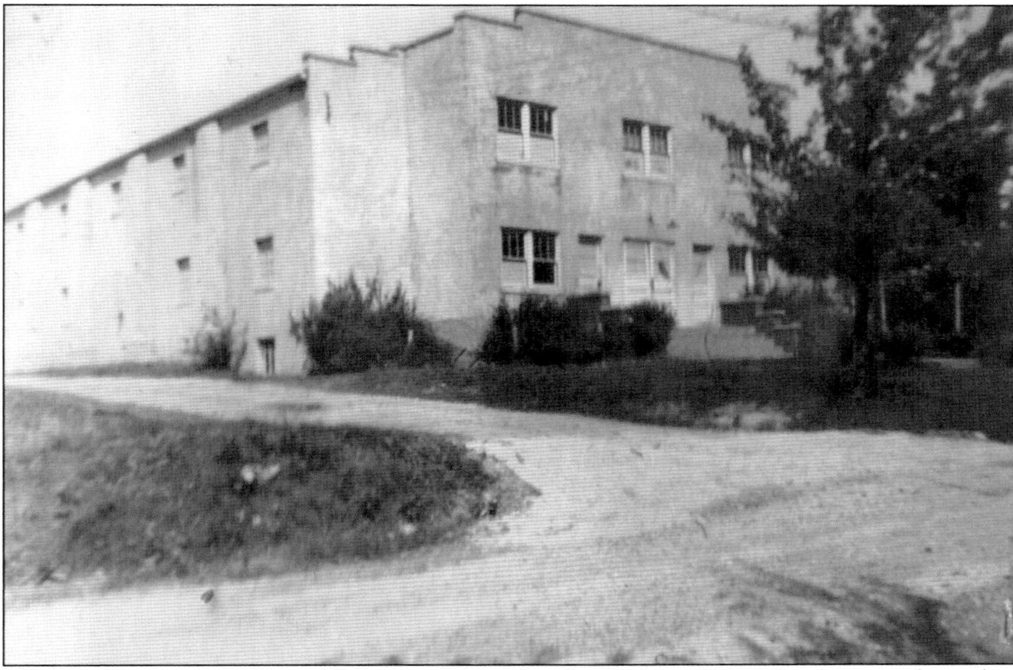

WALTON GYMNASIUM. A need for a new gymnasium for Walton High School was evident when the basketball teams had to play in an old tobacco warehouse. Built in 1929, the gym was behind the main school building and faced High School Court. (Courtesy of Russell Groger.)

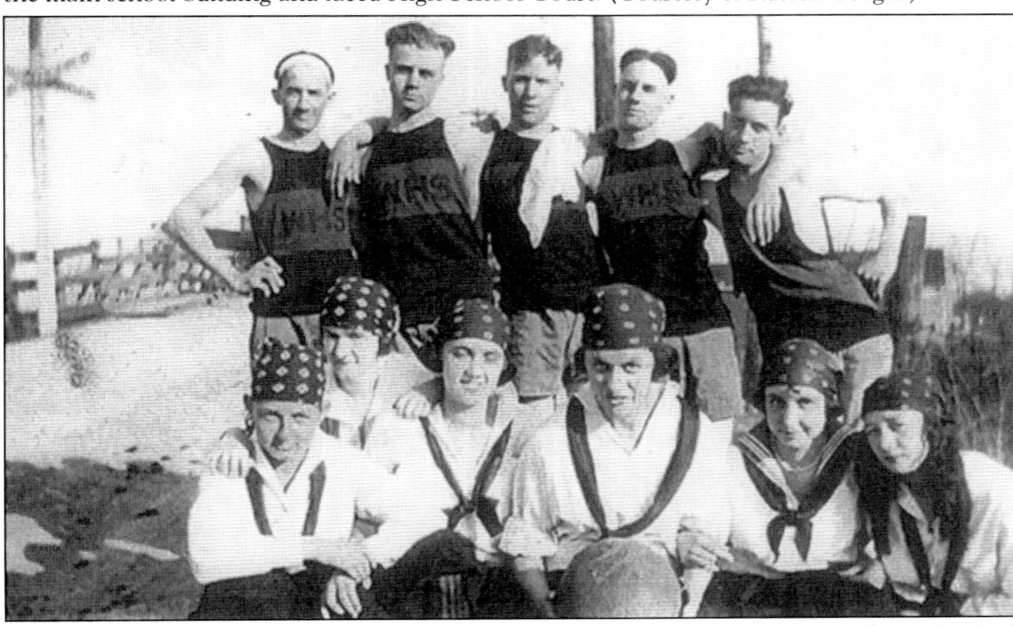

BASKETBALL TEAMS. The 1921 girls and boys basketball teams pose in front of the old High Street Bridge. Pictured from left to right are (first row) Sue Hance, Georgia Rouse Sulzberger, Mary Scott Chambers Grubbs, Ruth Roberts, Louise Jack Rouse, and unidentified; (second row) Phillip Bevarly, Dr. Harry Daugherty, Leon Childers, unidentified, and Asa Rouse. (Courtesy of Bernie Spencer, www.nkyviews.com.)

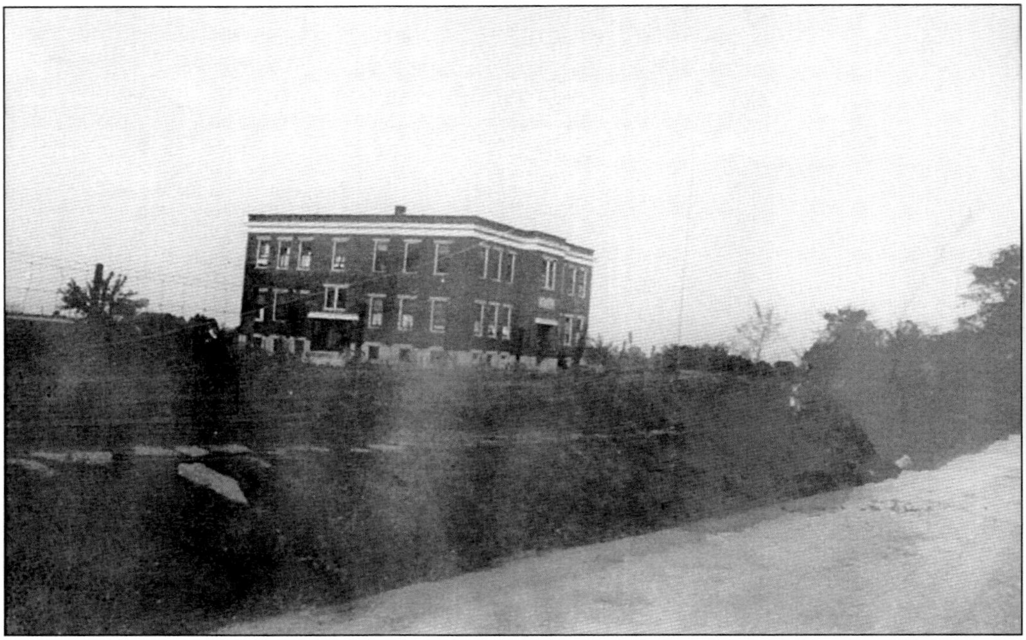

Verona High School. This faded photograph is an early view of the Verona High School. Built in 1914 on Walton-Verona Road, the school served the students of Verona until 1935, when it consolidated with Walton to become Walton-Verona Independent Schools. (Courtesy of the Kathleen Wiley Collection, Northern Kentucky University Special Collections.)

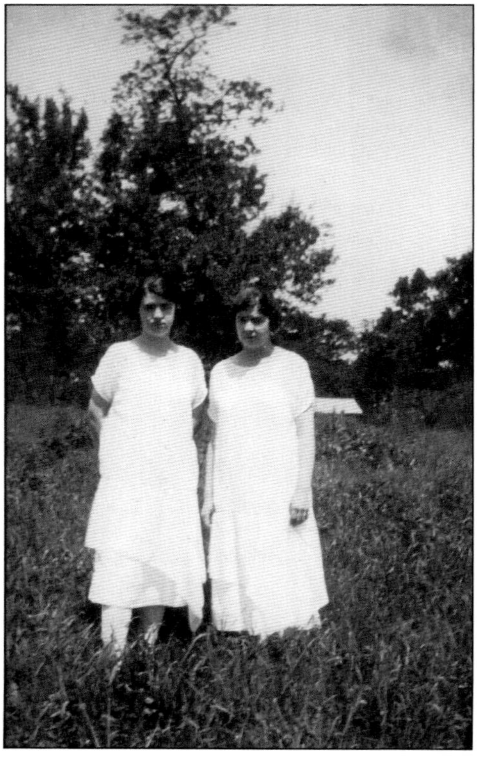

Teachers. The Chandler sisters, Effie and Agnes, were teachers in the Walton-Verona school system. Agnes married Roy Kenney of Beaver Lick, and their daughter Kathleen was also a teacher in the Walton-Verona schools. (Courtesy of Kathleen Wiley.)

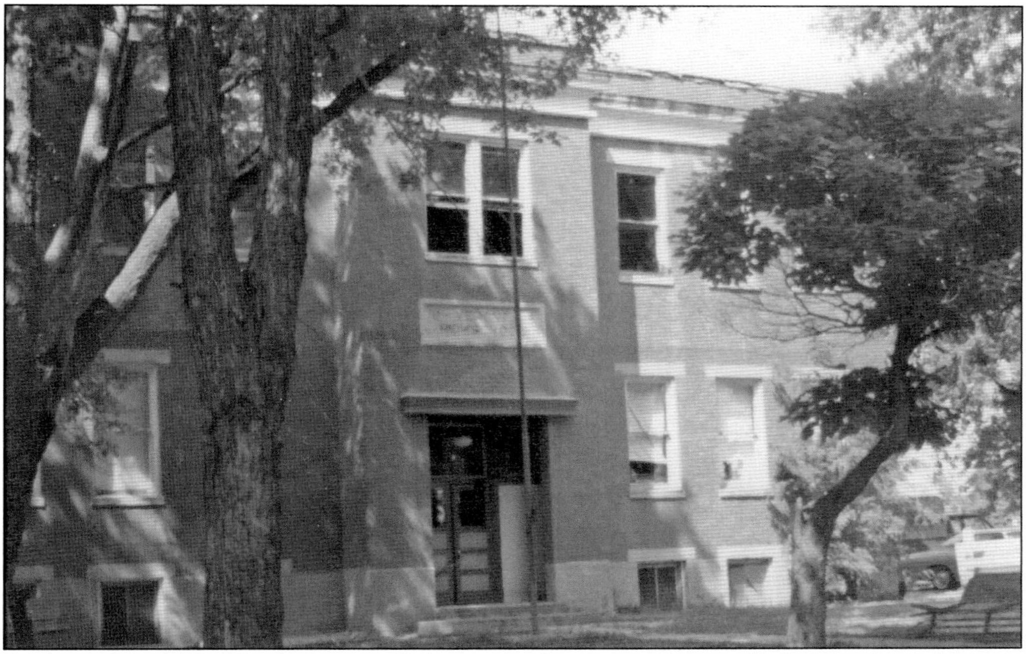

Another View. The above photograph shows a modern view of Verona High School. The building stands vacant just north of town, in disuse since the district consolidated with Walton. The 1935 graduating class was the last from Verona High School, since the districts consolidated in the fall of 1935. The principal, seated third from the left below, was W. F. Coop. (Above, courtesy of Paul Webster; below, courtesy of Bernie Spencer, www.nkyviews.com.)

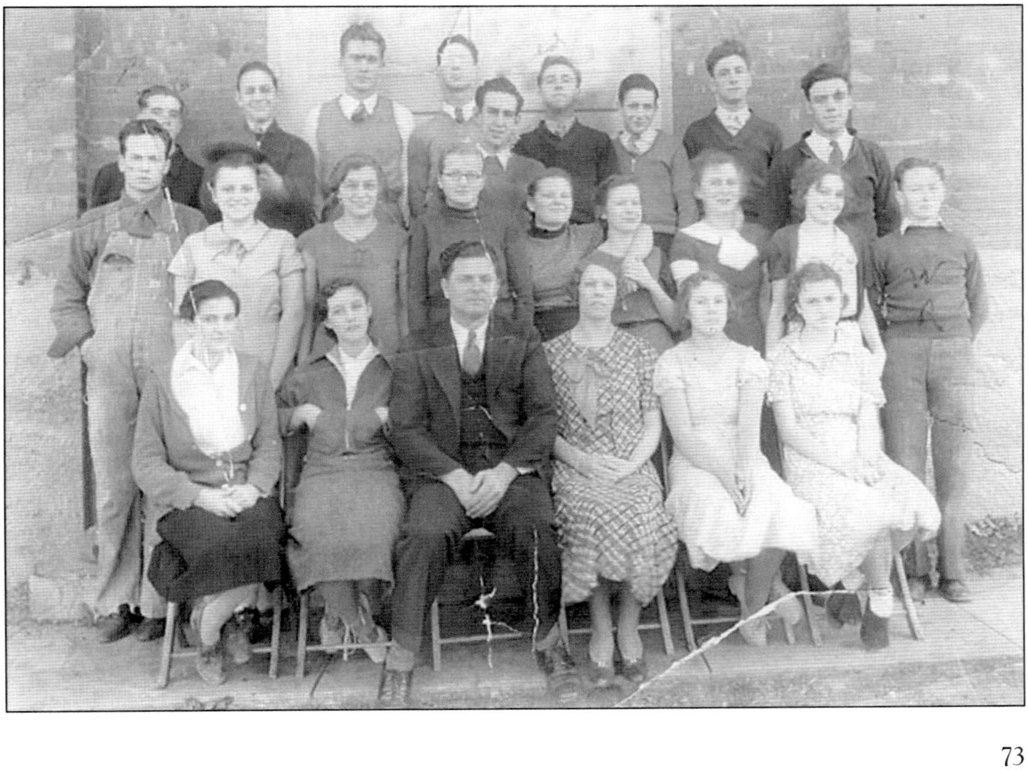

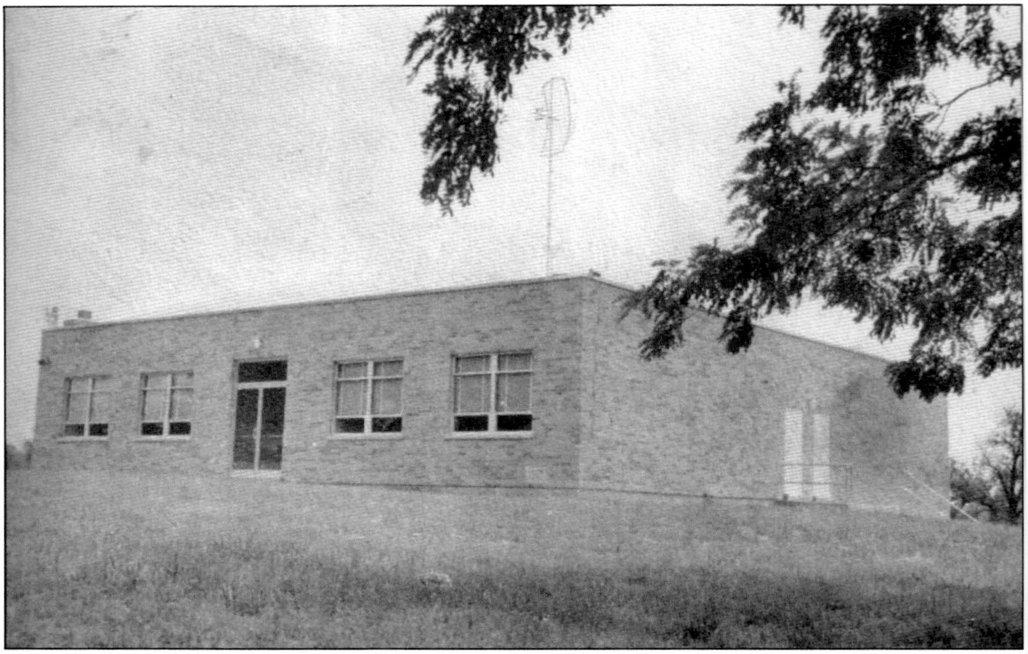

All Saints School. When All Saints Church was established as the parish for Walton-Verona in 1951, it contained two small classrooms to provide instruction for children. By the early 1960s, the classrooms were no longer able to hold the growing student body, and the men of the church joined together to plan for a new school. Dedicated in 1966, the new All Saints existed for only a few years before being closed, and it later reopened as St. Joseph's Academy by the Sisters of St. Joseph the Worker. (Courtesy of Mary Berkemeier.)

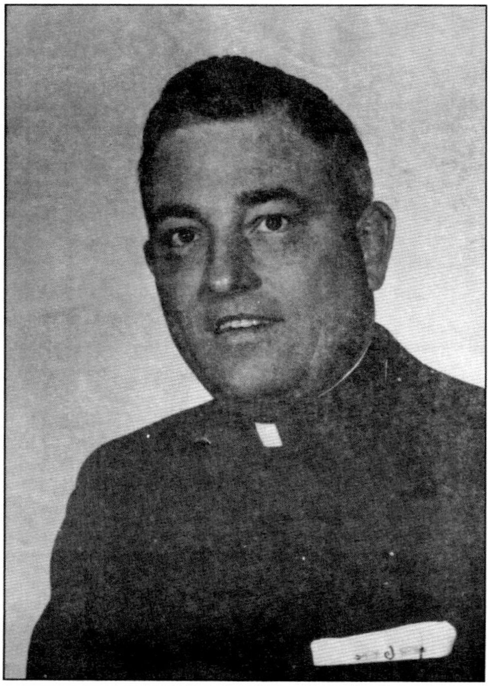

Forward Thinker. By 1962, the tiny classrooms at All Saint's Parish were bursting at the seams with students. Fr. Joseph Reuter met the problem head on by calling together the men of the parish to help solve the overcrowding problem. A building committee was formed and met with Father Reuter several times a week to make plans for a new school. The end result was the new All Saint's School, dedicated in 1966, a school that was later reopened as St. Joseph's Academy. (Courtesy of Mary Berkemeier.)

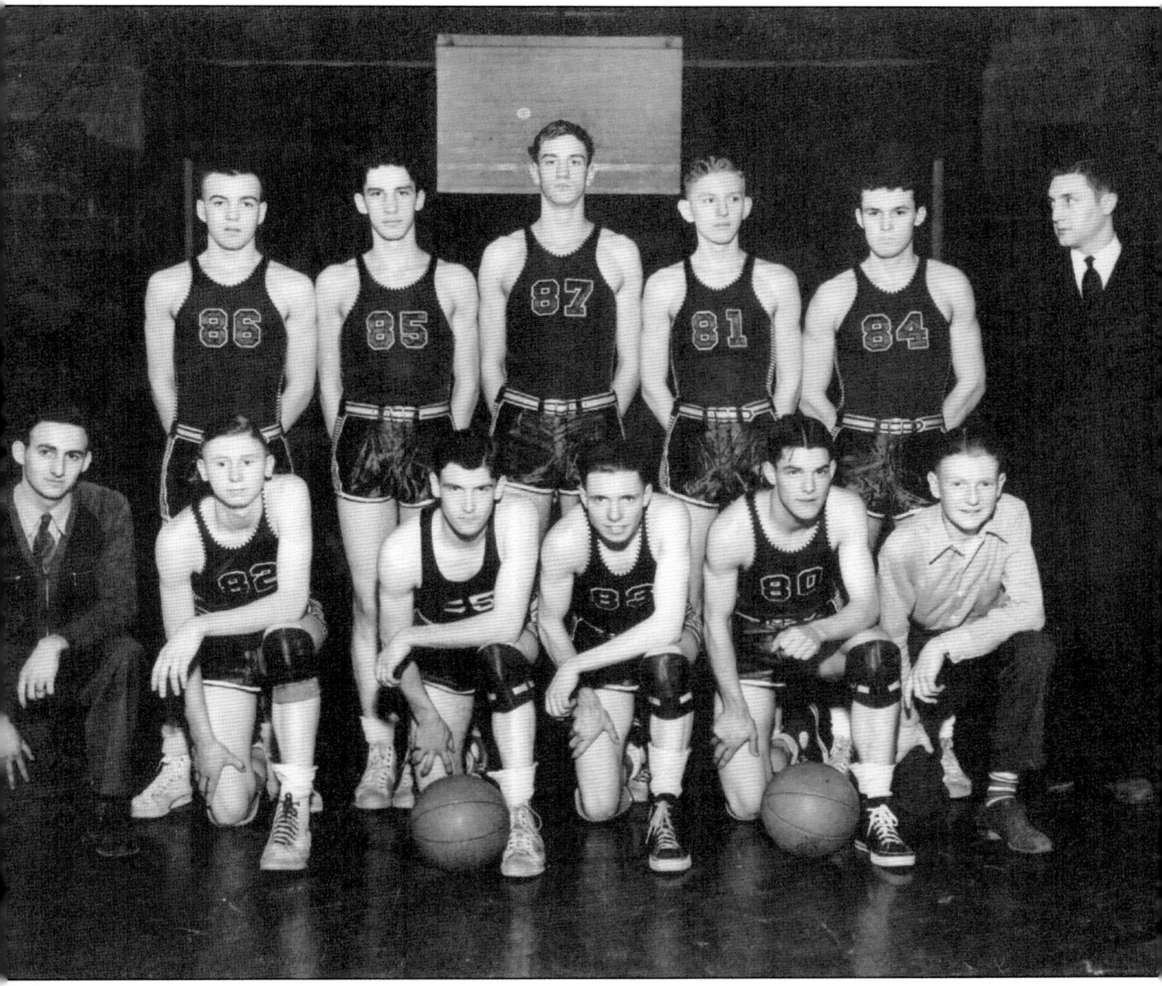

Walton-Verona Bearcats, 1942. The last time the Walton-Verona basketball team made the Kentucky state tournament was in 1942. Sadly, after the tournament was over, coach Lewis Shields was sent off to war ,where he was later killed in the Battle of the Bulge. The team, pictured from left to right, is (first row) manager James Dudgeon, Charles (Hunky) Holder, Cliff Ryan, Harry Mayhugh, Roy Coyle, and manager Jessie Thornton; (second row) Lawrence (Katie) Welsh, Stan McElroy, Truitt (Plucker) Demoisey, Russell Groger, Paul Simpson, and coach Shields. (Courtesy of Russell Groger.)

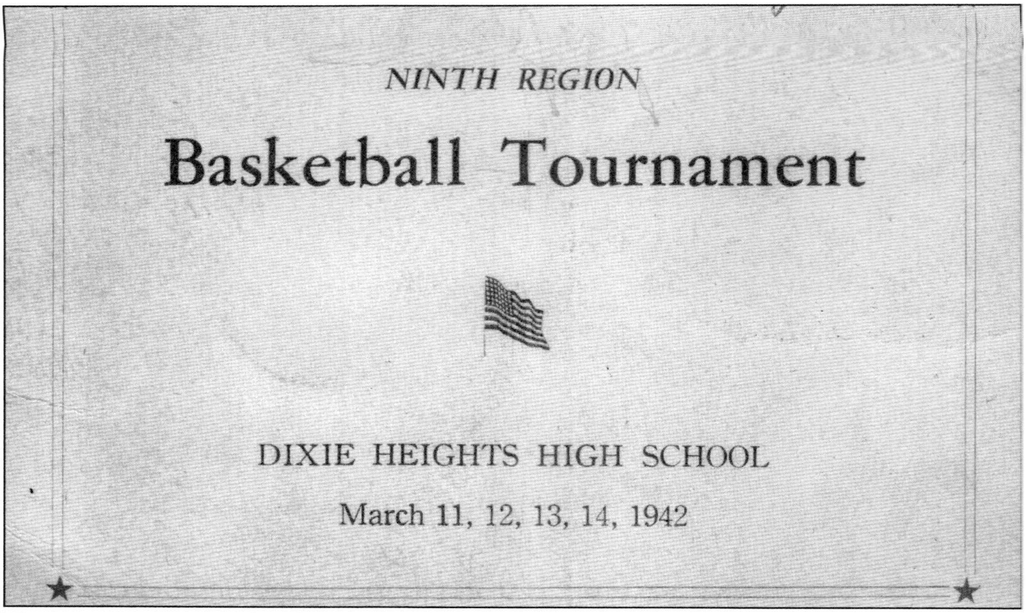
NINTH REGION

Basketball Tournament

DIXIE HEIGHTS HIGH SCHOOL

March 11, 12, 13, 14, 1942

TOURNAMENT. Pictured is the program from the Ninth Region Tournament, a tournament that featured perennial powerhouses such as Simon Kenton and Dixie Heights High Schools. For a small school like Walton-Verona to beat such opponents and go the state tournament was a major accomplishment on its own. Even though the team lost in the first round of the state tournament, that year was a great success for the basketball program. (Courtesy of Russell Groger.)

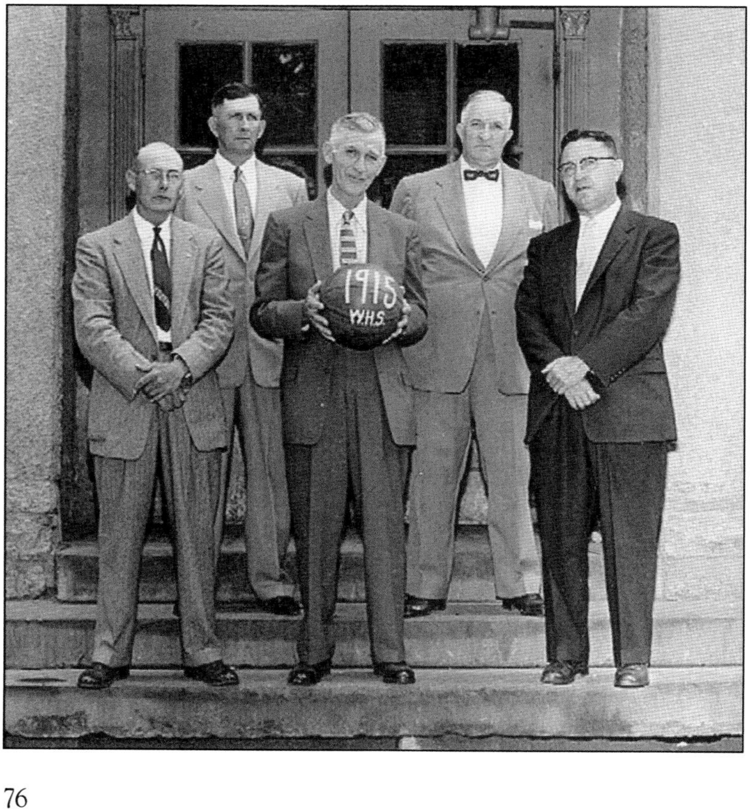

REUNION. A reunion of the 1915 basketball team took place in 1955. Roy Kenney (holding the basketball) joined teammates, from left to right, Kyle Nicholson, Lawrence McCart, W. Rice, and Dewey Benson to pose for the camera while standing on the steps of the gymnasium that was built years after they spent their playing time in tobacco barns. (Courtesy of the Boone County Public Library.)

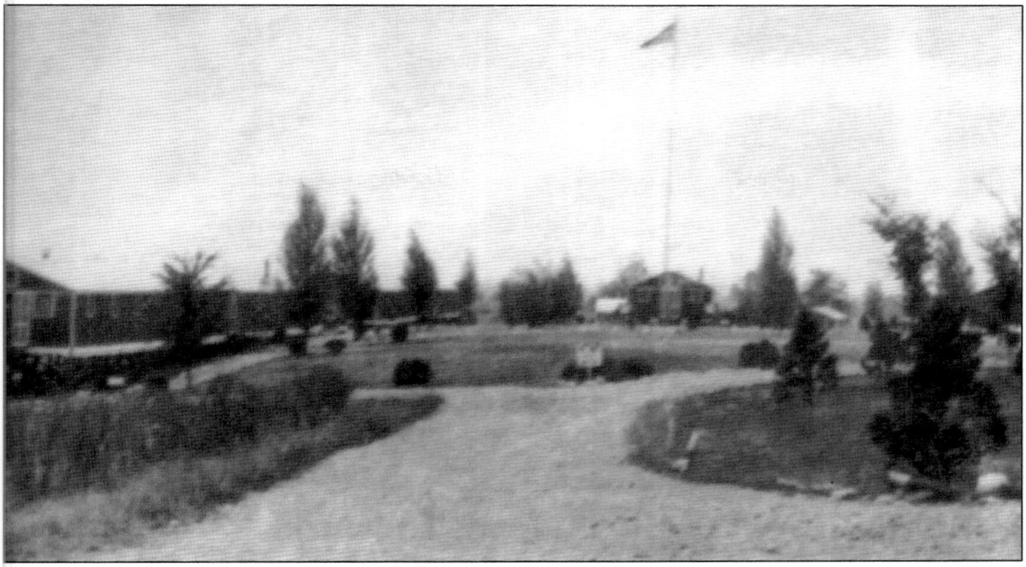

CCC Camp. The photographs on this page show the Civilian Conservation Corps camp, a group put together by the federal government during the Great Depression to provide jobs and training for young men. This camp was located at the end of present-day Alta Vista Drive facing School Road. After the corps abandoned the camp, it sat empty for many years, and the Walton-Verona school district eventually purchased it as the site for its new high school. (Both, courtesy of Russell Groger.)

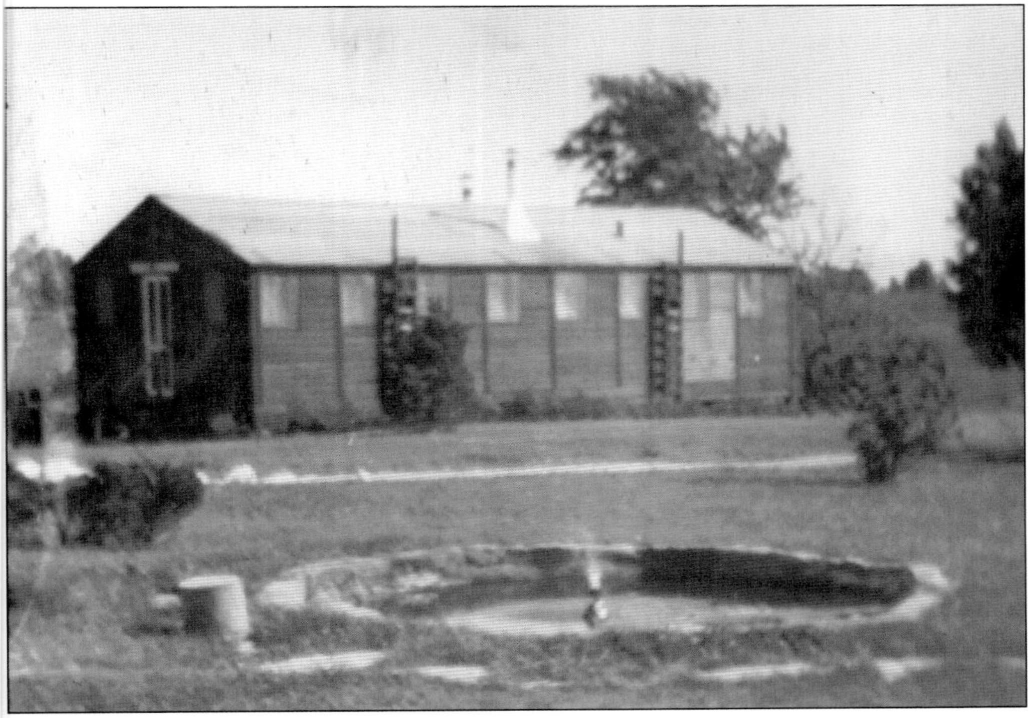

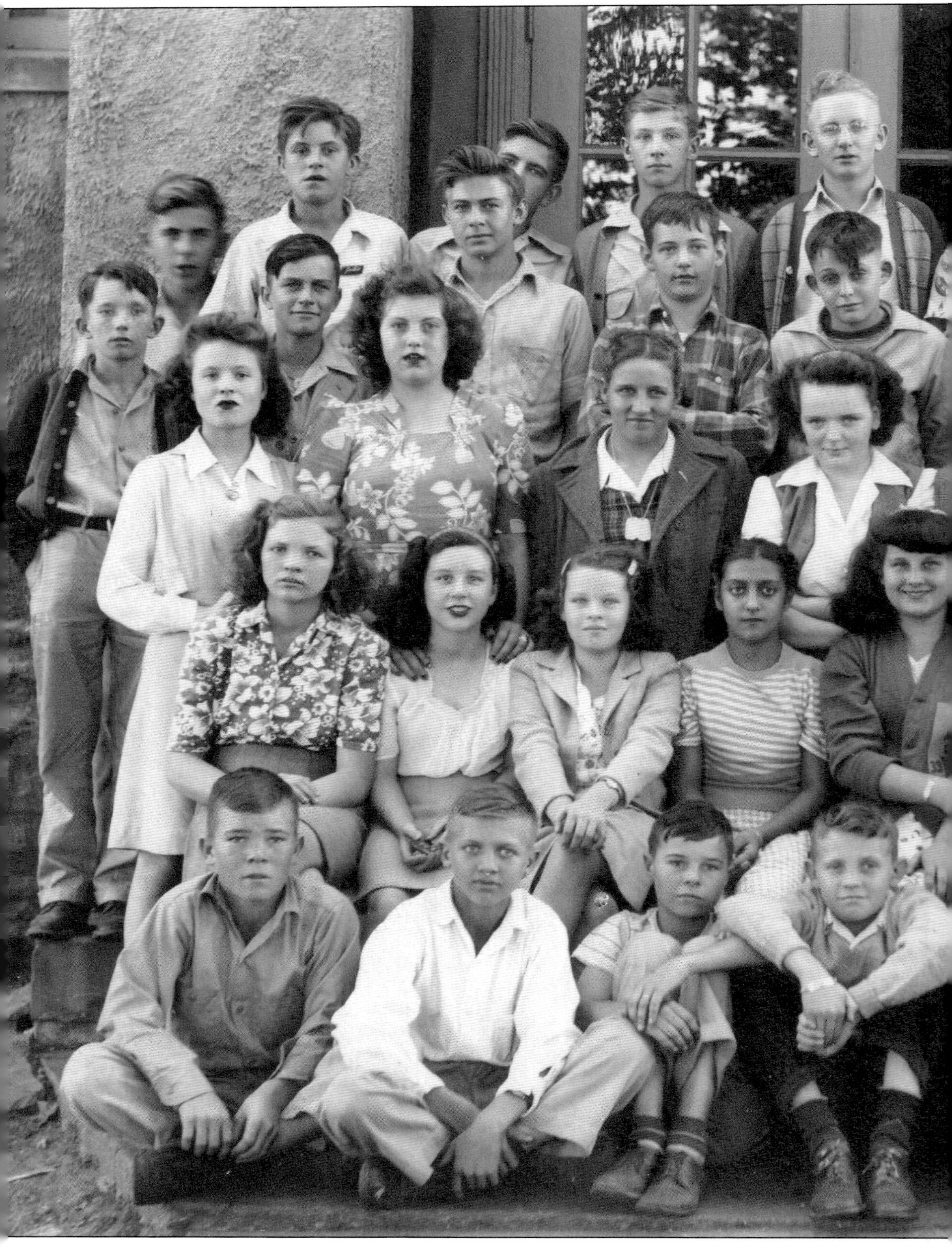

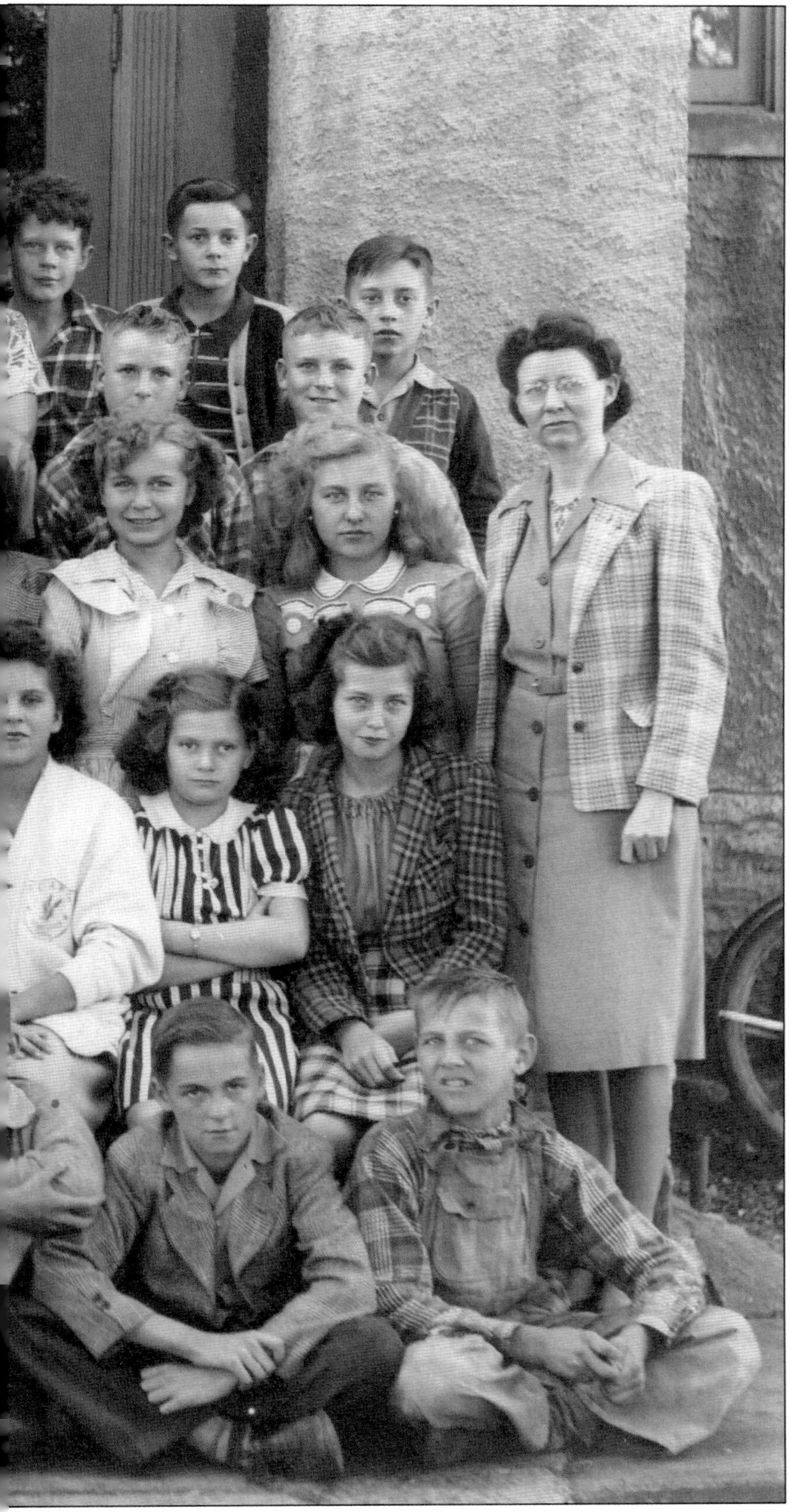

SCHOOL DAYS. Class pictures were part of the school experience, and this one from about 1947 is no exception. Longtime Walton residents will probably see many familiar names and faces. Pictured from left to right are (first row) C. Elmore, Charles Courtney, Wayne Menefee, Buddy Grubbs, Dennis Glacken, Gerald Dixon, and A. Linton; (second row) two unidentified, Patty Johnson, Ruth Northcutt, Louise Isbell, Wanda Caldwell, Betty Pennington, and Shirley Collins; (third row) Evelyn Runion, Alice Hiles, Mayme Brooks, Joyce McIntyre, Sue Messmer, Mary Howard, and Betty Lowell; (fourth row) Walter Leek, Gilbert Glenn, Carl Simmons, Maynard Meadows, Bob Hall, Tommy Leek, Don Woods, and Doug Woods; (fifth row) unidentified, Gene Simpson, Bubby Readnour, Mike Ryan, Elmer Groger, Don Rice, Tommy Pruett, Harvey Kennedy, and Jimmy Stephenson. Rebecca Sleet was the instructor. (Courtesy of Ruth Meadows.)

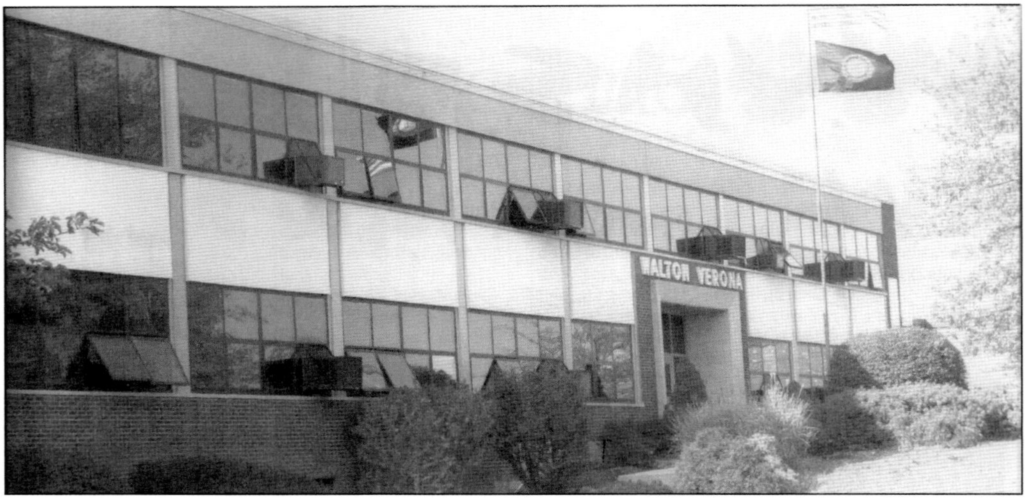

New School. By the 1950s, the Walton-Verona district was in dire need of a new high school building. The district secured funding to purchase the old CCC camp, and the new high school opened in 1954. A new elementary school was built in Verona in 1971. These schools served the district for many years, but population growth in both Walton and Verona, coupled with the district's reputation as one of the best in Northern Kentucky, made it necessary to expand to accommodate the growth. The new high school was opened in 2008, as an addition onto the old school that now serves a middle school, relieving the over-crowding at the elementary. Walton-Verona Independent Schools continues to be a desirable school district for young families, having for the second year in a row been named in the *U.S. News & World Report*'s top schools. (Both, courtesy of Walton-Verona Independent Schools.)

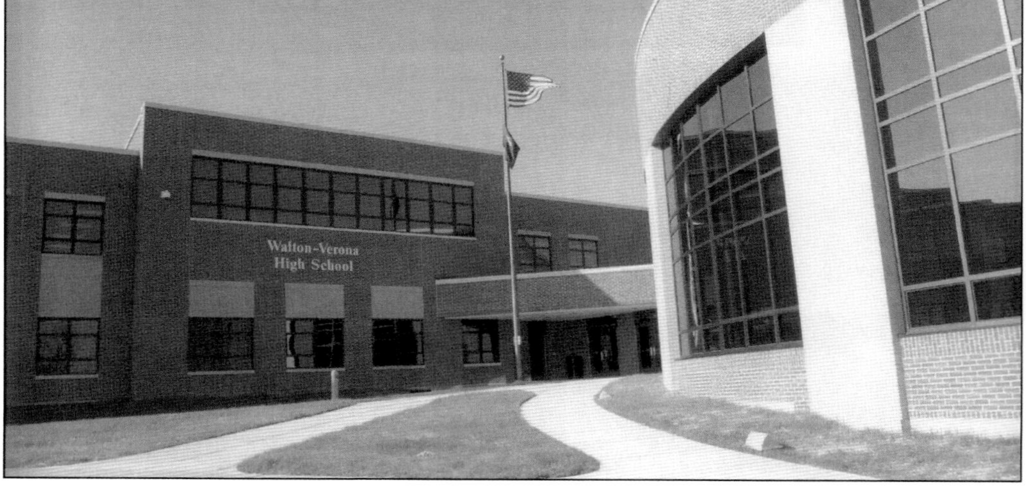

Five

People

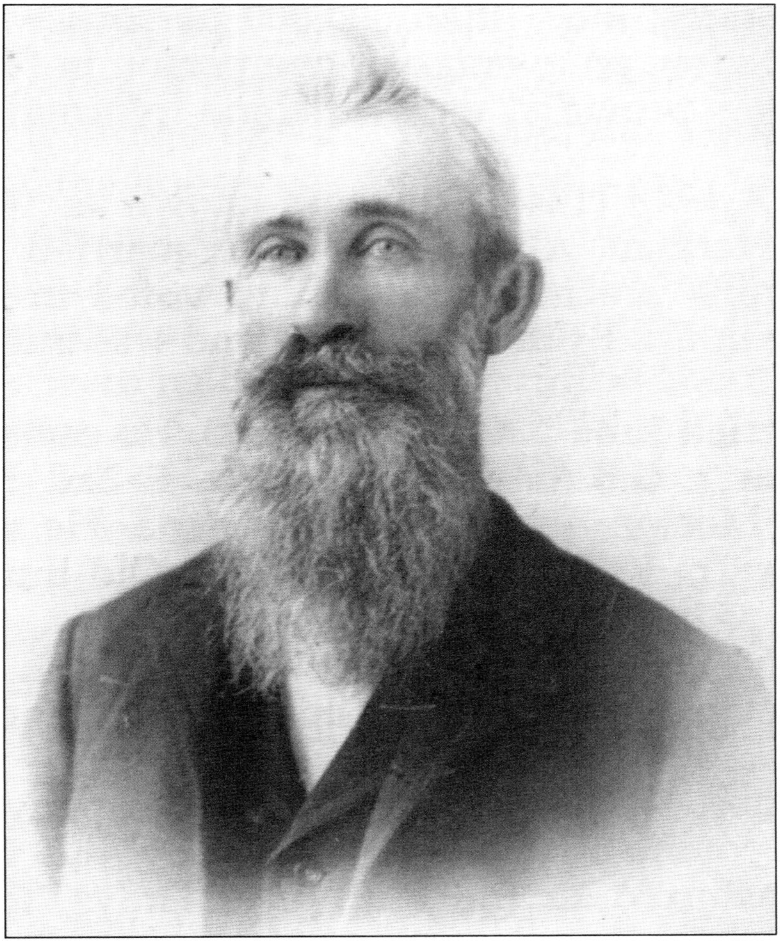

Confederate Soldier. Joseph Glenn enlisted in Company B of Jessee's Battalion Mounted Rifles CSA, signing up at Beaver Lick in 1862. In 1863, he was captured and sent to Vicksburg for an exchange. After the war, he settled in Walton, where he married and lived for many years. Glenn and his family are buried in Walton Cemetery. (Courtesy of the City of Walton.)

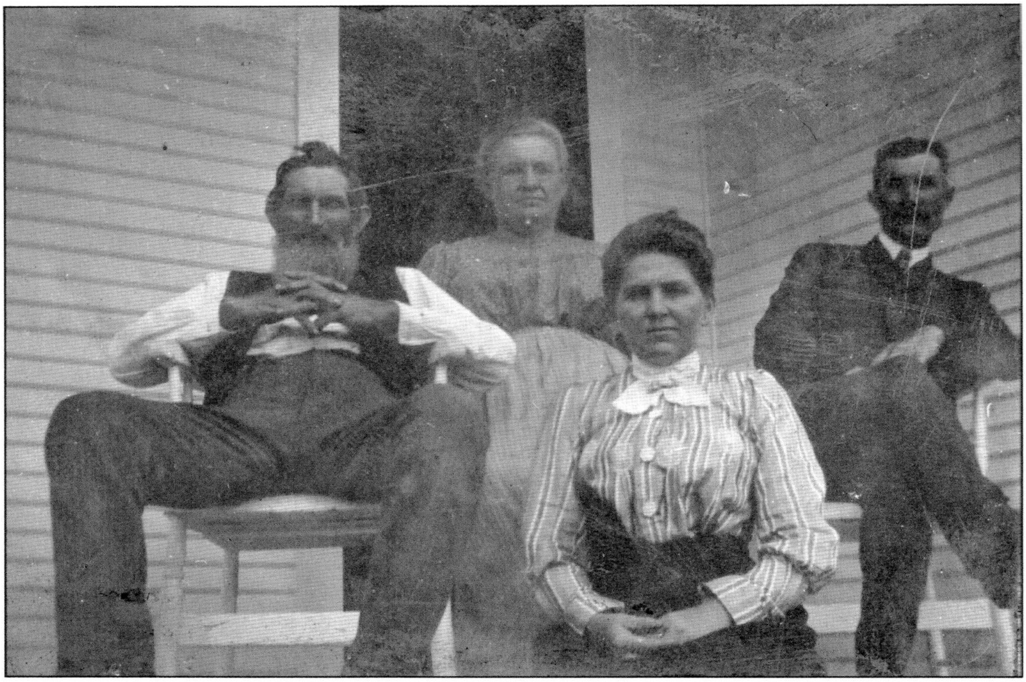

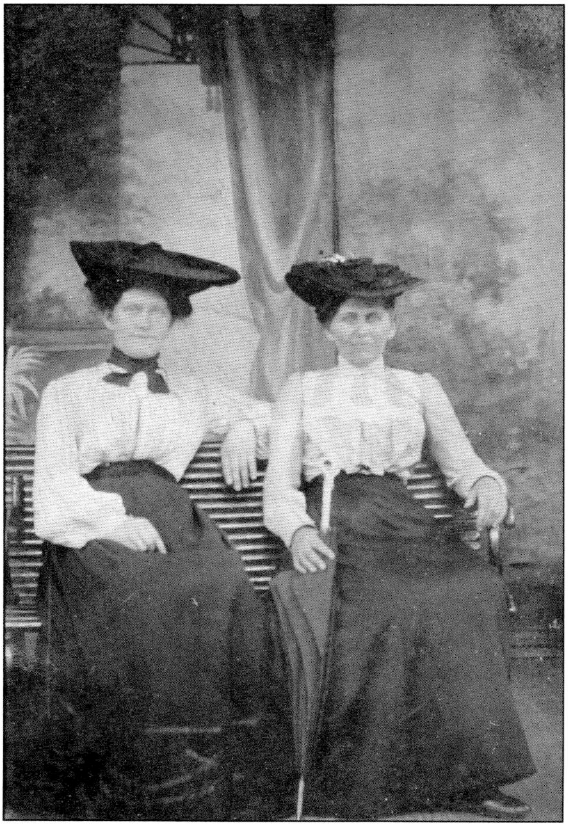

Taylor Family. Samuel Taylor owned a large farm between Beaver Lick and Richwood, near the Richwood Presbyterian Church and part of the Walton and Verona precinct. His daughter Belle married Thomas Jefferson Hutsell from Kenton County (pictured above). Belle Taylor gets stylish with her younger sister Stella in this *c.* 1900 photograph on a visit to Coney Island. Stella lived in the Walton precinct with her father, Samuel Taylor, on the 1900 census, but she died soon after at young age. (Both, courtesy of Kathleen Wiley.)

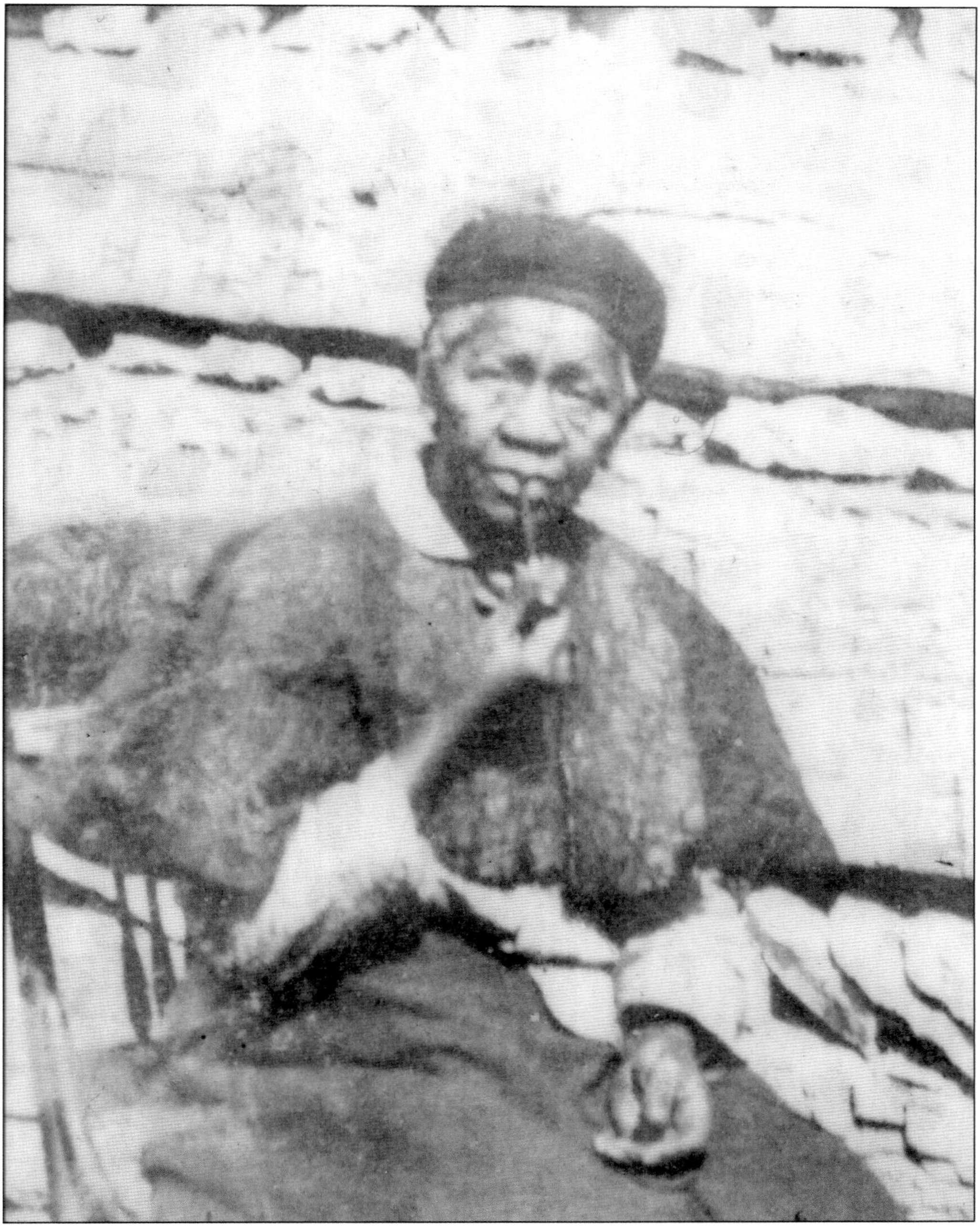

Betty Steele. The Steele family was an important part of the Zion Church community that grew up around Church Street after the Civil War. Aunt Betty was a freed slave who came to Walton with her husband to work, bought her own cabin, and raised her children. Her son Laton was an early deacon of the Zion Church, and his daughter Gladys married into the Ingram family, another stalwart church family. This photograph of Betty sitting in front of her cabin smoking a pipe was a common sight in the community, and she usually baked the bread for church communion. Betty died in 1923 at the age of 90, having lived a long and eventful life. (Courtesy of Zion Baptist Church.)

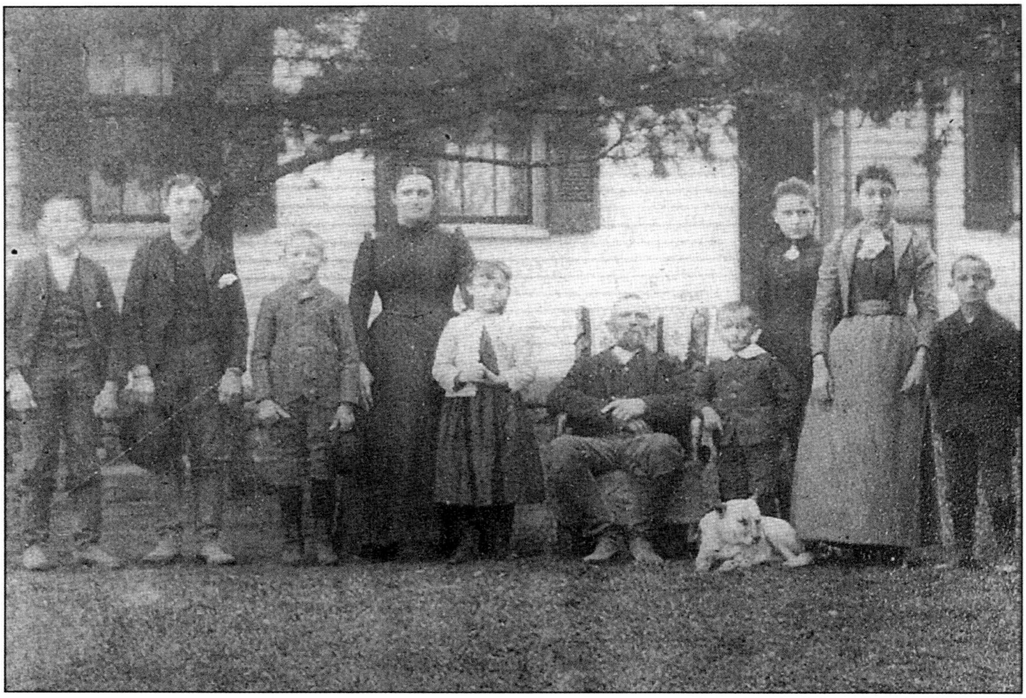

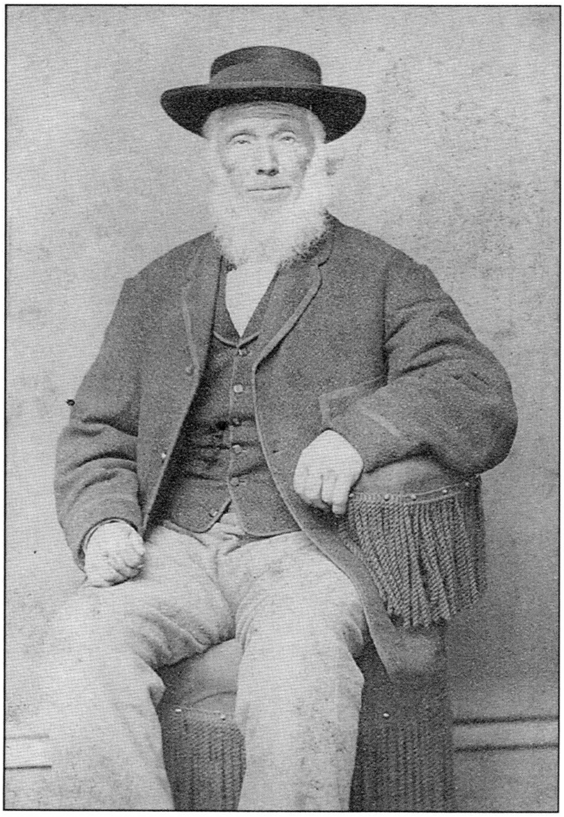

PERCIVAL FAMILY. This faded photograph of the Ira Percival family c. 1890 was taken in front of the old Percival homestead near Walton. The Percival family owned a large amount of land from the end of Cruise's Creek Road out toward Banklick Creek in Kenton County. Ira's brother Orrin was vice president of the Walton Deposit Bank, his other brother Henry was sheriff of Kenton County, and Ira himself had been a hotel keeper in Walton (the same location as the present-day Waltonian) until it burned, killing his young son. Ira and his second wife, Sarah Baker, lived on the farm on Percival Road, raising a large family until Ira's death in 1899. Orrin Percival Sr. (pictured at left) was the patriarch of the Percival family, and the family homestead he built in the mid-19th century still stands on Walton-Nicholson Road, the original log cabin recently discovered intact while the owners were doing renovations. (Both, courtesy of Margaret Percival Armstrong.)

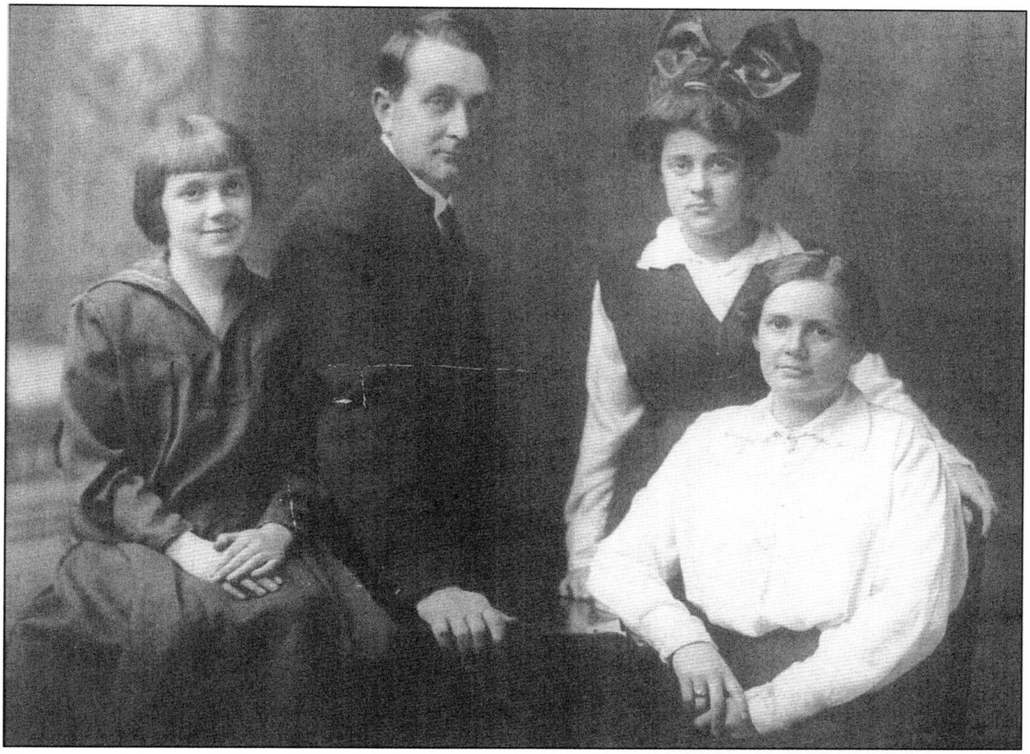

CHAMBERS FAMILY. When C. Scott Chambers moved his family to Walton from Petersburg, Kentucky, little did he know that it was the beginning of the longest-running business in Walton. Pictured from left to right are the young family, Mary Scott, C. Scott, Aleen, and Alta (Terrill) Chambers. Later on the Chambers would adopt another child, Ella Mae, making their family complete. (Courtesy of Janice Grubbs.)

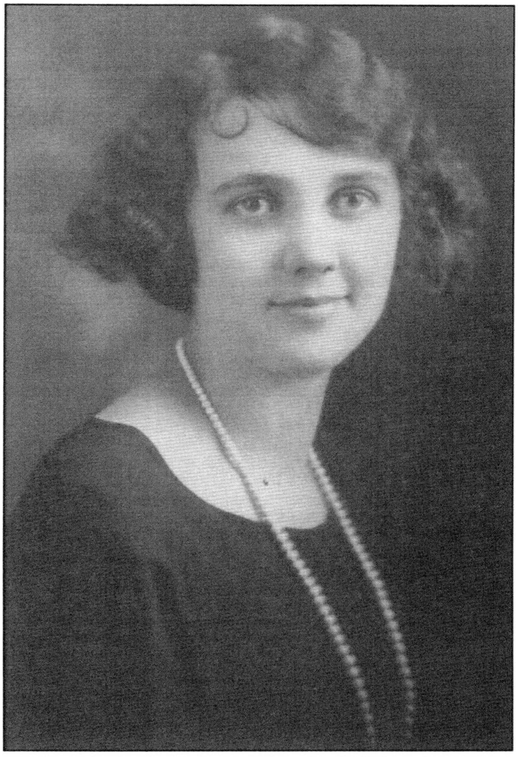

FATHER'S FOOTSTEPS. Young Mary Chambers became interested in the funeral business at an early age, conducting her first service at the age of 13. When she was old enough, she took the train to Cincinnati to attend the embalming school, and after she graduated, she became the first licensed female funeral director in Kentucky. The connector road from Interstate 75 to Main Street is named Mary C. Grubbs Highway after this female pioneer. (Courtesy of Janice Grubbs.)

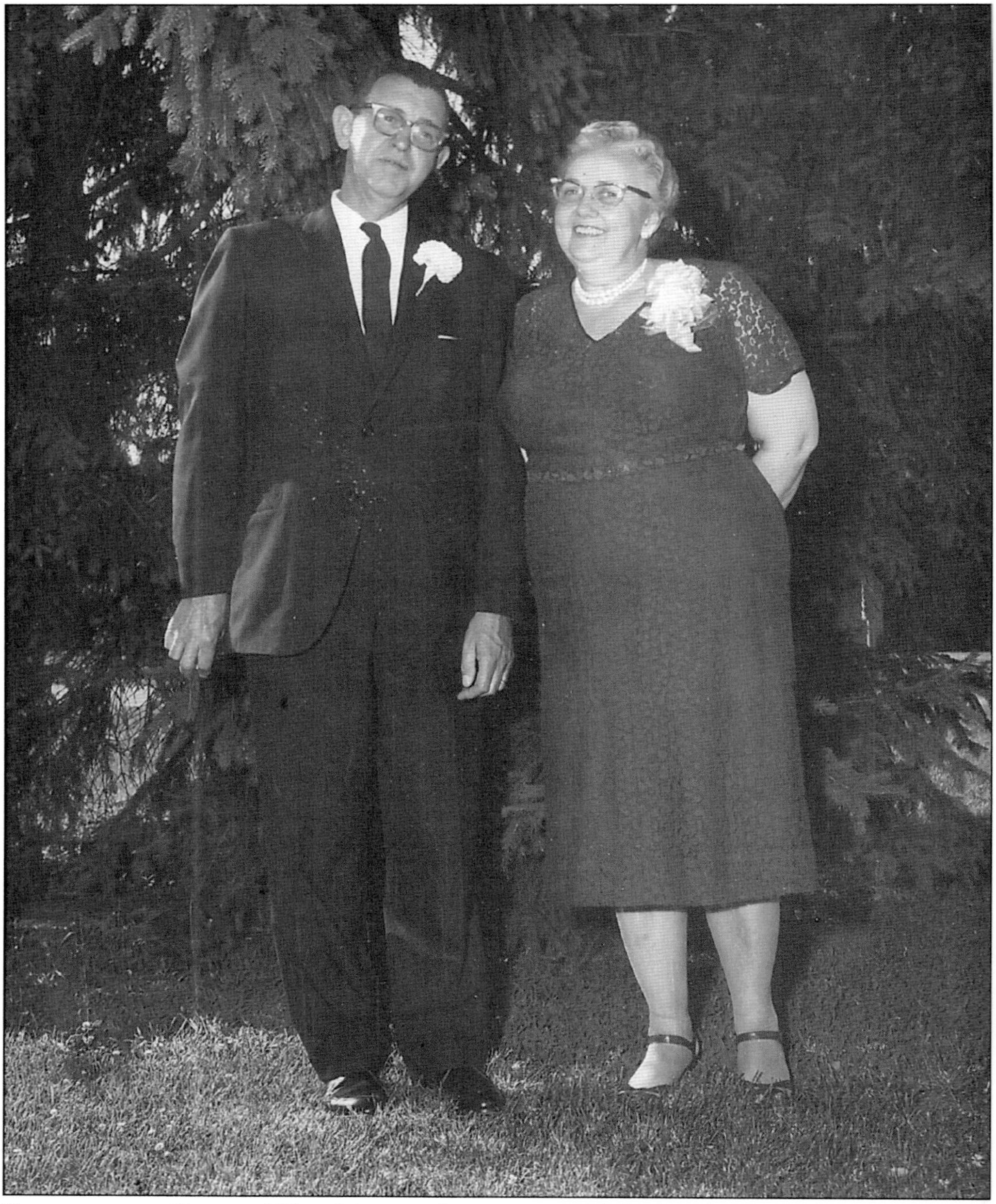

CHAMBERS AND GRUBBS. When Mary was becoming established in the funeral business, she met and married Wallace Grubbs. Grubbs soon developed an interest as well, becoming a licensed director in order to join his wife in their business venture. The Chambers and Grubbs Funeral Home was originally run out of a small brick home on North Main Street, and Grubbs, seeing the need for more room, arranged to have the beautiful home built at its current location on the corner of Alta Vista Drive and Main Street. (Courtesy of Janice Grubbs.)

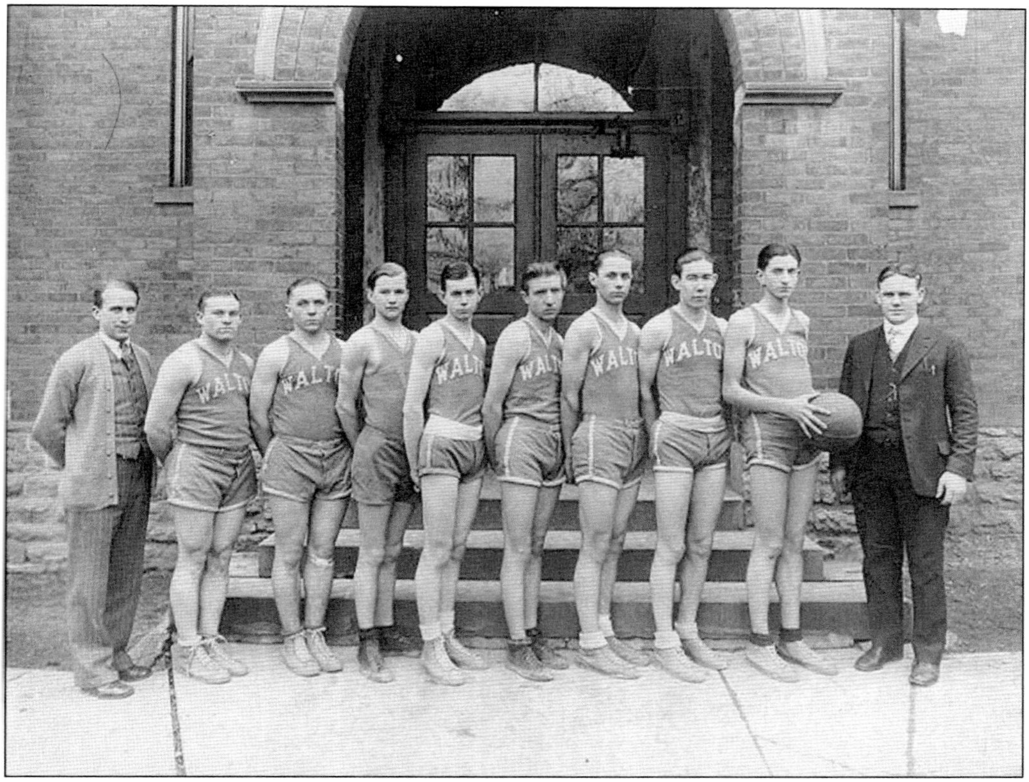

Basketball Great. John "Frenchy" DeMoisey had the distinction of being one of the legendary coach Adolph Rupp's first recruits for the University of Kentucky. Even though he played for a small school, he caught Rupp's eye, and Rupp convinced him to attend Kentucky. DeMoisey had planned on attending Duke University, but after listening to what Rupp had to say, decided to stay close to home. A multisport player, DeMoisey also played for the university baseball team, having been a member of the 1929 Boone County League champions. In the 1928 team photograph, DeMoisey is holding the basketball, and looks little like the player he became a few years later under the guidance of Adolph Rupp. DeMoisey was an All-SEC selection in 1933 and 1934 and was named an All-American in 1934 while serving as captain of the Kentucky Wildcat team. (Above, courtesy of Bernie Spencer, www.nkyviews.com; right, courtesy of Ruth Meadows.)

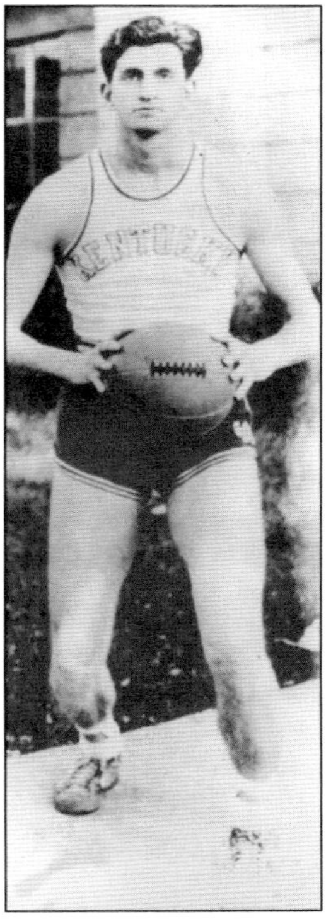

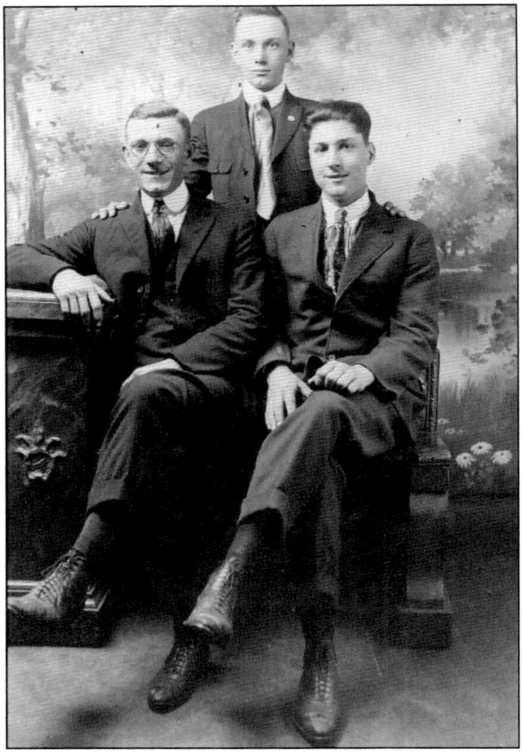

DASHING YOUNG MEN. These young men from Verona make a dashing trio in this *c.* 1920 photograph. All were from prominent Verona families with backgrounds in farming and retail. Pictured from left to right are a Mr. Kennedy, Howard McClure, and John William Powers. (Courtesy of Paul Webster.)

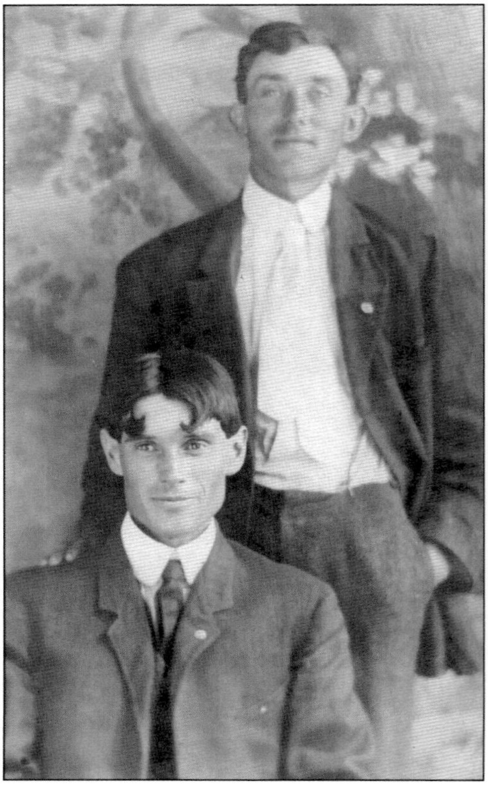

MORE DASHING YOUNG MEN. The Osborne brothers pose for the camera in another *c.* 1920 photograph, proving that Walton could produce handsome young men as well as Verona. The Osborne family lived on High School Court in Walton. (Courtesy of Ruth Meadows.)

WALTON POSTMISTRESS. Mildred Cleek served the citizens for many years working for the U.S. Postal Service, moving up from an assistant to head postmistress in the 1960s. She served in that capacity until 1979. (Courtesy of Bernie Spencer, www.nkyviews.com.)

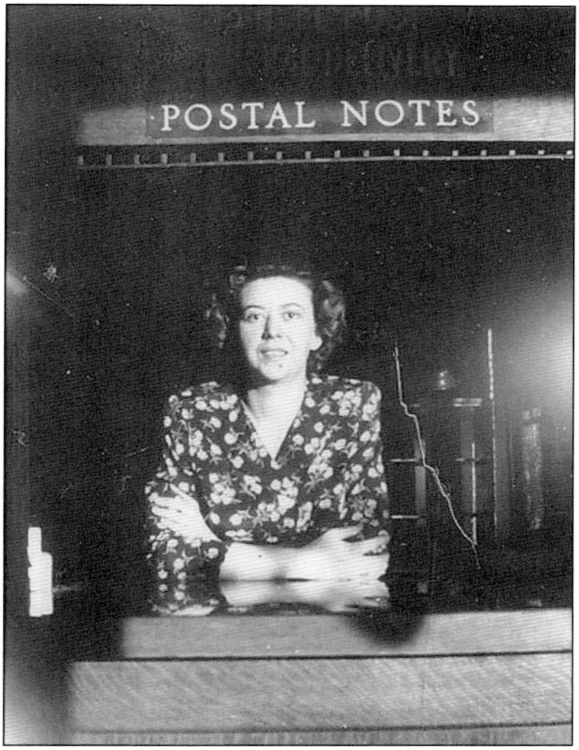

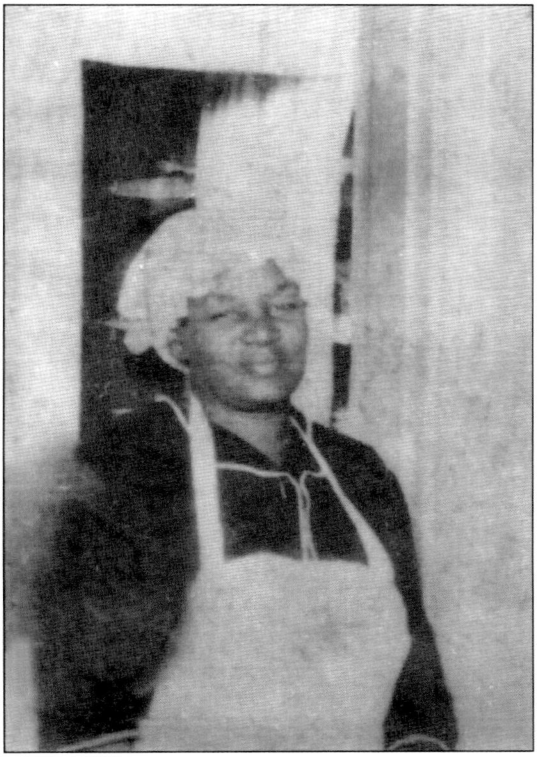

AUNT LOU JOHNSON. This faded photograph shows Lou Johnson while at work. She was the first cook for the old Phoenix Hotel in Walton and was an active member of the Zion Baptist Church community. (Courtesy of Zion Baptist Church.)

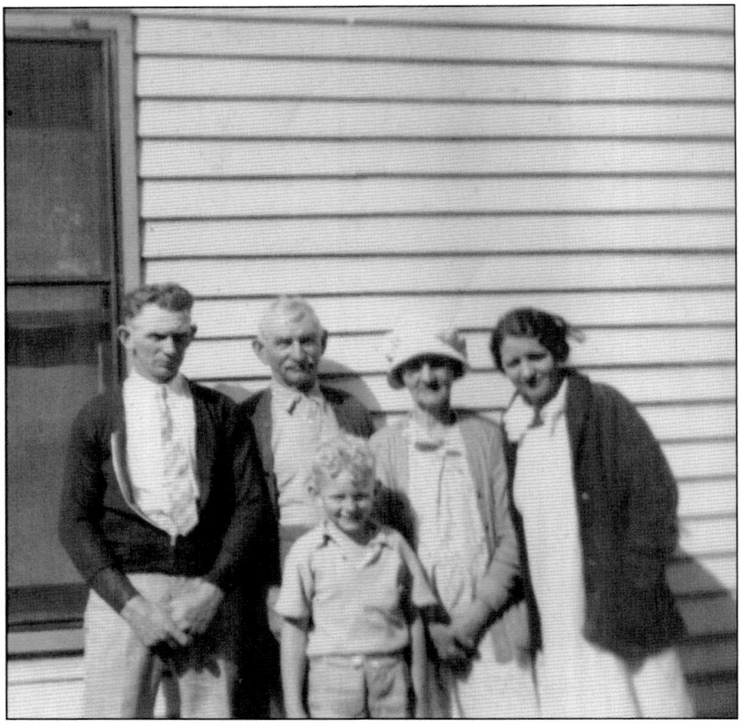

GROGER FAMILY. The Groger family, originally from Kenton County, moved south to a farm just outside of Walton. Later on Gilbert Groger (pictured at far left) would help launch Groger Truck Line, a company that served the Walton area for almost 70 years. (Courtesy of Russell Groger.)

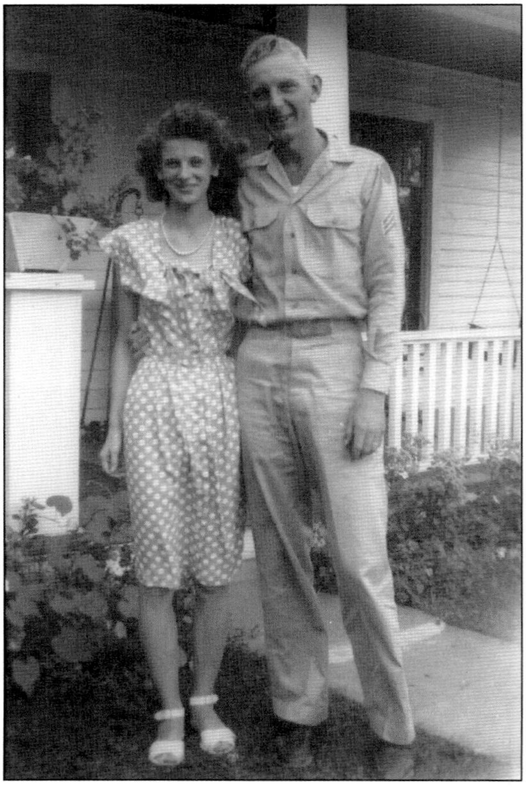

NEXT GENERATION. Russell Groger not only helped run the family business, but he also found time to be fire chief of Walton. He previously played on the 1942 basketball team that made the state tournament. Pictured here are Groger and his wife, Alberta, who is from nearby Independence. (Courtesy of Russell Groger.)

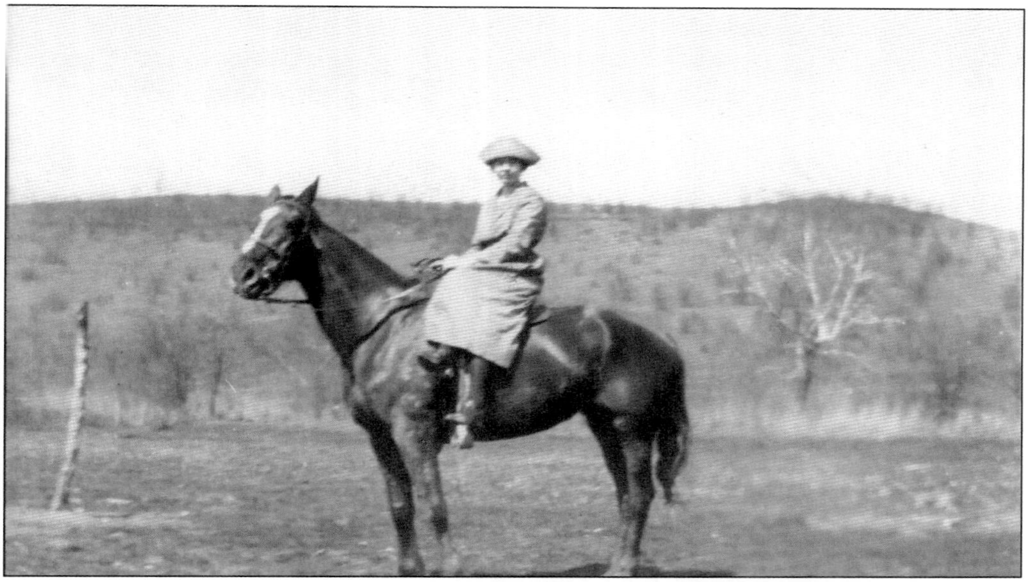

A TALENTED COUPLE. Agnes Chandler was a teacher for Boone County Schools and spent some time teaching at Verona. She shows her grace and elegance while on horseback in this *c.* 1920 photograph. Her husband, Roy Kenney, was from Beaver Lick and graduated from Walton High School, where he played basketball for the 1915 Bearcats. Kenney is shown at right working in his barn on their farm on Beaver Road. He also had a variety of interests, including photography and tennis, and could be seen playing tennis on the court he put in his yard. (Both, courtesy of Kathleen Wiley.)

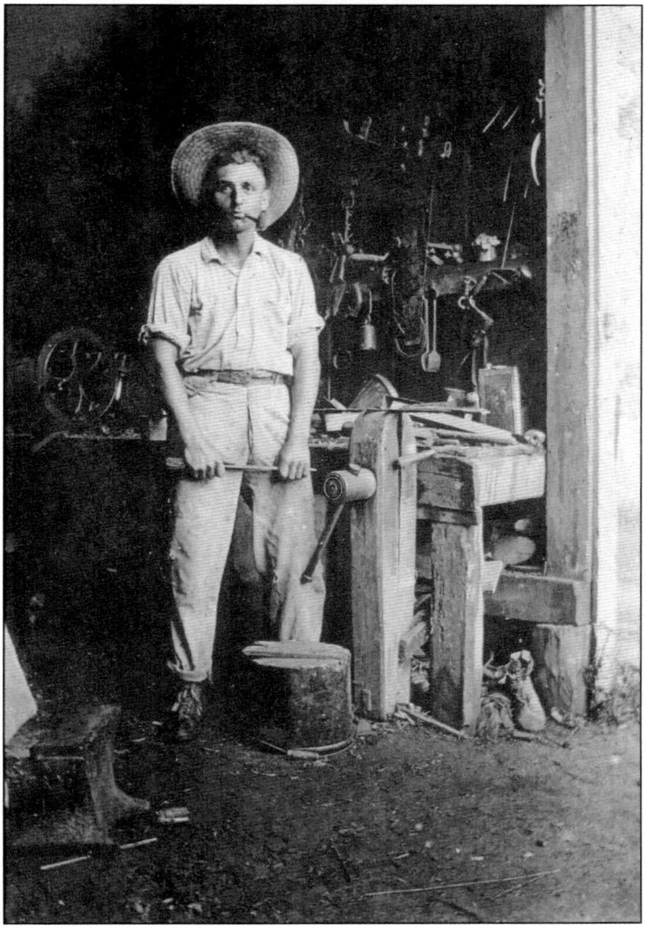

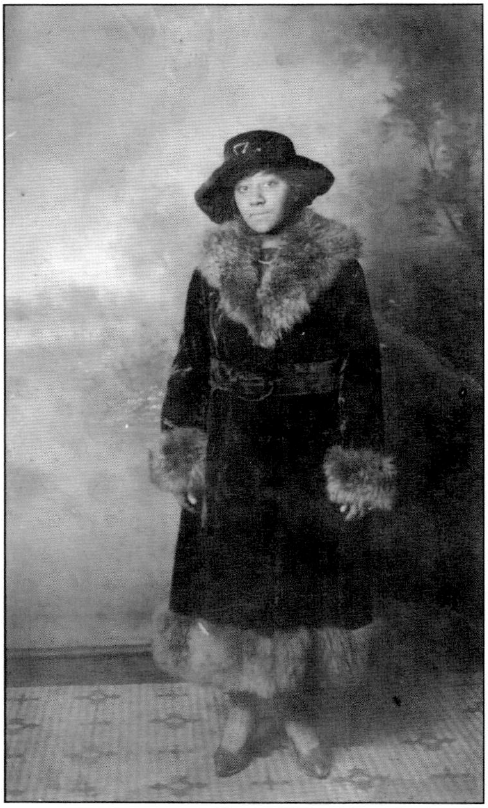

Strike a Pose. Martha Johnson (left) and Amelia Dixon show off their fashion sense in these *c.* 1920 photographs. The Johnson family was an integral part of the Zion Baptist Church community. Amelia was the daughter of Steve and Amanda Brown and lived on Church Street. She later enlisted as an aviation cadet in the Women's Corps during World War II. (Both, courtesy of Zion Baptist Church.)

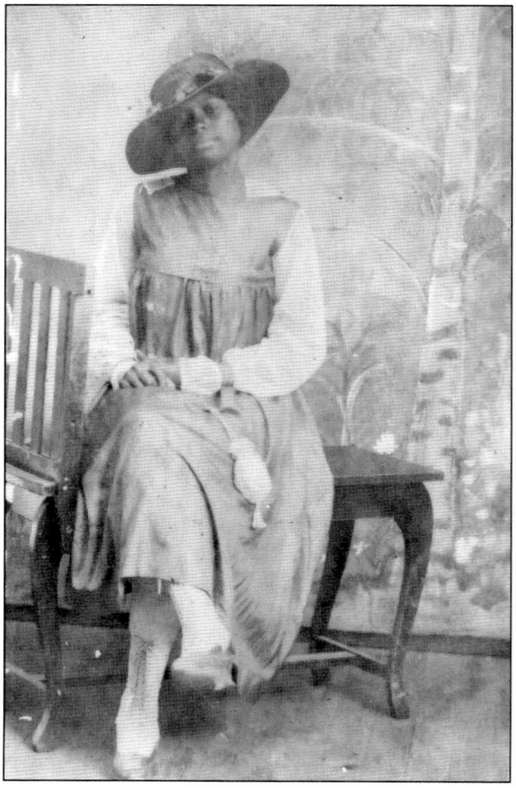

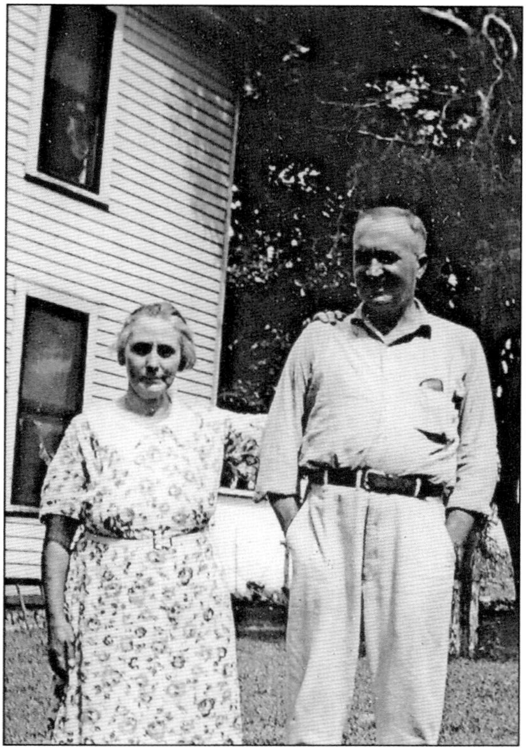

Happy Couple. Edwin and Mary Percival Johnson pose in the side yard of their home on North Main Street in Walton. Edwin Johnson was the son of Rev. LaFayette Johnson, earliest pastor of the First Baptist Church, and Frances Mullins Johnson. Johnson spent his life as a farmer and a conservation officer. Mary Johnson was the daughter of Ira and Sarah Baker Percival. (Courtesy of Margaret Percival Armstrong.)

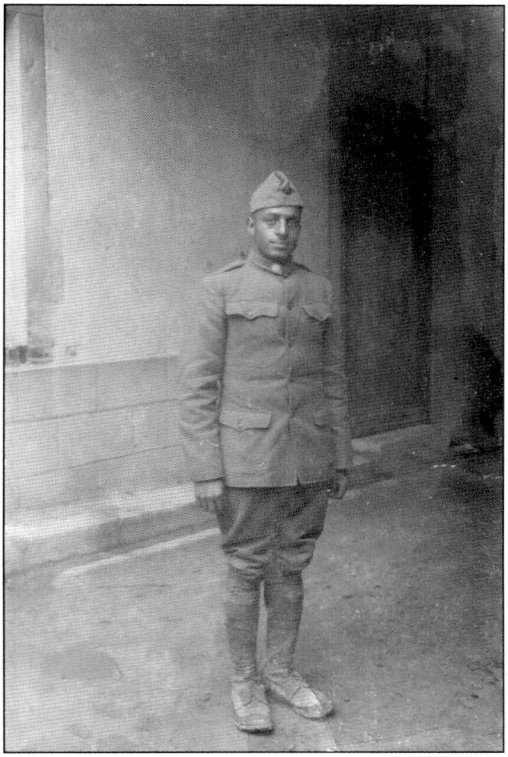

Proud Soldier. Jesse Sechrest poses for the camera in his military uniform during World War I. Sechrest was originally from the Mount Zion area, just over the Grant County line. He married Mary Sleet from Beaver Lick, and they were active in the Zion Baptist Church until her untimely death in 1933. He then moved from the area, spending the rest of his life in Covington, Kentucky. (Courtesy of Zion Baptist Church.)

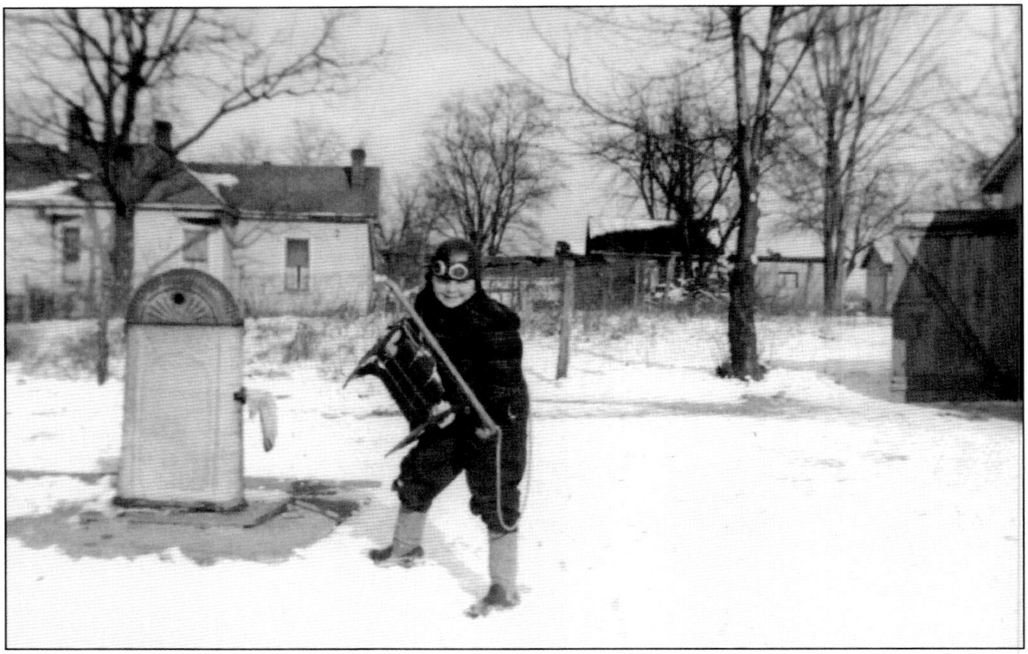

Playtime. Billy Wynn gets ready for some sledding in this 1930s photograph. The backyard was behind the houses on North Main Street next door to Tom Percival's home. Billy later joined the navy during World War II, eventually becoming a member of the air force during college. He served in Korea and Vietnam. (Courtesy of Charlie "Hunky" Holder.)

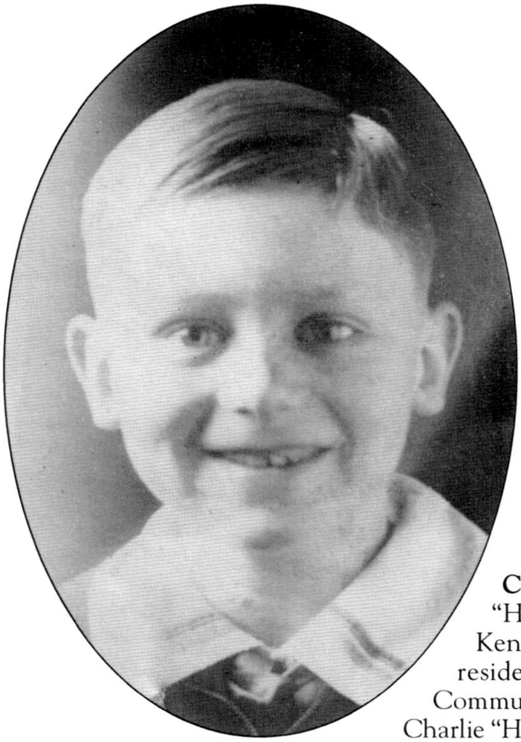

Cute Kid. Charlie Holder, forever known as "Hunky," moved to Walton from Vanceburg, Kentucky, as a young child. A lifelong Walton resident, Holder worked for many years for the Community Public Service Company. (Courtesy of Charlie "Hunky" Holder.)

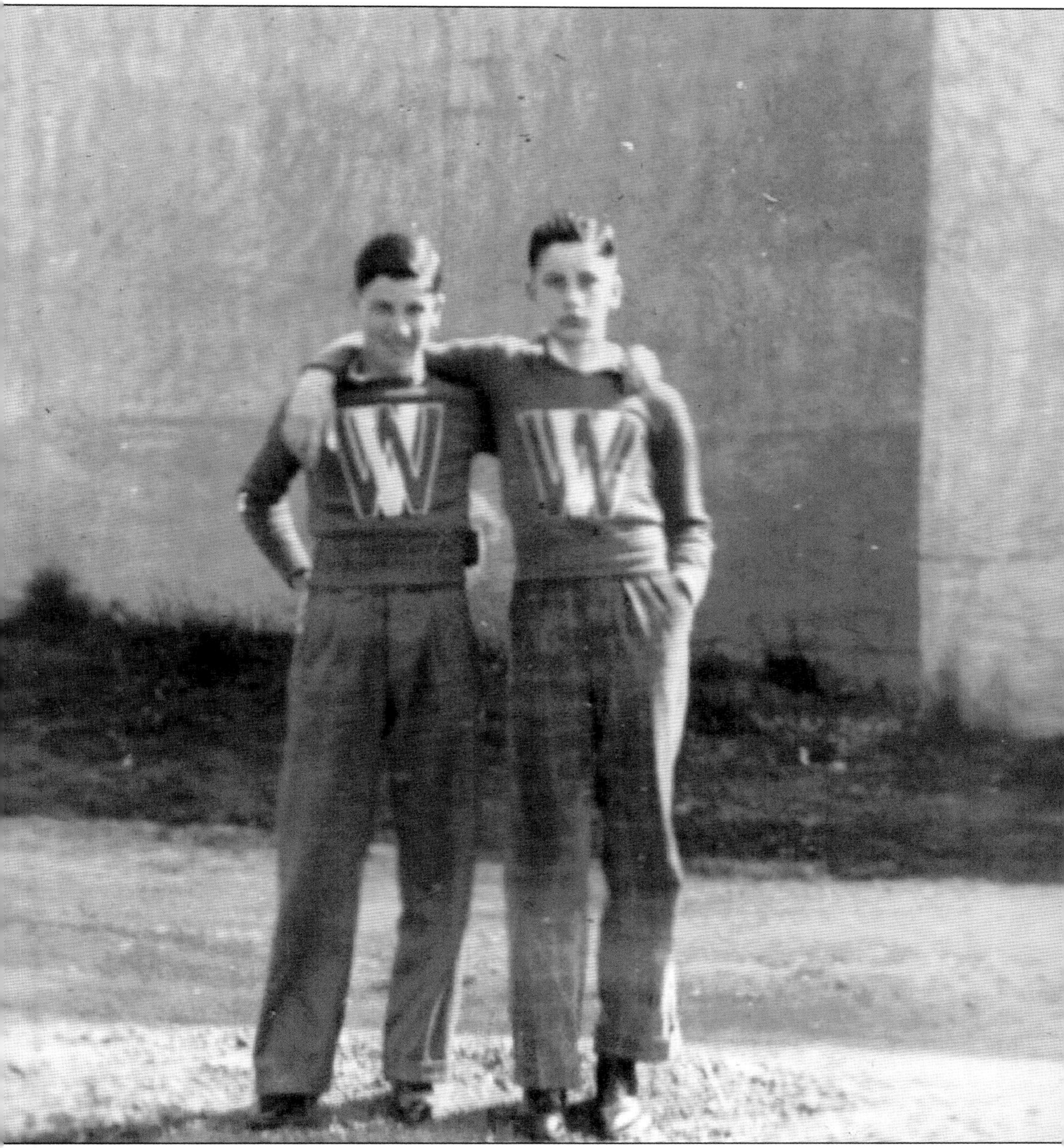

Best Buddies. Cliff Ryan and Stanley McElroy pose in front of the school gymnasium in this late-1930s photograph. Walton and Verona schools had consolidated in 1935, and the boys are proudly wearing their sweaters with the new logo. Ryan and McElroy played for the high school basketball team that went to the state tournament in 1942. The McElroy family had several business interests in town, and Ryan later owned Ryan's Hardware and Dry Goods. (Courtesy of Russell Groger.)

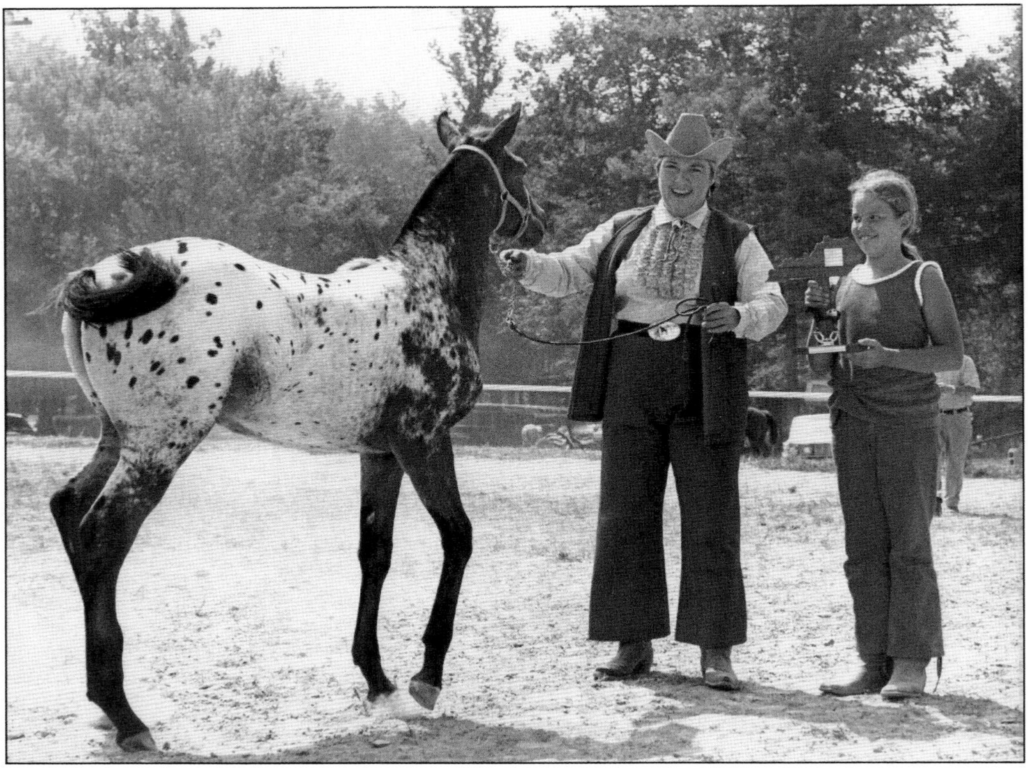

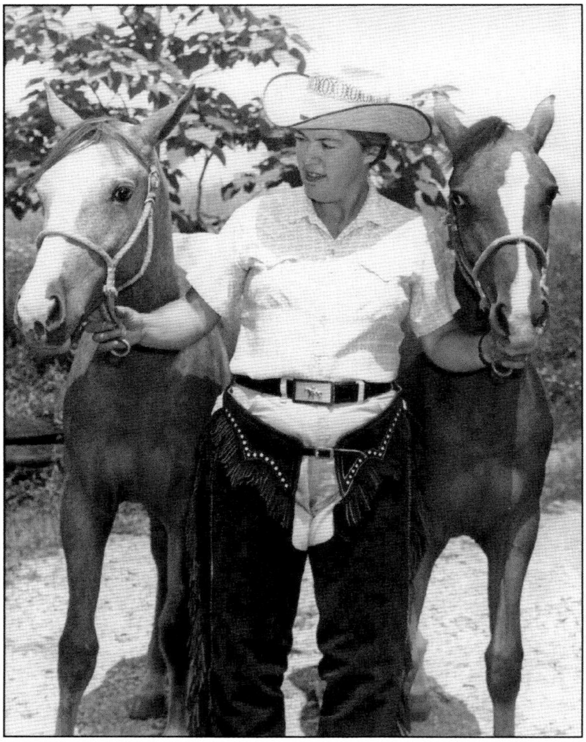

Award Winner. Pat Scott is recognizable to most people for her career as a pitcher with the All-American Girls baseball team during the 1940s. She was inducted into the Baseball Hall of Fame in 1989. After her playing days were over, Scott obtained a zoology degree from the University of Kentucky and spent many years in the medical field. Always a horse lover, she followed her dreams and opened her own business, M-Bar-S Farm, training registered Appaloosa horses. These photographs show Scott with some of her beloved horses. (Both, courtesy of Pat Scott.)

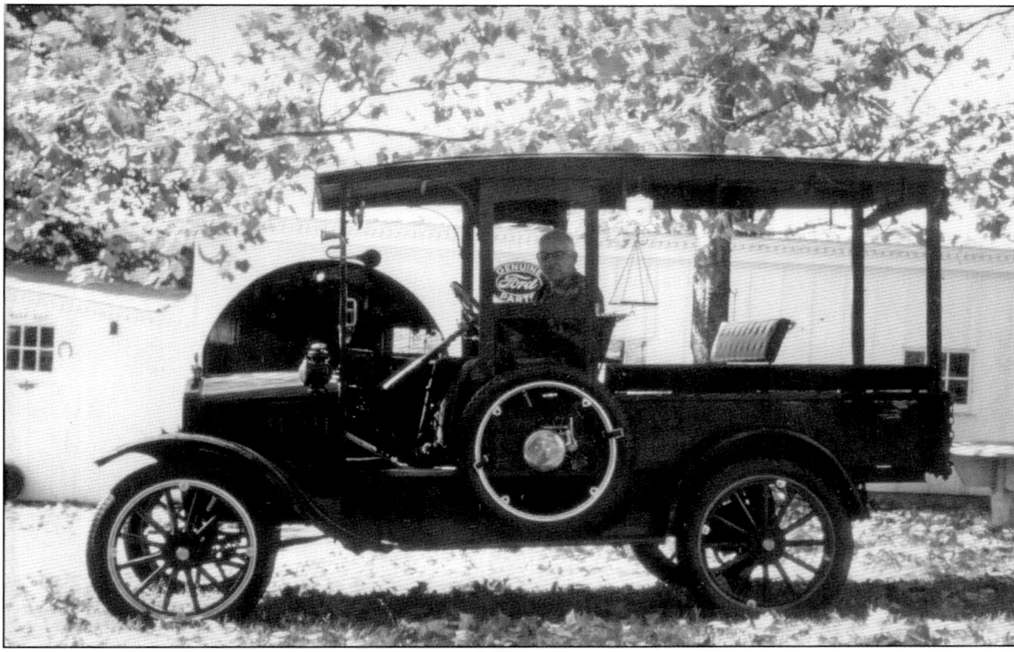

Antique Lovers. Col. John Gault and his wife, Madeline, share a laugh in the front yard of their Federal-style mansion (at right). Colonel Gault spent his life in Walton doing what he loved, collecting and selling antiques and restoring his home, the old Abner Gaines house, to its prior beauty after years of neglect. Especially fond of antique cars, he amassed quite a collection that he stored in a big garage behind the house. He is pictured above in one of his beloved antique cars, and the garage is the building with the old Ford sign on it. (Both, courtesy of Johnny Gault.)

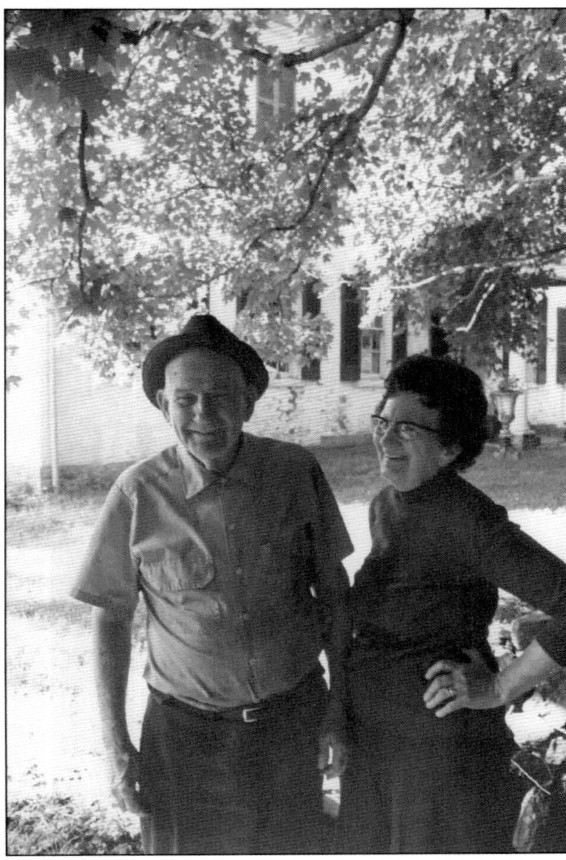

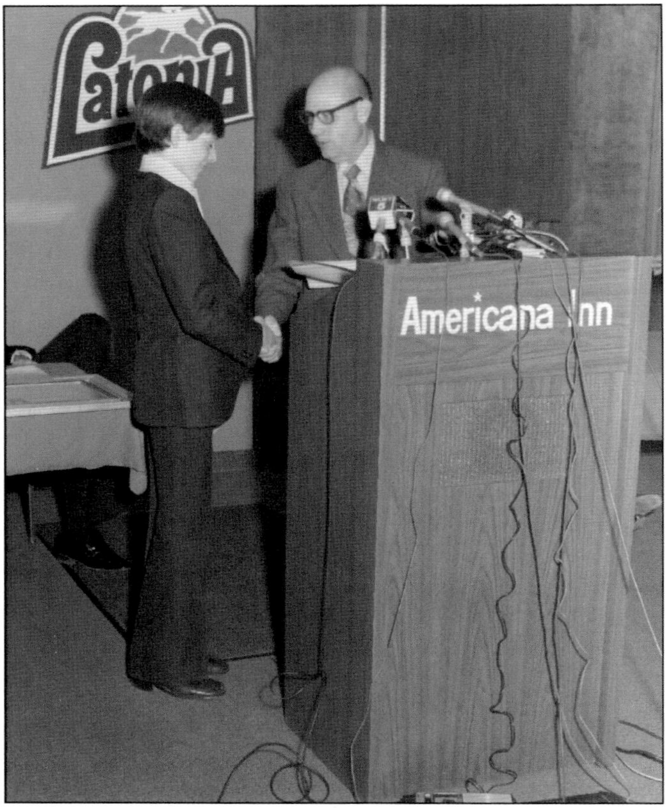

THE WINNING BEGINS. This photograph of Steve Cauthen was taken in the days before winning the Triple Crown. Cauthen began racing as a young teenager at the Churchill Downs track in Louisville, Kentucky, and River Downs across the river in Cincinnati, Ohio. Cauthen is pictured here with Walton mayor Sam Gamble in April 1, 1977, the official Steve Cauthen Day in Boone County. (Courtesy of Ruth Meadows.)

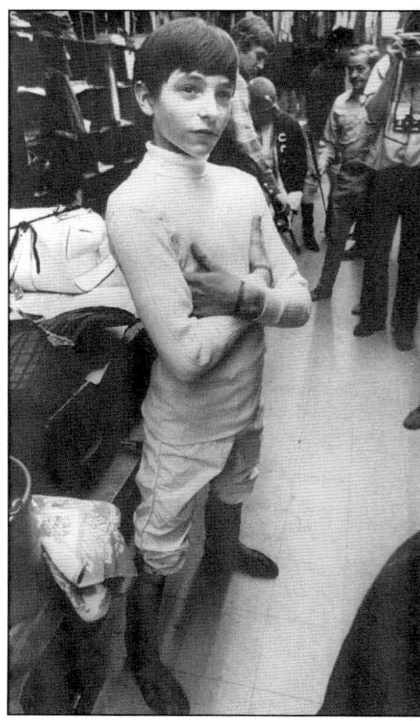

GRACE UNDER PRESSURE. Taken just days before the 1978 Belmont Stakes, the third race of horse racing's Triple Crown, jockey Steve Cauthen displays his focus and determination while under immense media scrutiny and mounting pressure to win the Triple Crown. Cauthen was successful in his quest, guiding Affirmed to a photo-finish win over his rival Alydar in what is regarded as one of the most exciting racing events ever recorded. (Courtesy of the Kenton County Public Library, Covington, Kentucky.)

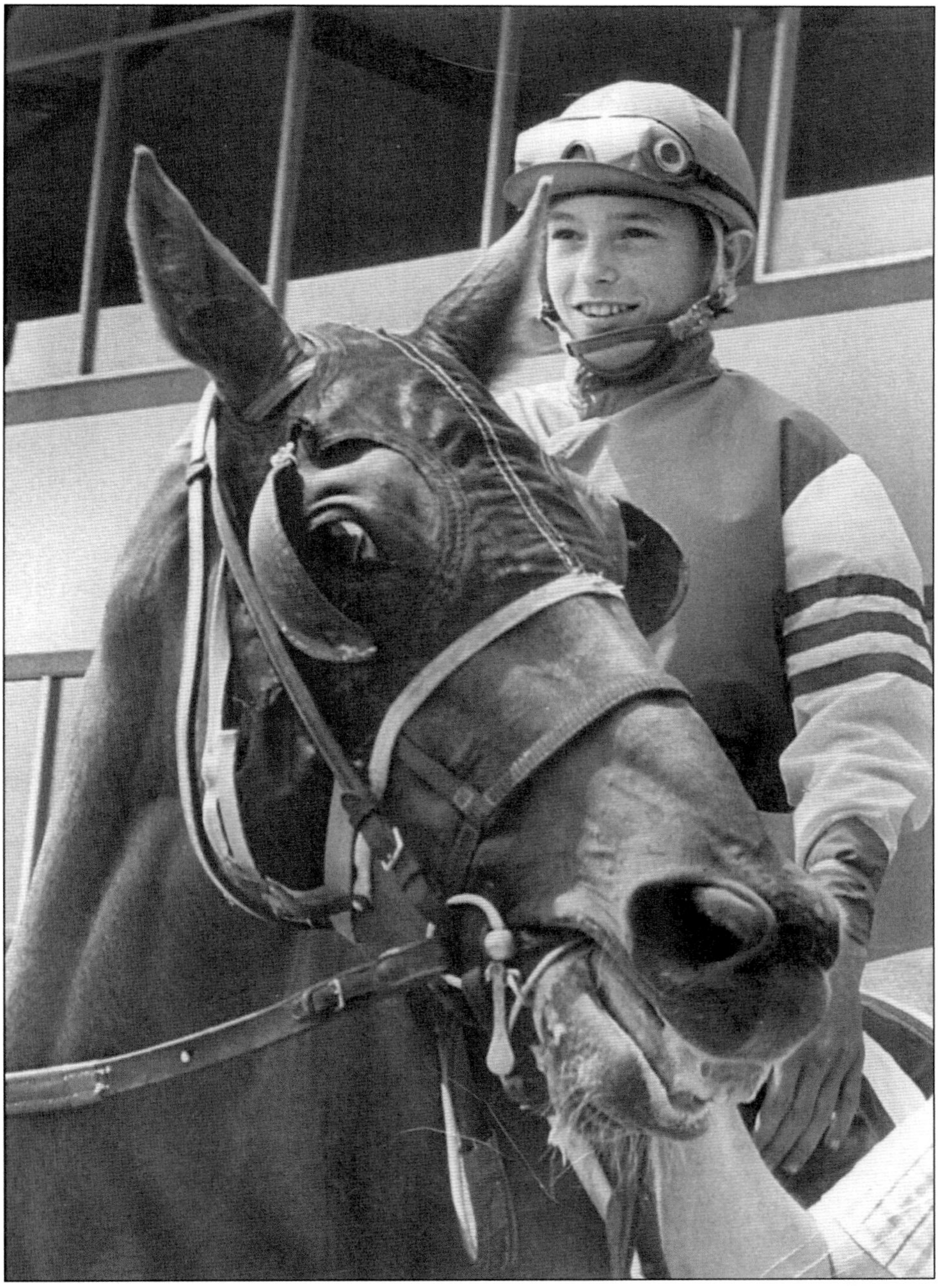

Racing Legend In 1977, seventeen-year-old Steve Cauthen won 447 horse races and was named *Sport's Illustrated*'s Sportsman of the Year, beating out icons Muhammad Ali and Reggie Jackson for the honor. The next year, Cauthen mounted a two-year-old colt named Affirmed for the first time, establishing a special partnership with the young horse that carried them to the ultimate prize in horse racing, the Triple Crown. After his historic win, Cauthen raced for many years in England before returning home to the Walton-Verona area, establishing a horse farm, raising a family, and becoming a vital member of the community. (Courtesy of the Kenton County Public Library, Covington, Kentucky.)

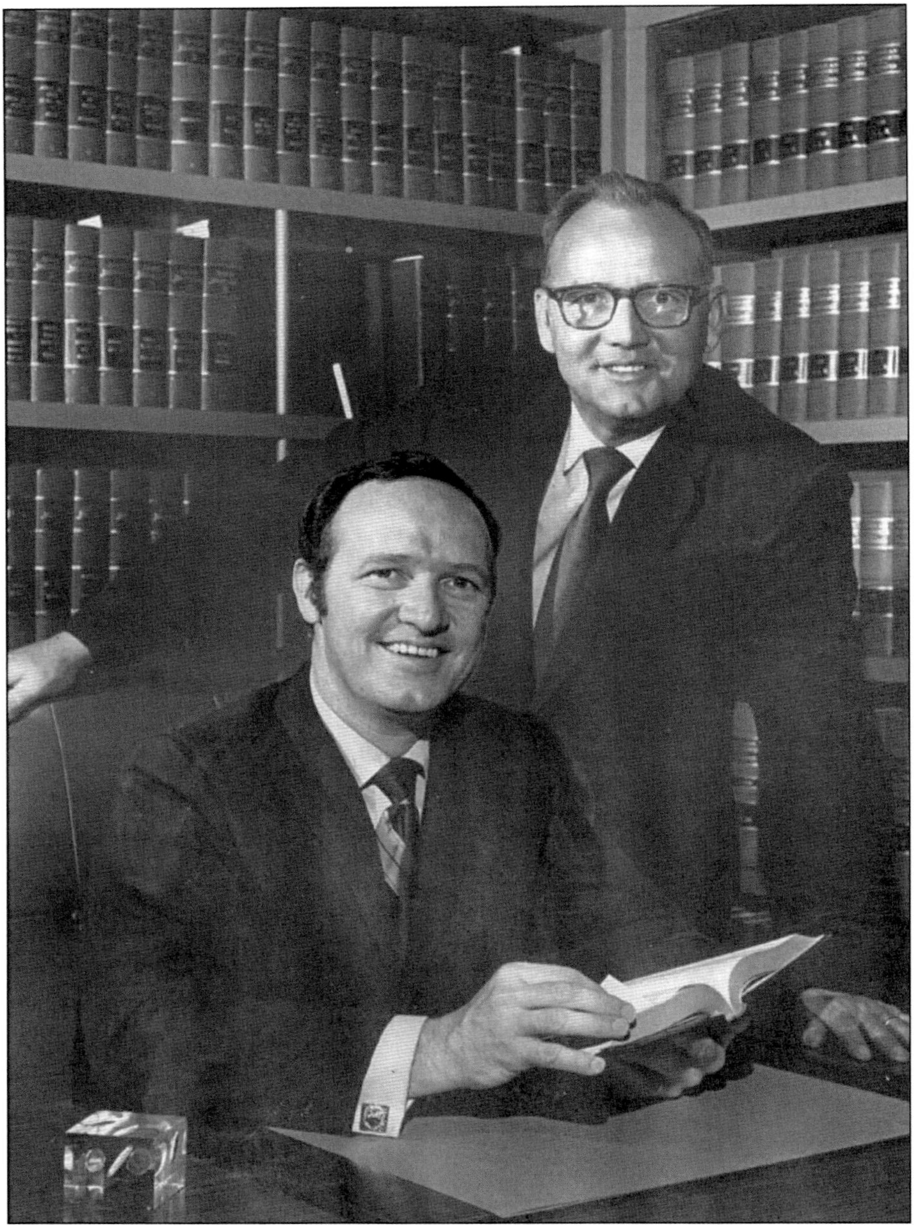

WALTON RESIDENTS. Asa Rouse (left) and his brother Jack pose for the camera in this early-1970s photograph. The law office surroundings are fitting since Asa was a successful attorney and Boone County trail commissioner, and Jack was a Boone County police court judge. Sons of William Wendell and Sara Louise Jack Rouse, their ancestors founded the Rouse Brothers' Mill in the late 19th century. The brothers are lifelong Walton residents, and the next generation maintains the Rouse and Rouse law firm in downtown Walton. Jack is known as the local expert on Boone County's role in the Civil War, devoting many years to researching the unknown heros from the county. The brothers' love of history and vast knowledge of the city's past are important contributions to preservation of that history for future generations. (Courtesy of the Kenton County Public Library, Covington, Kentucky.)

Six

Around the Community

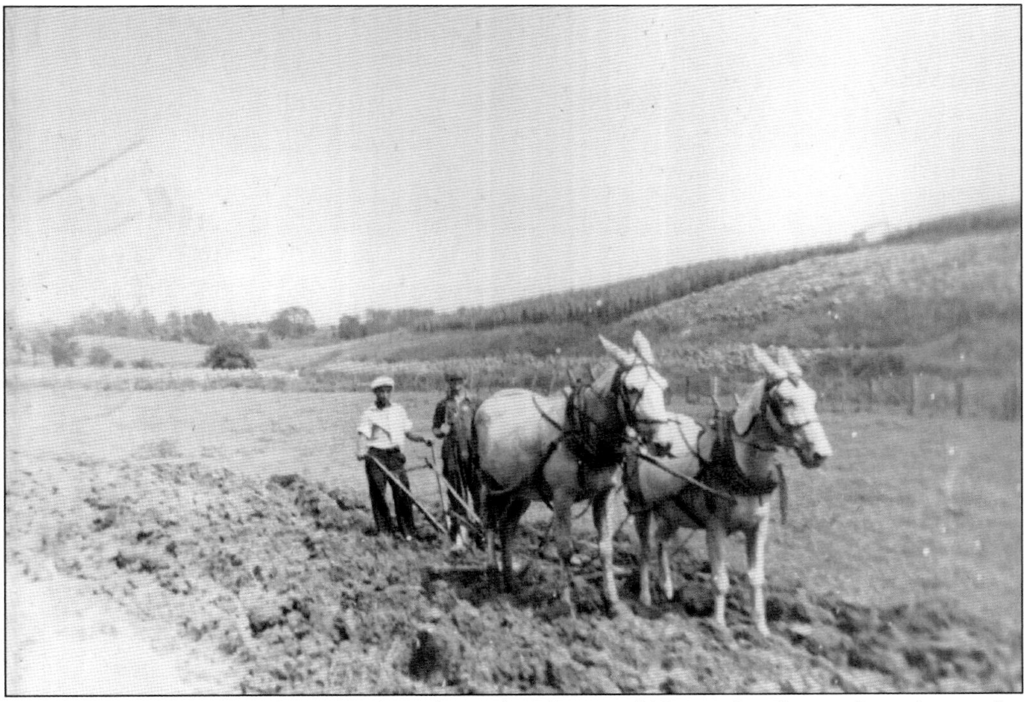

Farming Community. The typical resident of Walton and Verona lived on a farm during the 1800s and into the 1900s, providing not only their own food, but also goods to be shipped into the city. The railroad greatly increased these shipments, improving the quality of life for local farmers. The scene in this photograph was of the Groger farm, located on Chambers Road just north of Walton, a familiar sight to anyone traveling through the area. (Courtesy of Russell Groger.)

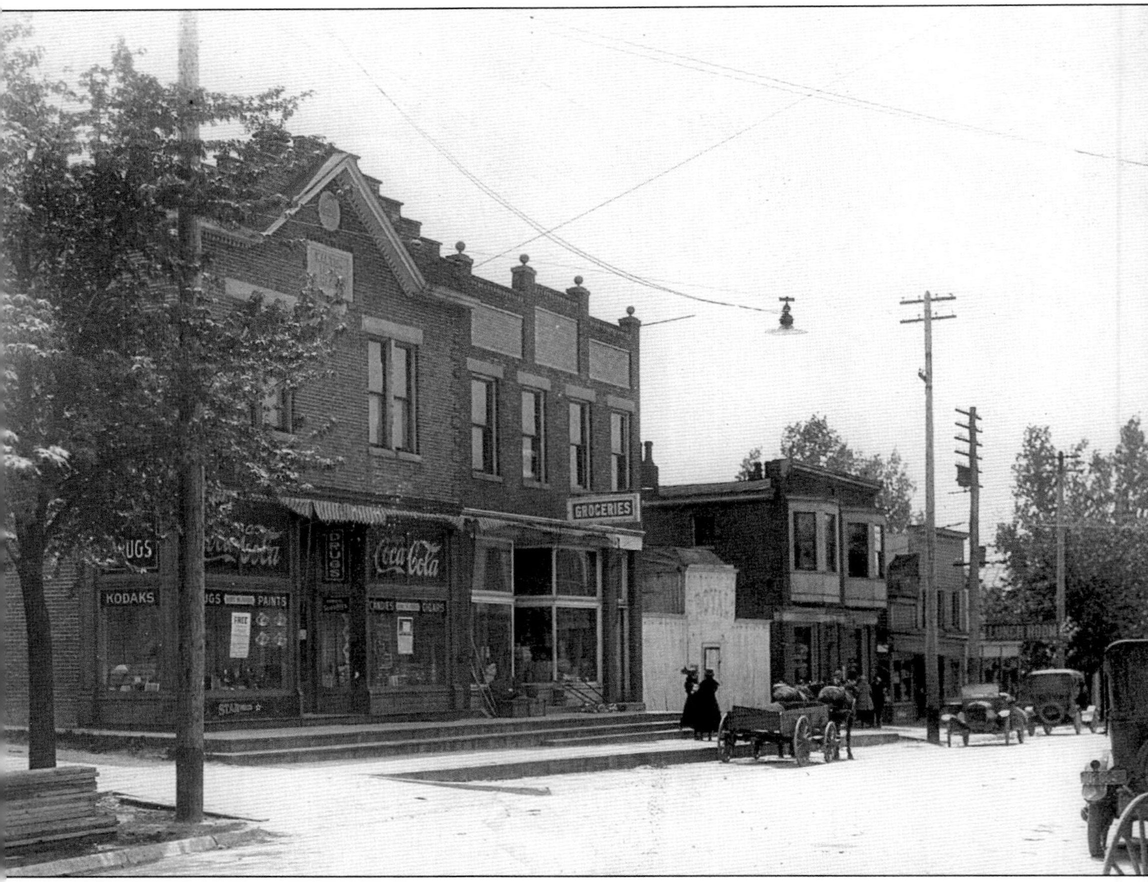

CORNER OF HIGH AND MAIN. Two women stop to chat in this photograph from about 1920. Notice the mix of cars and buggies in front of the shops. Jones Drugstore is on the corner, and the odd storefront the women are standing in front of was probably the entrance to the Air Dome, an outdoor theater that found great popularity in the early part of the century. Turning on High Street by the drugstore, the old bridge across the Cincinnati Southern tracks connected the center of town with the main residential area of Walton at the time. (Courtesy of Bernie Spencer, www.nkyviews.com.)

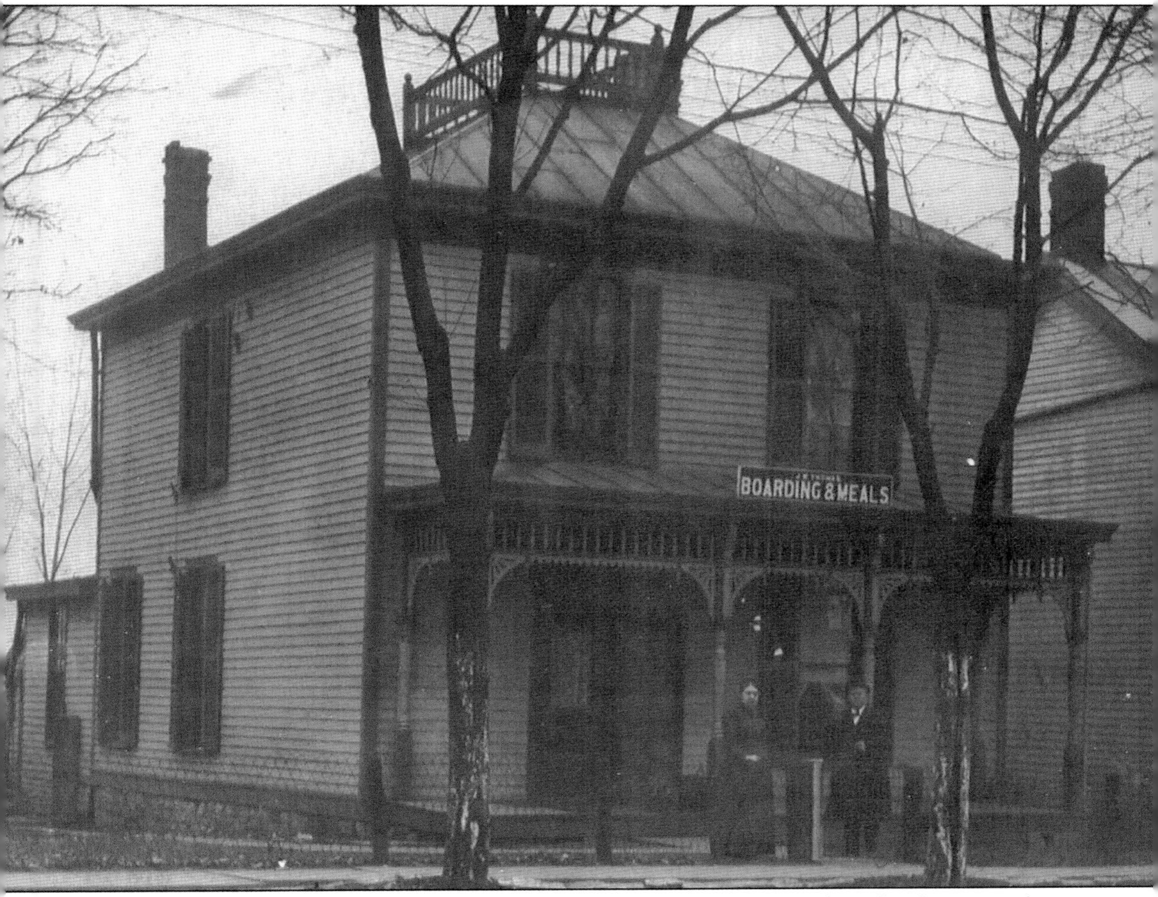

Boardinghouse. Down the street from the Air Dome, Mag Thomas ran a boardinghouse in the early 1900s. Its proximity to the Louisville and Nashville Depot made it an attractive destination for travelers and newcomers. This photograph shows Thomas standing in front of the house with an unidentified gentleman. Later on this same house was known for being the home of Professor Gordon, a popular teacher in town. The house still stands directly across the street from the Boone County Public Library. (Courtesy of Margaret Percival Armstrong.)

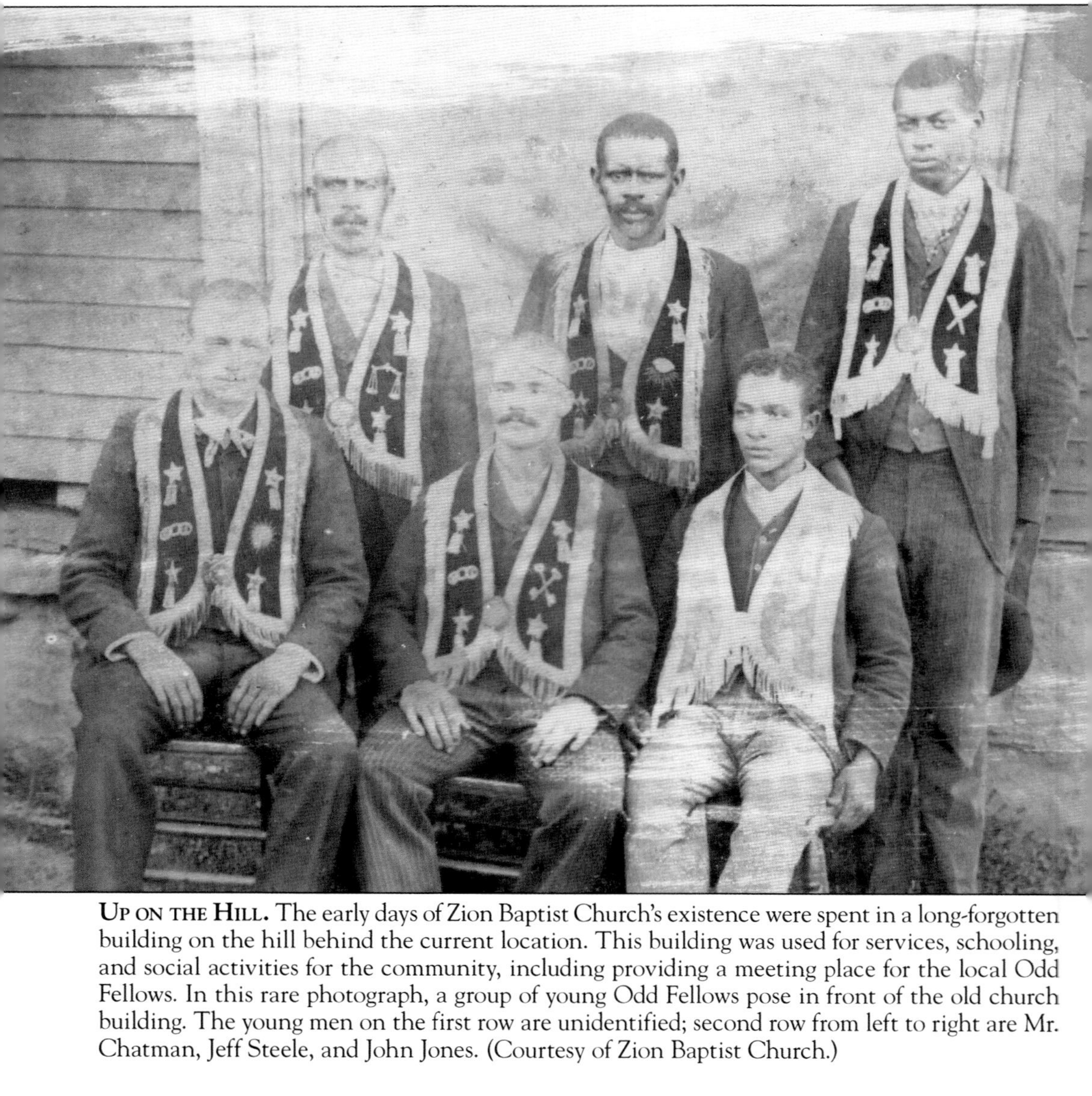

Up on the Hill. The early days of Zion Baptist Church's existence were spent in a long-forgotten building on the hill behind the current location. This building was used for services, schooling, and social activities for the community, including providing a meeting place for the local Odd Fellows. In this rare photograph, a group of young Odd Fellows pose in front of the old church building. The young men on the first row are unidentified; second row from left to right are Mr. Chatman, Jeff Steele, and John Jones. (Courtesy of Zion Baptist Church.)

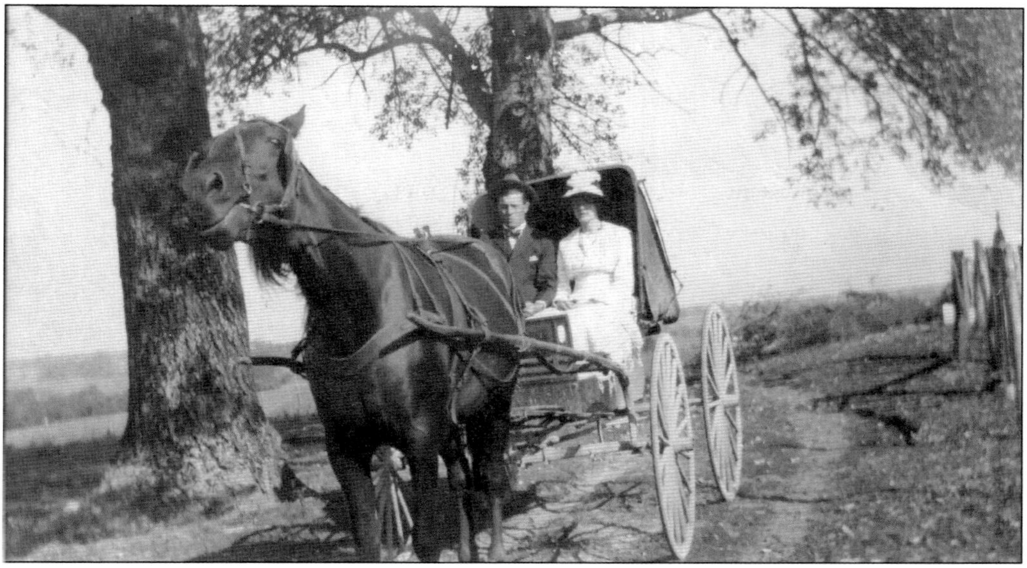

Out for a Ride. John Marshall McClandless and his wife, Emma Jump, take a ride through the hills of Verona in their buggy dressed in their Sunday finest in this early-1900s photograph. McClandless was a local farmer and resided on Verona-Mudlick Road. (Courtesy of Ruth Meadows.)

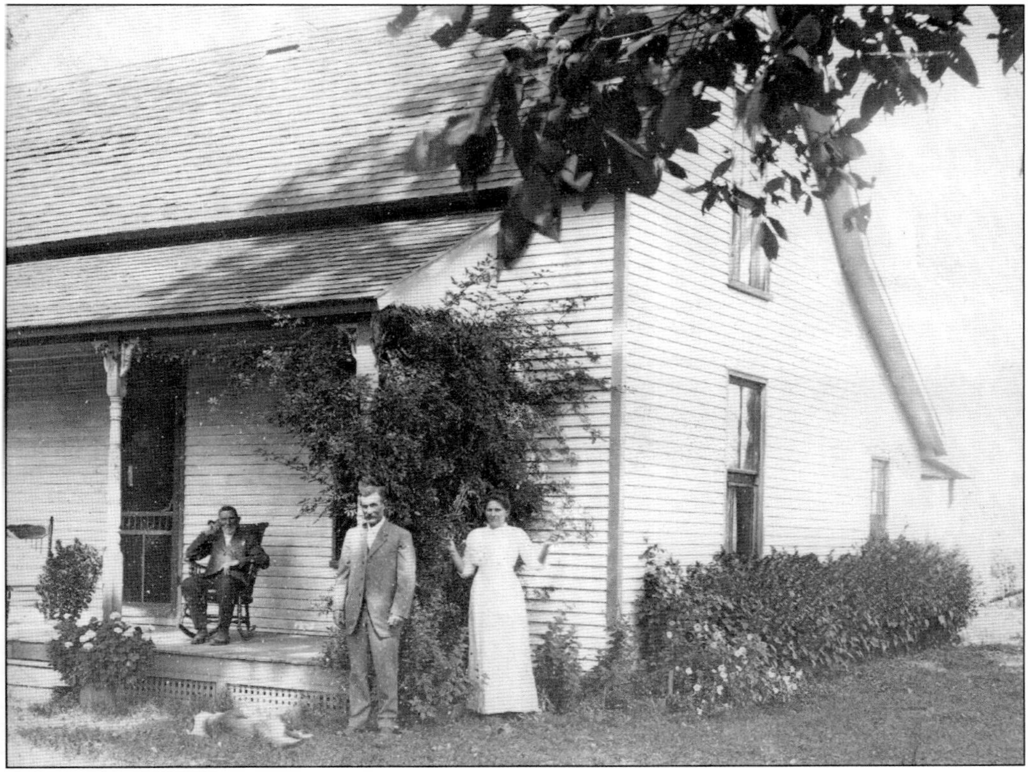

Under the Shade Tree. Samuel Taylor, Jeff Hutsell, and Belle Taylor Hutsell take time to pose for the camera in this early-1900s photograph, while their dog enjoys the shade from the afternoon sun. Taylor owned a large farm on Beaver Road near Richwood. (Courtesy of Kathleen Wiley.)

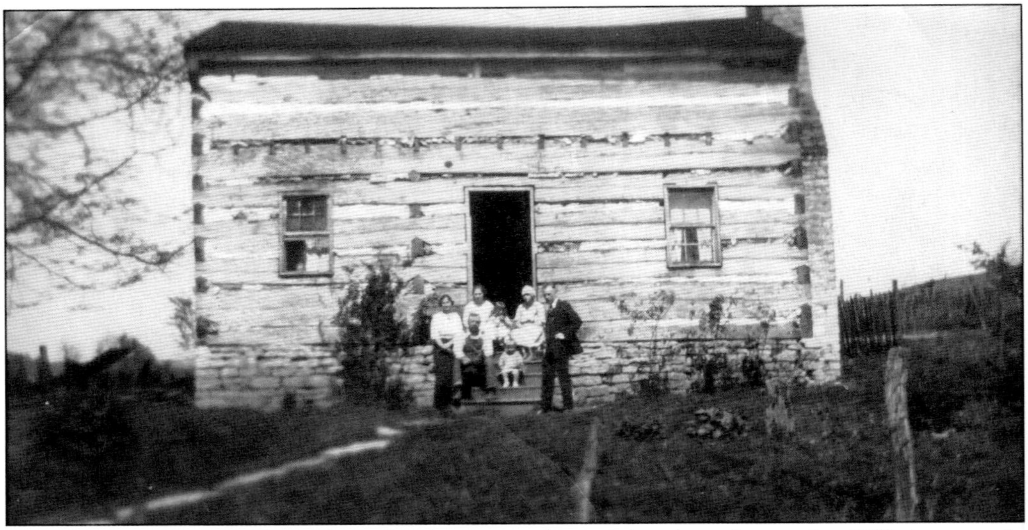

The Old Homestead. The Webster family poses in front of their log cabin in this 1923 photograph. The family lived just south of Verona. (Courtesy of Paul Webster.)

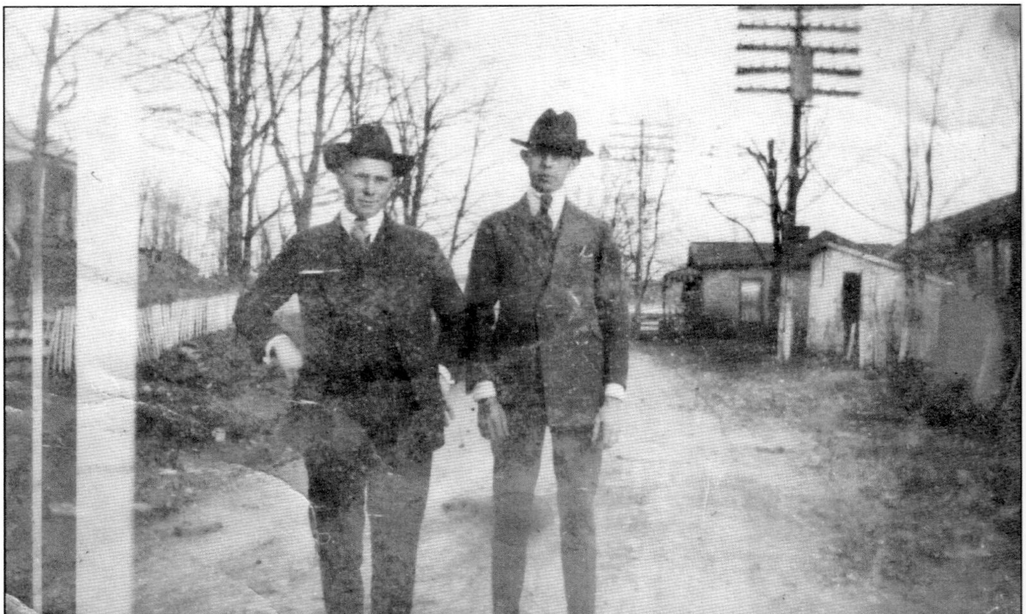

Beaver Lick. Two unidentified young men stand in the road to smile for the camera in this early-1900s photograph. Beaver Lick was a tiny community featuring a few shops, a church, and a school at the crossroads of Beaver, Union, and South Fork Roads. (Courtesy of Ruth Meadows.)

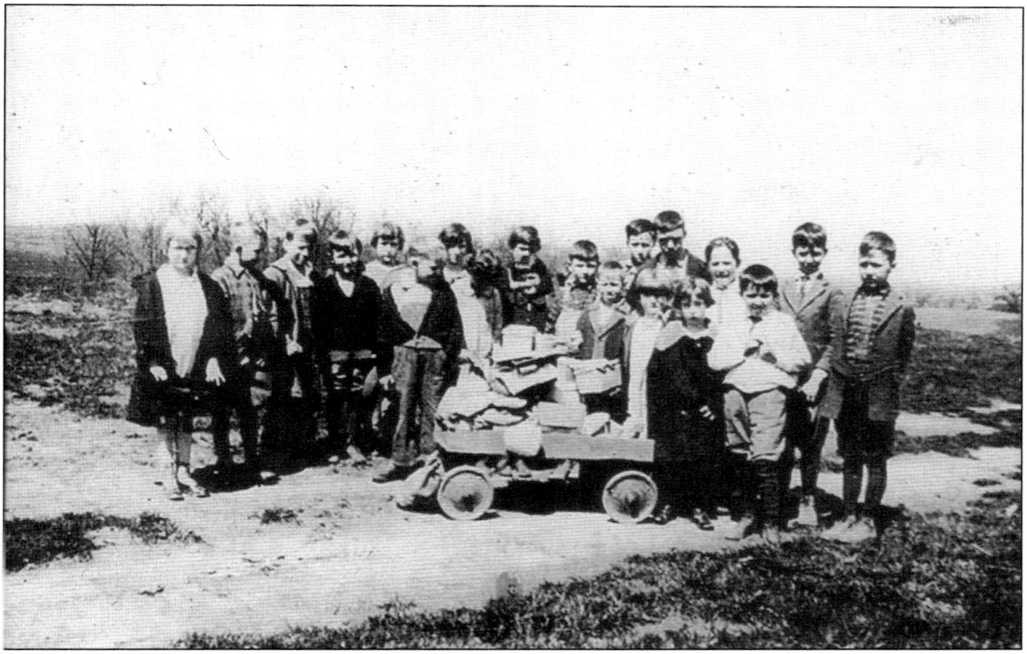

Supply Wagon. Young Verona school students stand proudly beside their overflowing wagon full of school supplies in this undated photograph. They are standing in the field behind the old Verona school. (Courtesy of the Kathleen Wiley Collection, Northern Kentucky University Special Collections.)

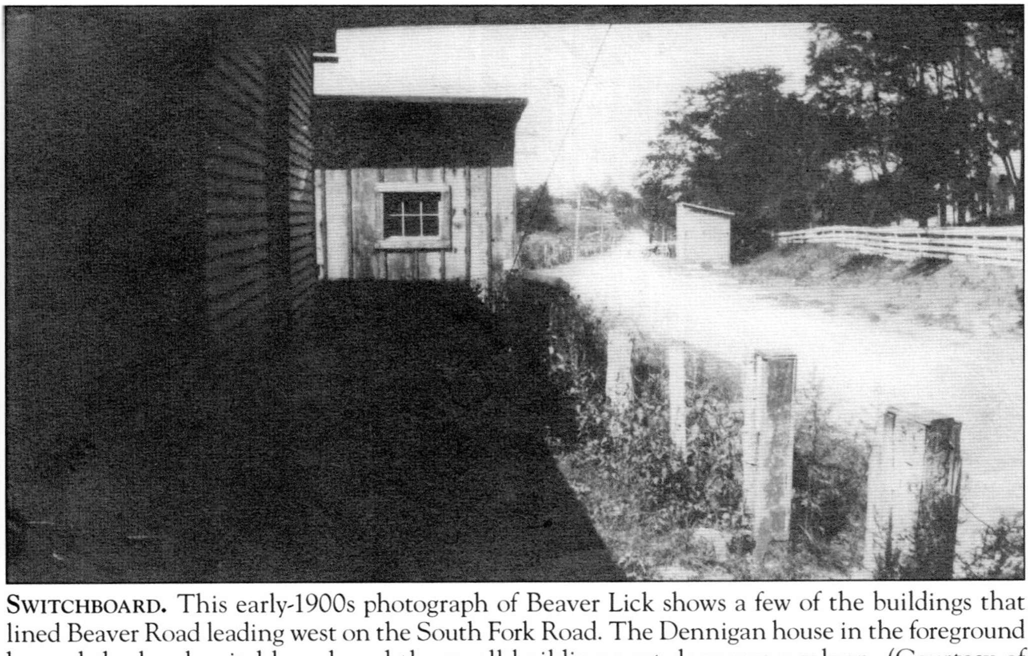

Switchboard. This early-1900s photograph of Beaver Lick shows a few of the buildings that lined Beaver Road leading west on the South Fork Road. The Dennigan house in the foreground housed the local switchboard, and the small building next door was a saloon. (Courtesy of Ruth Meadows.)

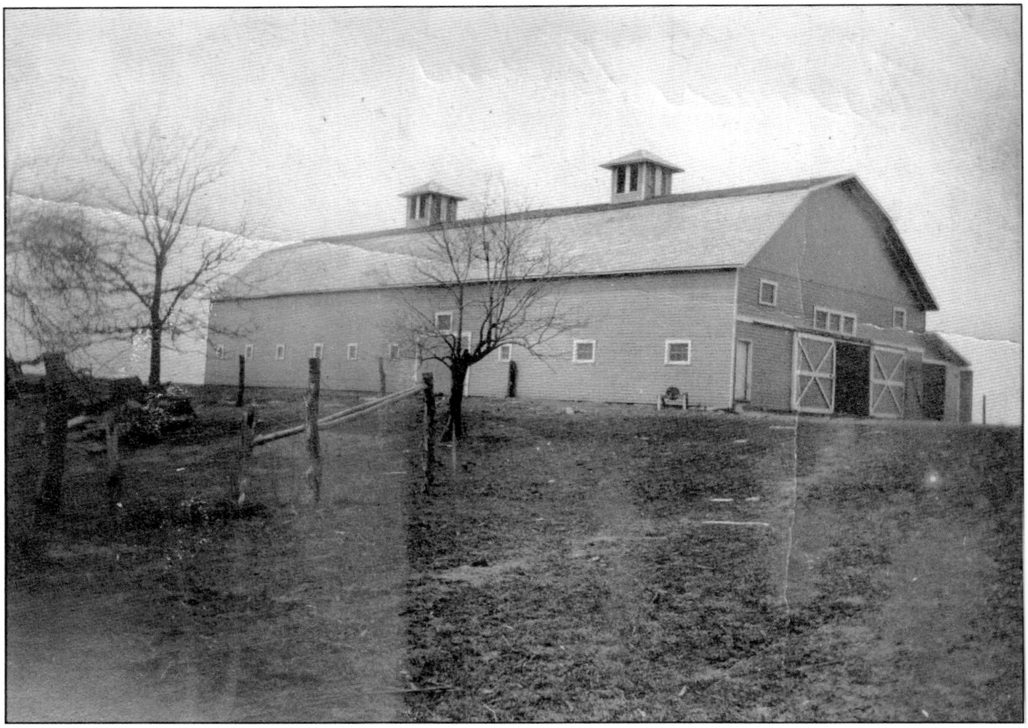

VERONA BARNYARD. A large barn is the focal point of this early-20th century Verona farm. A typical scene for one of these barns was slaughter time, when the farmers would process the hogs for their meat, ensuring a fresh supply of pork to feed their families. Hog season typically started around the first week of November (notice the snow on the ground), and farmers who owned a large amount of hogs would sell the excess to drovers, who sent the hogs to slaughterhouses in nearby Cincinnati for processing and packaging to sell to the city dwellers. (Both, courtesy of Ruth Meadows.)

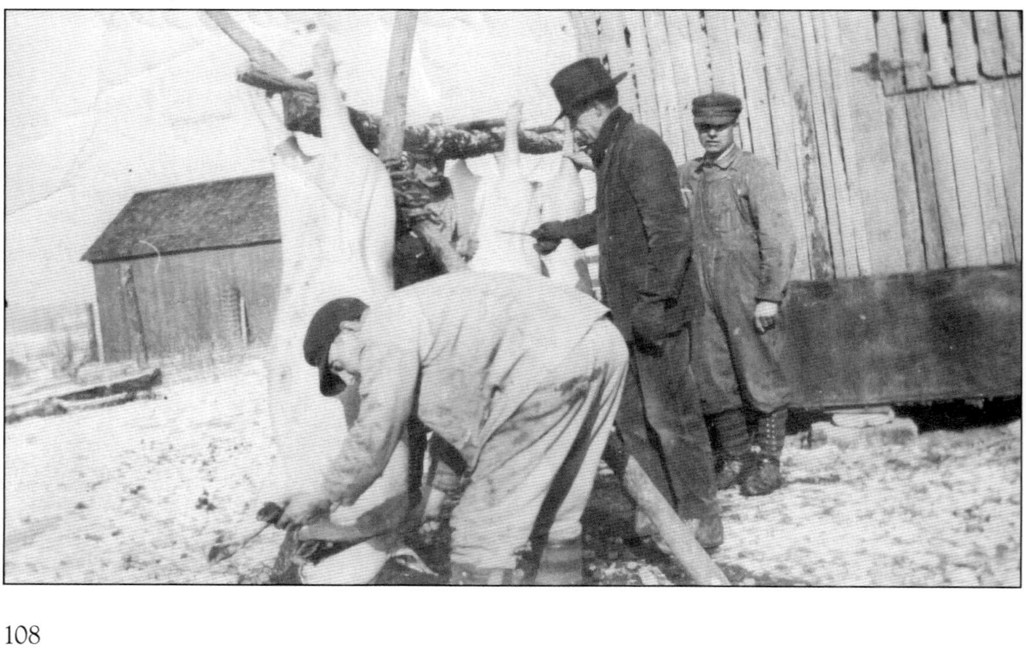

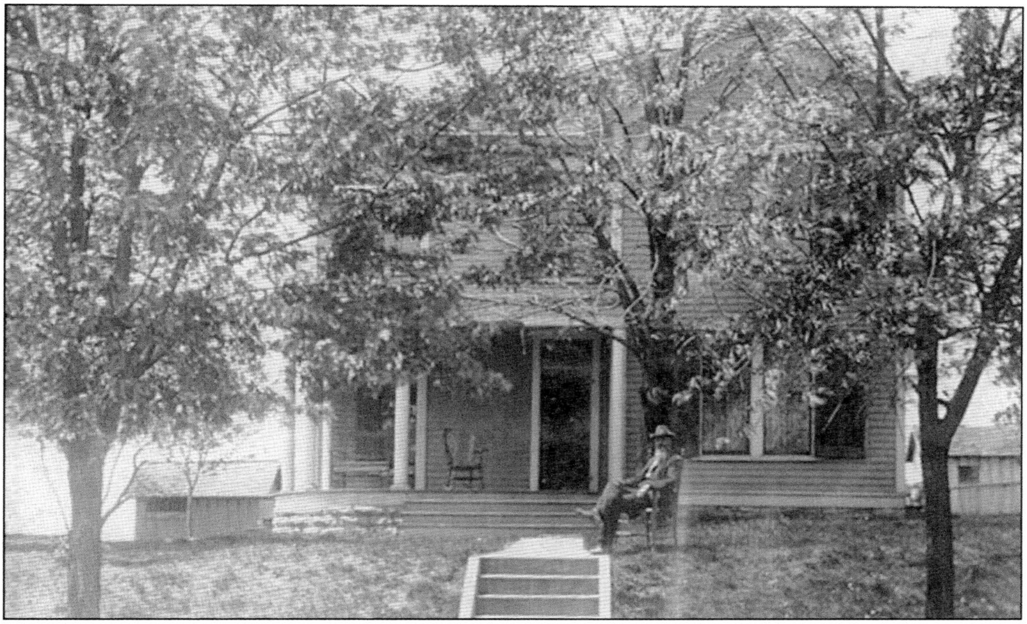

Time to Relax. A. M. Rouse takes a break from the mill to enjoy the sunshine in his front yard. His house was located across the street from the mill at the corner of old Verona Road (Needmore Street) and Main Street. Rouse owned the Rouse Brothers' Mill with his brother R. W. Rouse. (Courtesy of Bernie Spencer, www.nkyviews.com.)

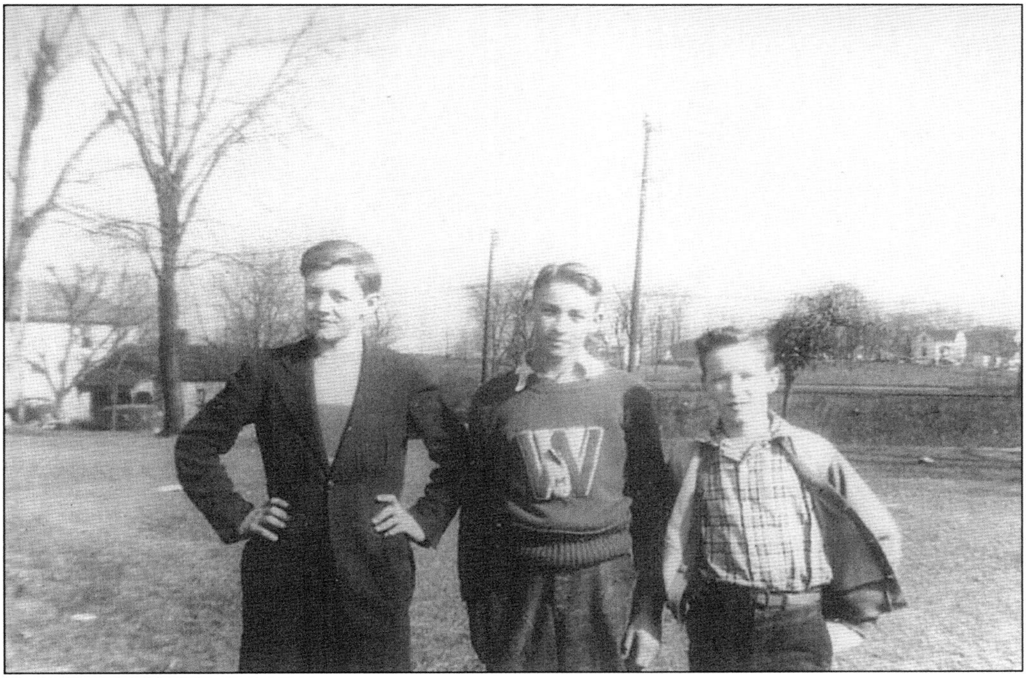

Another Generation. Jack Rouse, Kenneth Johnson, and Asa Rouse enjoy an afternoon in this *c.* 1942 photograph. Jack and Asa are the grandsons of A. M. Rouse, co-owner of the Rouse Brothers' Mill. (Courtesy of Bernie Spencer, www.nkyviews.com.)

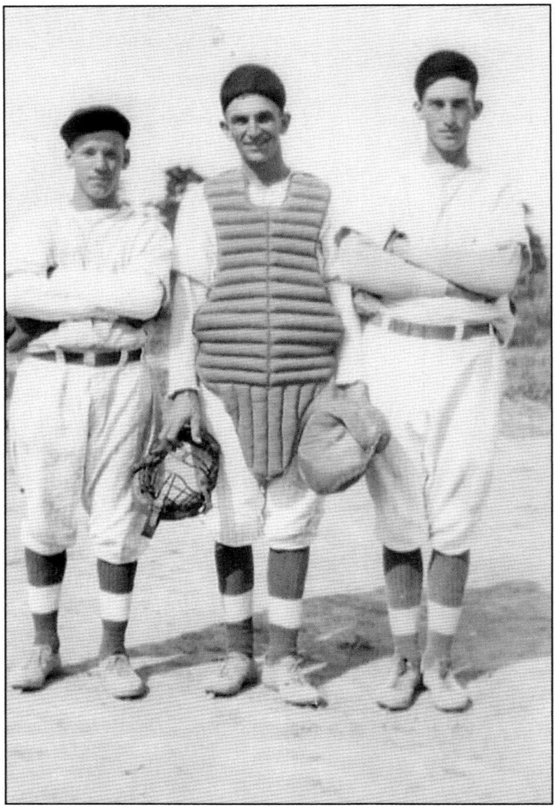

Baseball Fever. Local baseball leagues were in their heyday during the 1920s and 1930s, and most towns put together teams that offered good competitions and entertainment for large crowds of citizens. This 1929 team from Walton was part of the Northern Kentucky Semi-Pro League and the Boone County League that featured teams from Hebron, Petersburg, Burlington, Union, and Belleview. The Walton team beat Belleview that year for the county championship. The baseball leagues remained popular until World War II. A lot of games were played at Big Bone Park near Union, as shown in this photograph of S. Jack, R. Brown, and C. Afterkirk getting ready for a big game. All three young men were from the Beaver Lick area. Below, players are, from left to right, (first row) Hinges, Zimmer, Miller, Ross, K. Johnson, and R. Johnson; (second row) Dudgeon, Benson, DeMoisey, Hartman, and Glenn. (Both, courtesy of Bernie Spencer, www.nkyviews.com.)

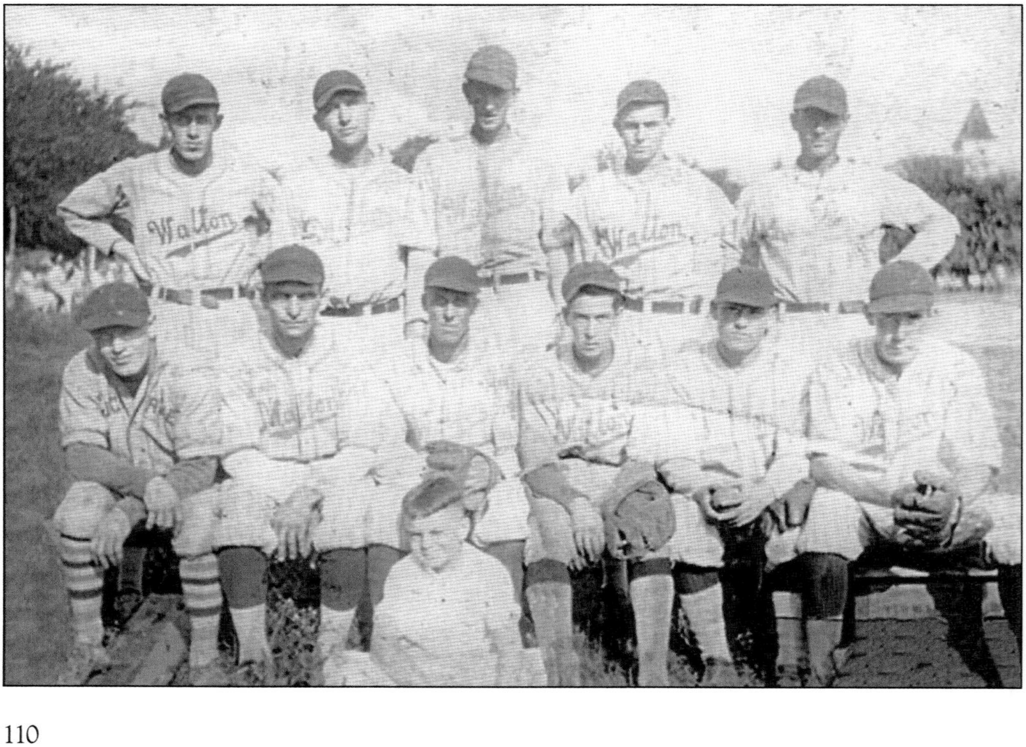

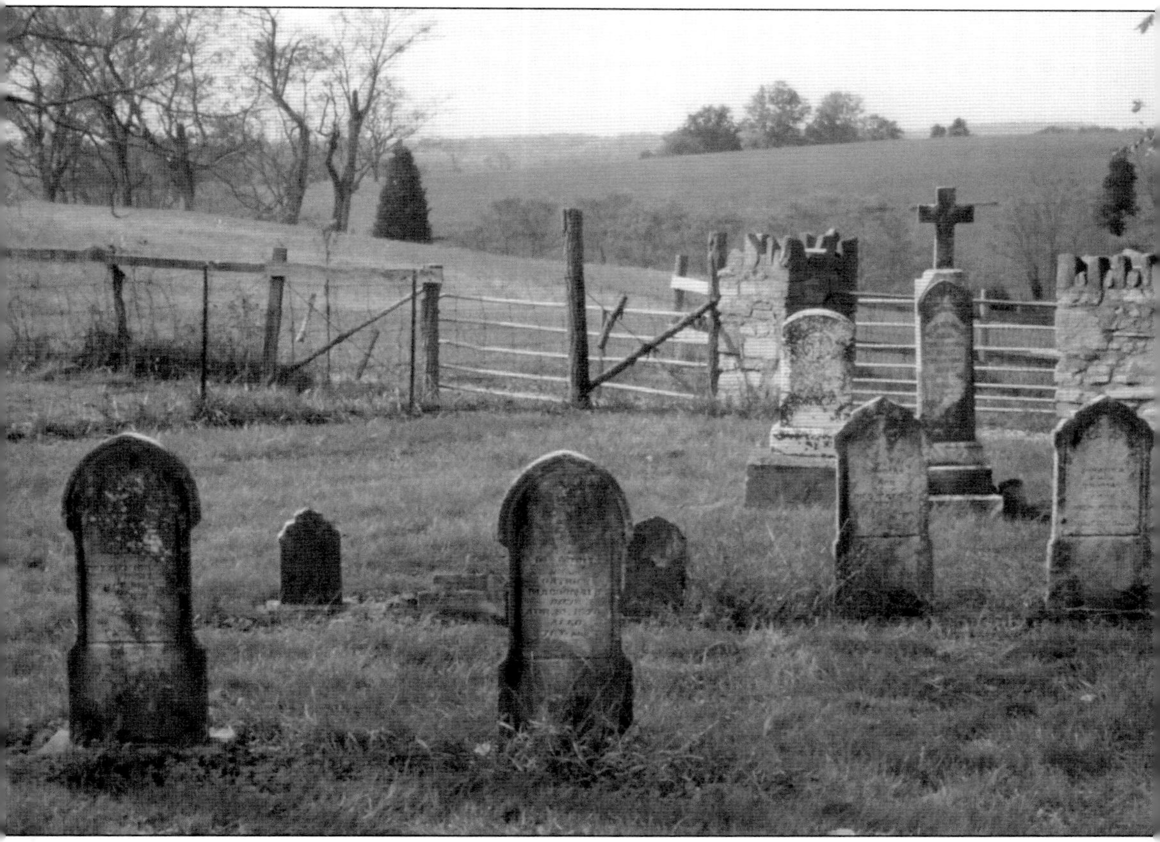

Carr Cemetery. Before the advent of large public cemeteries, a common sight in the rural landscape was the family cemetery. The Carr Cemetery in Verona sits just off Verona-Mudlick Road west of Brown Road. It is not visible from the road, so most passersby are unaware of the rural beauty that is the backdrop to this old cemetery. The Carr family, Irish farmers who came to the Verona area in the mid-19th century, established themselves in the Irish Catholic community. The headstones in the foreground of Patrick and Mary MacDonald (neighbors of the Carrs) date to 1870; Thomas Carr (died 1875) and his wife, Johanna, are buried directly behind them. This cemetery is one of the lucky ones; old family cemeteries are often abandoned and lost, victims of the passage of time, descendents moving out of the area, and the expansion of the suburban population. (Courtesy of Mary Berkemeier.)

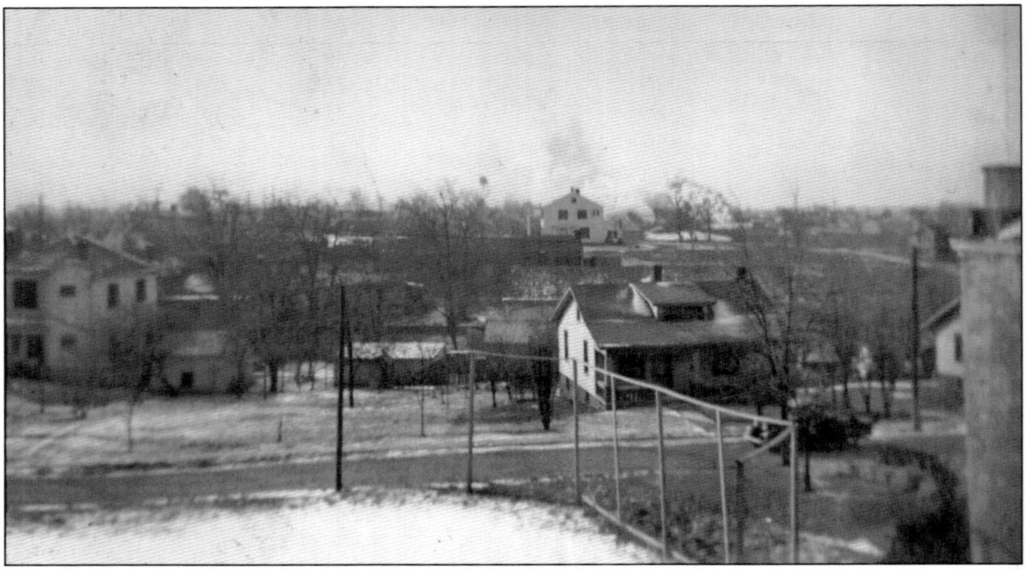

UPSTAIRS VIEW. This 1940s photograph was taken from a window of the old Walton-Verona High School facing High School Court, overlooking the tennis court. The corner of the gym can be seen to the right, and in the distance, the Chambers and Grubbs Funeral Home stands in an open field beside Alta Vista Drive. As people began moving off the family farms and into town, the open landscape around the funeral home became a desirable residential neighborhood when the new high school was built nearby. (Courtesy of Russell Groger.)

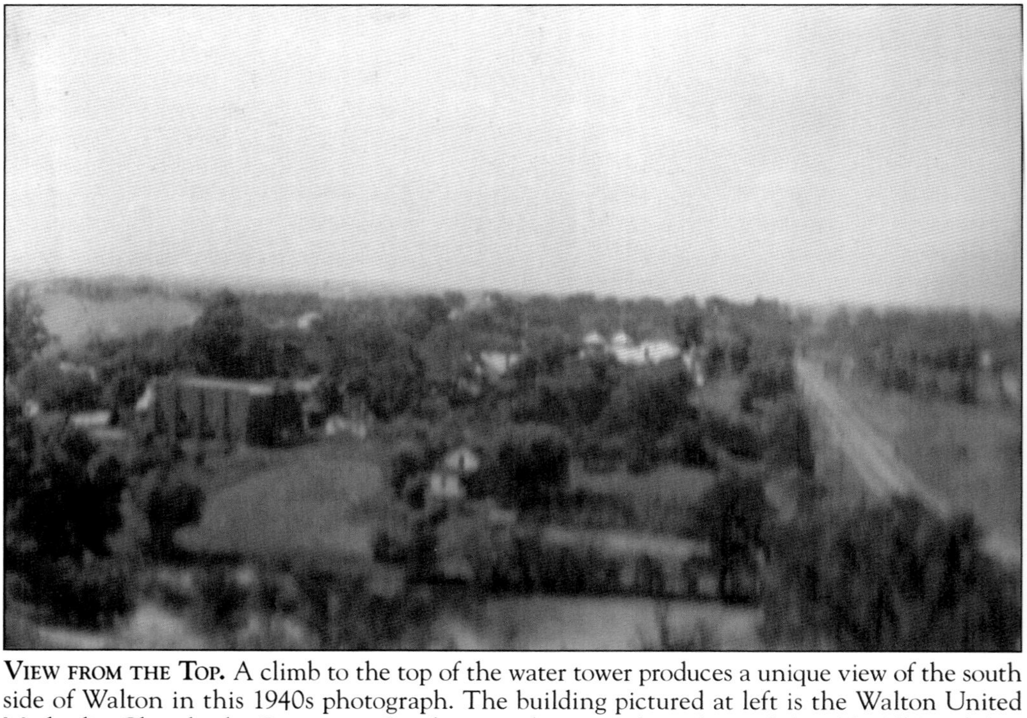

VIEW FROM THE TOP. A climb to the top of the water tower produces a unique view of the south side of Walton in this 1940s photograph. The building pictured at left is the Walton United Methodist Church, the Cincinnati Southern tracks are to the right, and the old Mill Pond that served the Rouse Brothers' Mill is in the foreground. (Courtesy of Russell Groger.)

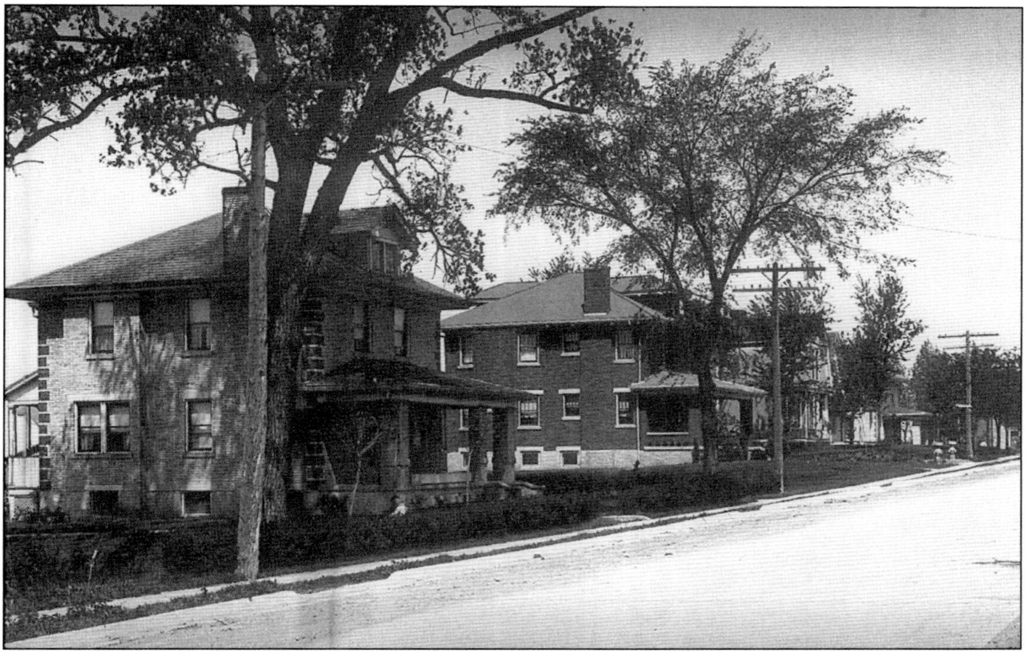

HISTORIC DISTRICT. These beautiful homes line South Main Street in Walton. Designated as a National Historic District, this residential area preserves the architecture and quality of workmanship from a different era. Residents participate in the city's annual Christmas on Main, when they open their decorated homes to the public for tours. Nearby, construction continues on the new Walton Towne Center, a stark contrast to the historic ambience of this neighborhood. (Courtesy of the Boone County Historic Preservation Review Board.)

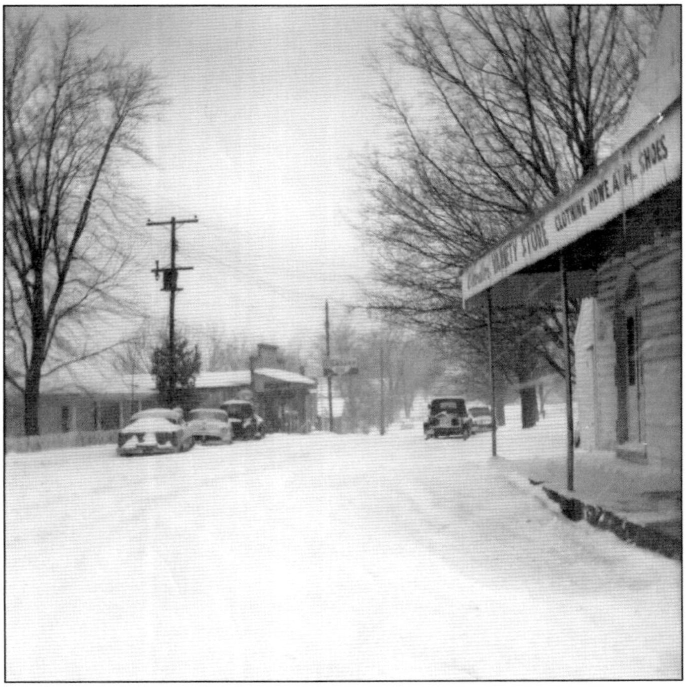

SNOWED IN. These vehicles will probably not be moving much in this 1966 photograph. Looking west on Verona-Mudlick Road, Chandler's Variety Store is pictured on the right and the Verona Garage is on the left. The Renaker house is beside the garage. (Courtesy of Paul Webster.)

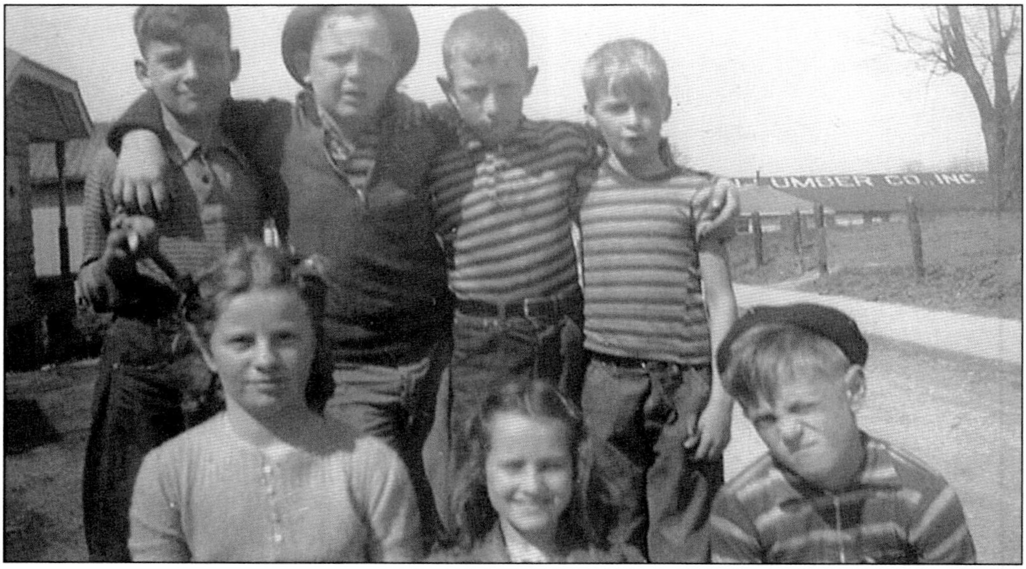

BUDDIES. A group of youngsters take time from their activities to pose for the camera in this 1930s photograph. Pictured from left to right are (first row) Wanda Dixon, unidentified, and Dyke Vest; (second row) Jimmy Isbell, Billy Wynn, James Smith, and Gerald Dixon. Jimmy Isbell later became a Walton firefighter and was killed on duty in December 1947. The Walton Lumber Company is located beside the Louisville and Nashville tracks across from the old depot site. (Courtesy of Bernie Spencer, www.nkyviews.com.)

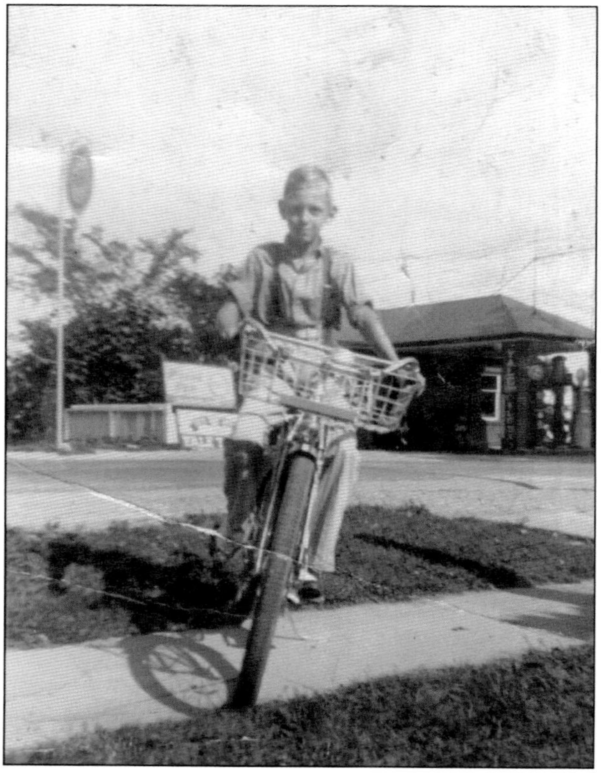

A BOY AND HIS BIKE. Young Russell Groger sits still on his bicycle long enough for a photograph. Taken during the 1930s, behind him is Jimmy Falls's gas station at the corner of Alta Vista Drive and Main Street. The site is currently the location of Taylor's Barbershop. (Courtesy of Russell Groger.)

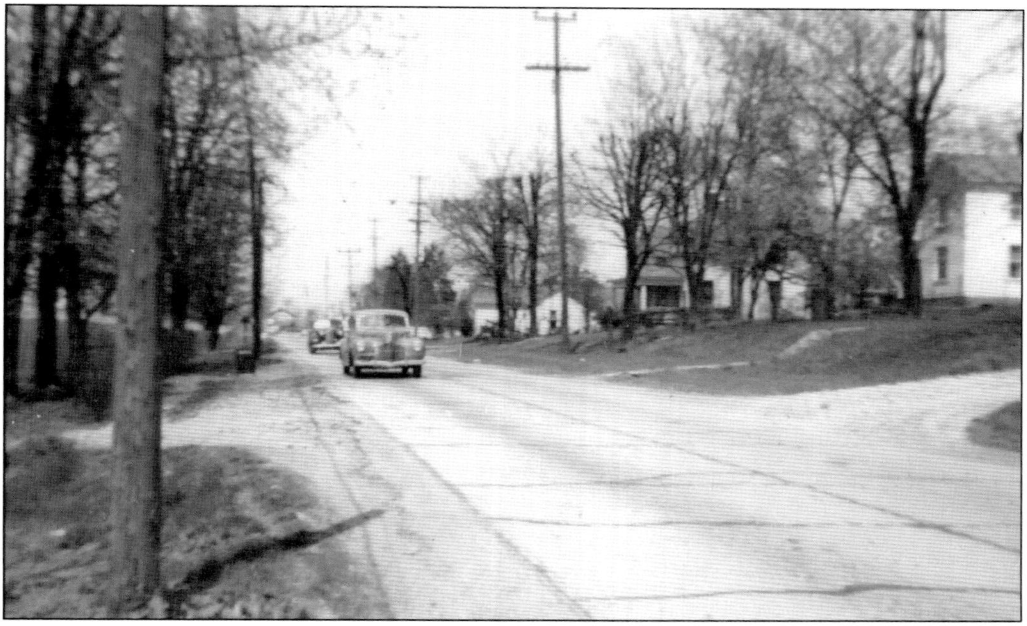

Chevrolet or Ford? Cars coming into Walton were the subjects of a popular game with local children. Sitting beside the road, each child would guess what kind of vehicle would be next to come down the street. This location is looking north across from the current Mr. G's Deli on North Main Street. (Courtesy of Charlie "Hunky" Holder.)

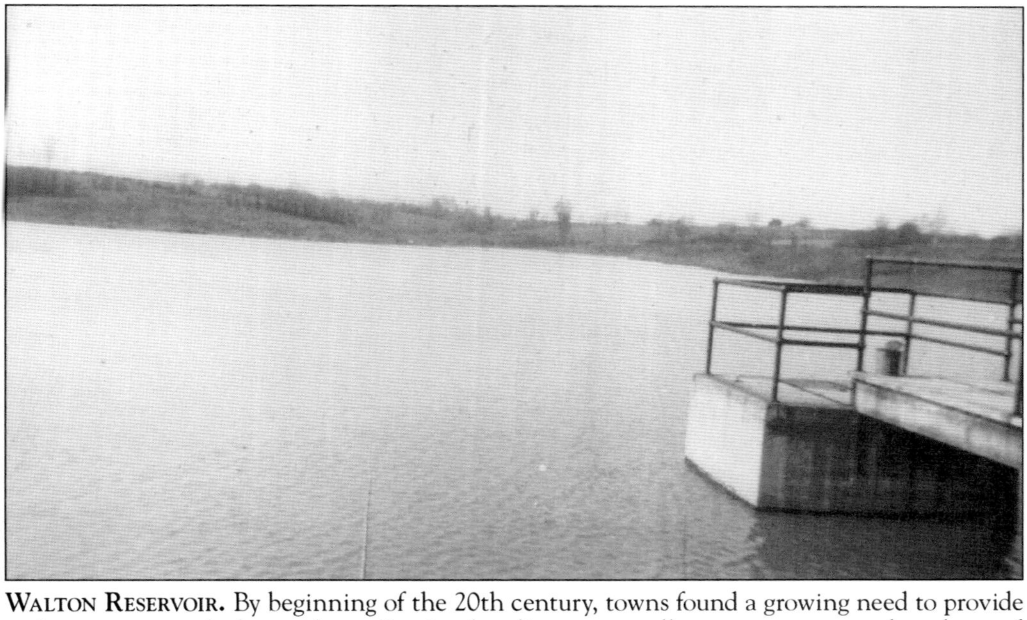

Walton Reservoir. By beginning of the 20th century, towns found a growing need to provide a clean water supply for residents. Previously reliant on a well system, numerous droughts and devastating fires due to the lack of water made it necessary to build a reservoir system. This 1940s photograph shows the size the Walton Reservoir. The reservoir was located at the end of Church Street near the county line. (Courtesy of Russell Groger.)

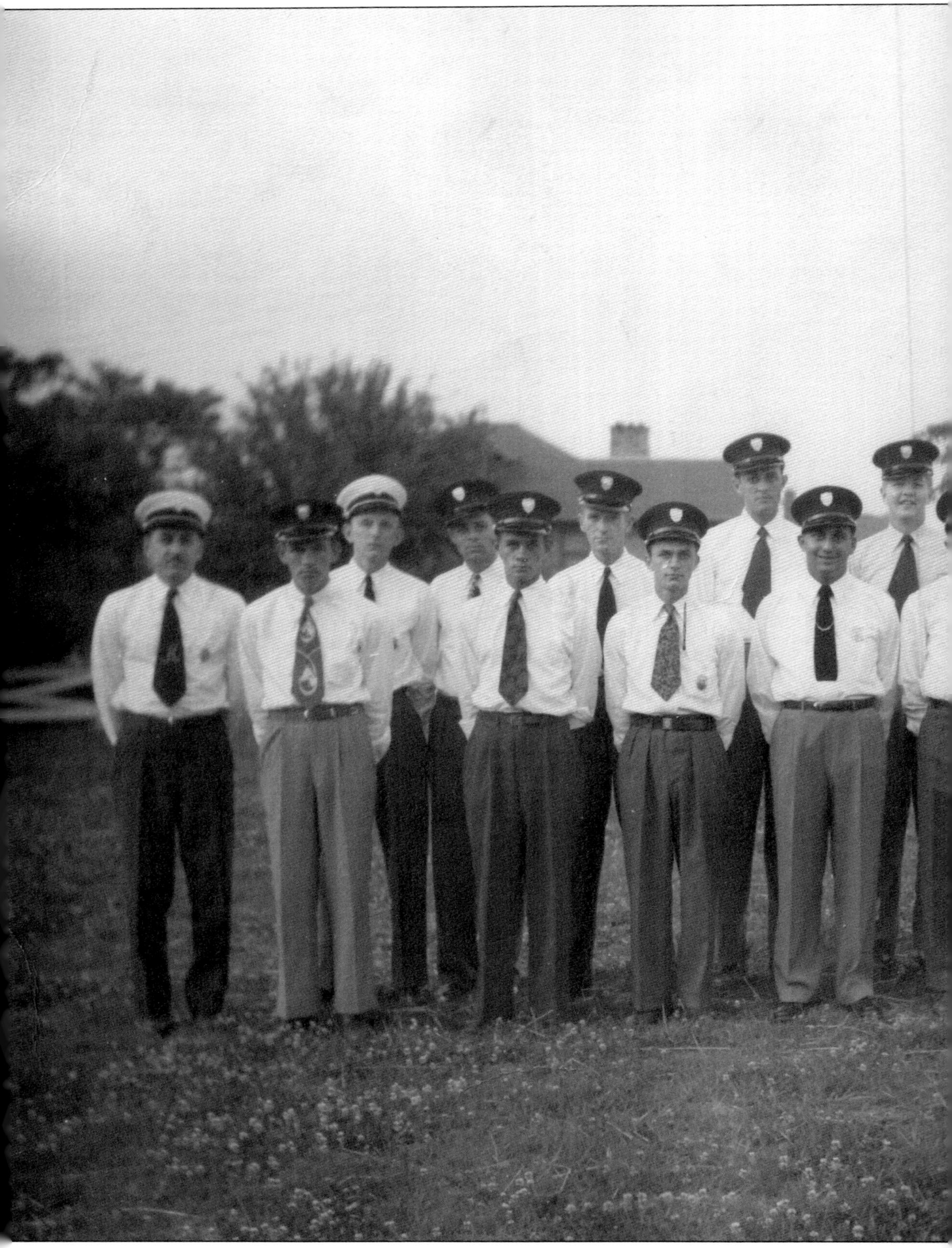

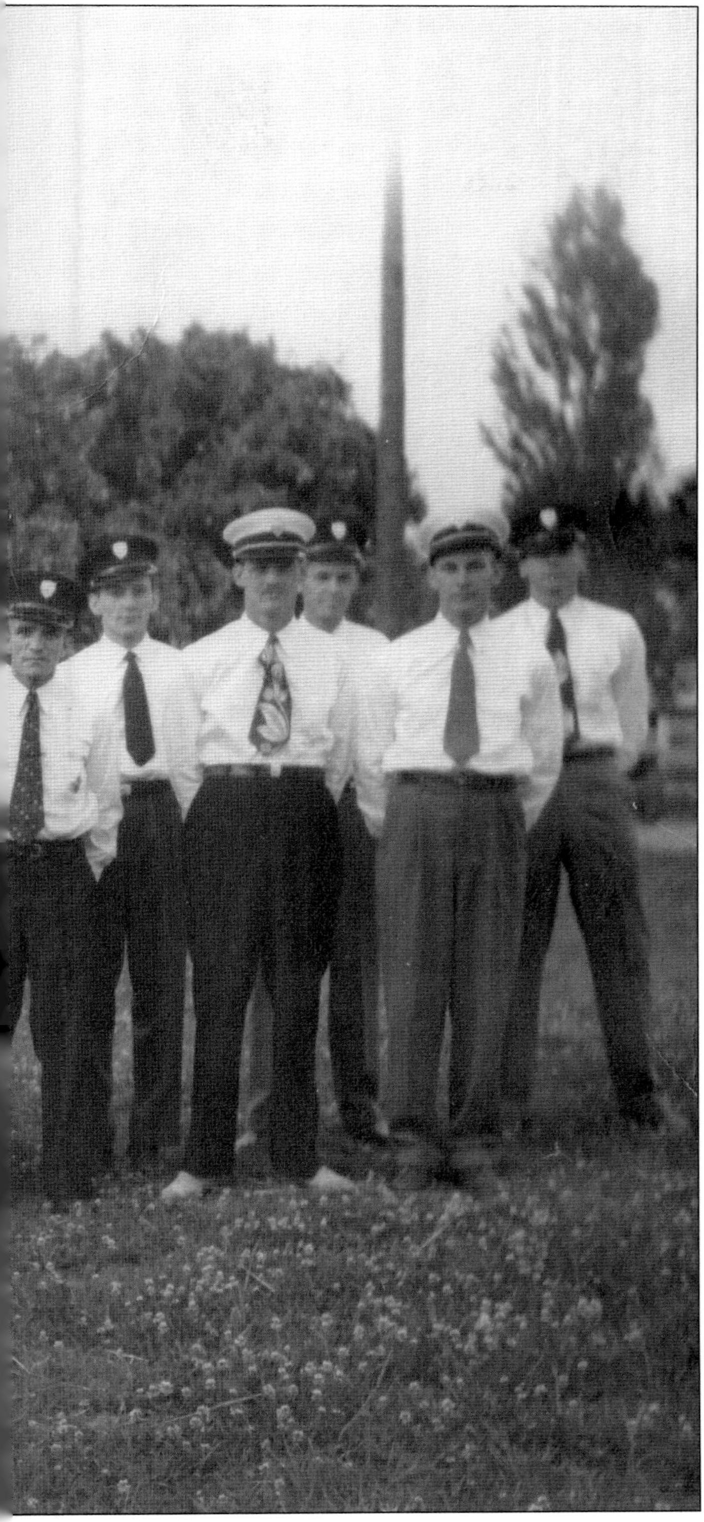

WALTON FIRE DEPARTMENT. Typical of small towns in the late 19th century, Walton's fire department started out as a bucket brigade, dowsing structure fires by throwing buckets of water on them. By the beginning of the 20th century, the town installed a new hand-powered pump that utilized cisterns placed strategically throughout the town. By 1920, a new Model T fire engine was obtained by the city, and over the years newer and better trucks were obtained to serve the town and surrounding area. In the mid-1940s, a group of young men decided to join together and form the Walton Volunteer Fire Department, dedicating themselves to the safety of the citizens of Walton. (Courtesy of Mary Birkemeir.)

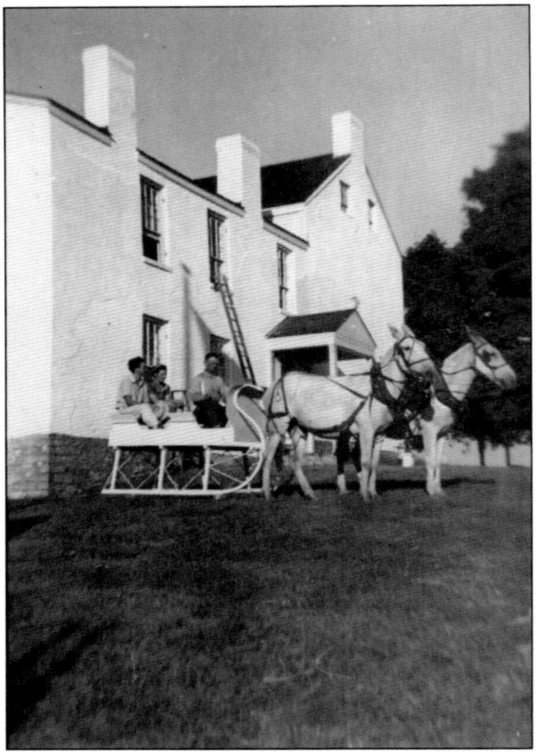

No Snow. The Gault family checks out their sleigh and mule team in this c. 1940 photograph. Unfortunately they are not going to get very far, since there is no snow on the ground. Gault bought the property in 1937 and began extensive renovations that were still being finished at the time of this photograph, as evidenced by the ladder in the background. (Courtesy of Johnny Gault.)

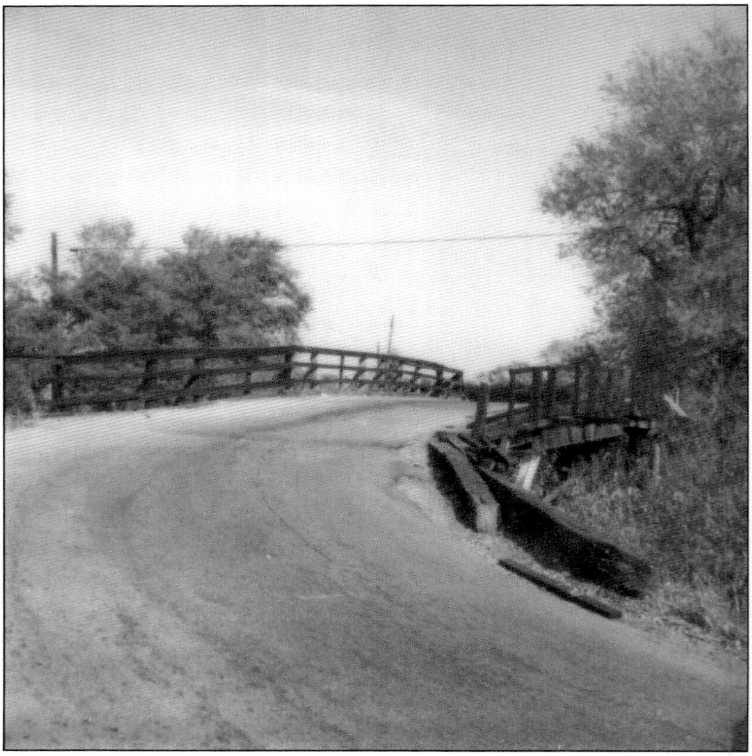

Old Southern Bridge. Just north of the Gaines house, this rickety old bridge over the Cincinnati Southern Railroad connected the Walton-Nicholson Road with the old turnpike. Used for many years past its prime, it was the site of numerous accidents because of the 90-degree turn onto the turnpike and increased traffic through the area. It was finally retired when a new bypass road was built over the tracks to connect to Dixie Highway. (Courtesy of Johnny Gault.)

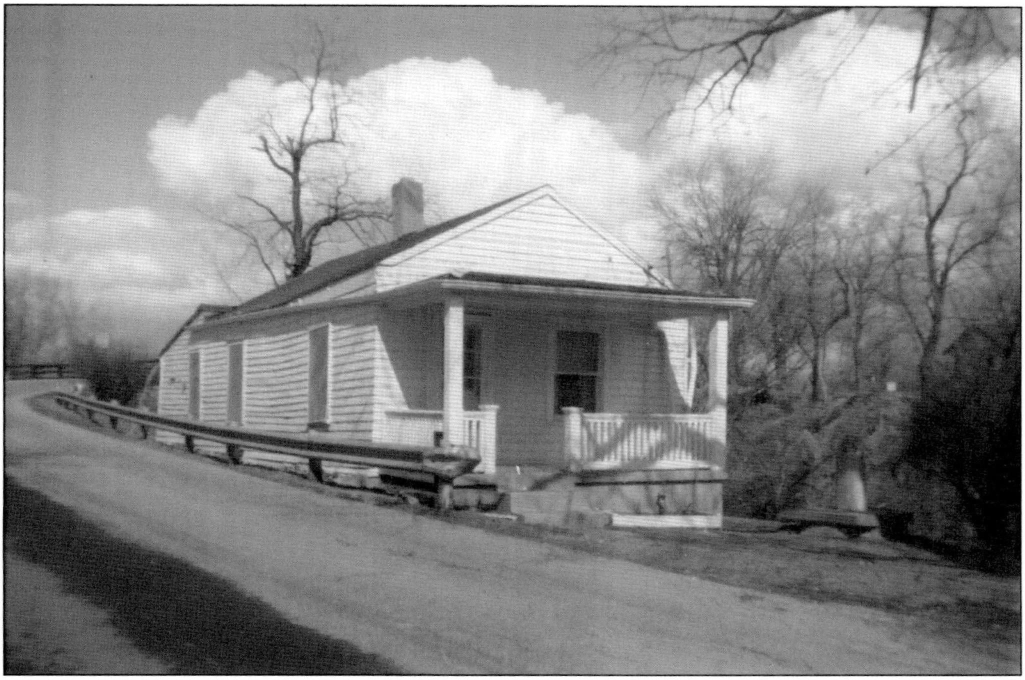

Tollhouse. The tollhouse for the Covington and Lexington Turnpike was just a few yards north of the Gaines house. The back section of the house pictured here was the original building, added onto in later years for residential use. It was located at the turn onto the old bridge, and the drop off behind the well leads down to the tracks. The later view is of the abandoned house after traffic was routed on Dixie Highway behind the Gaines house, and this section of the road was closed to traffic. The house was later torn down, and all that remains is the crumbled concrete base of the well; the road now disappears into a patch of trees. (Both, courtesy of Johnny Gault.)

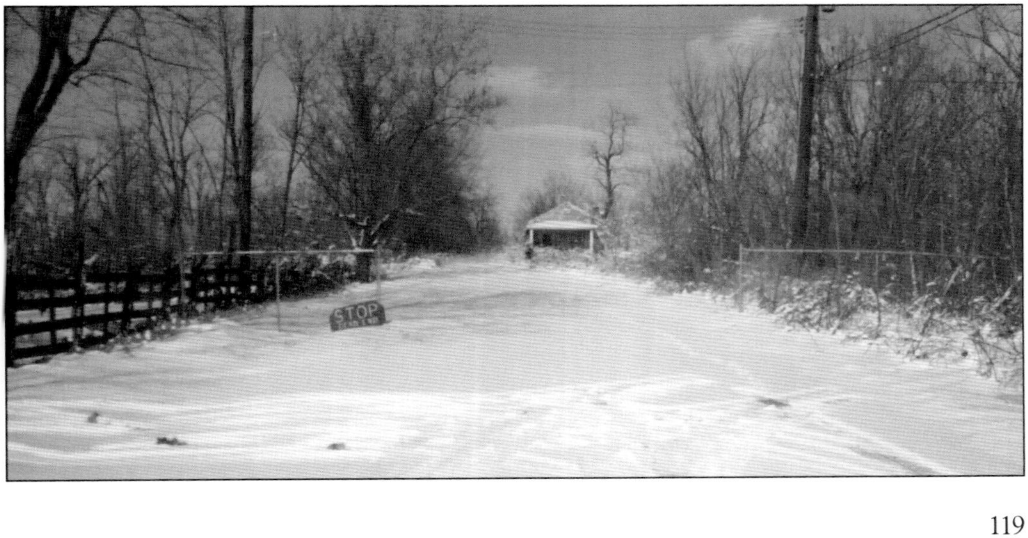

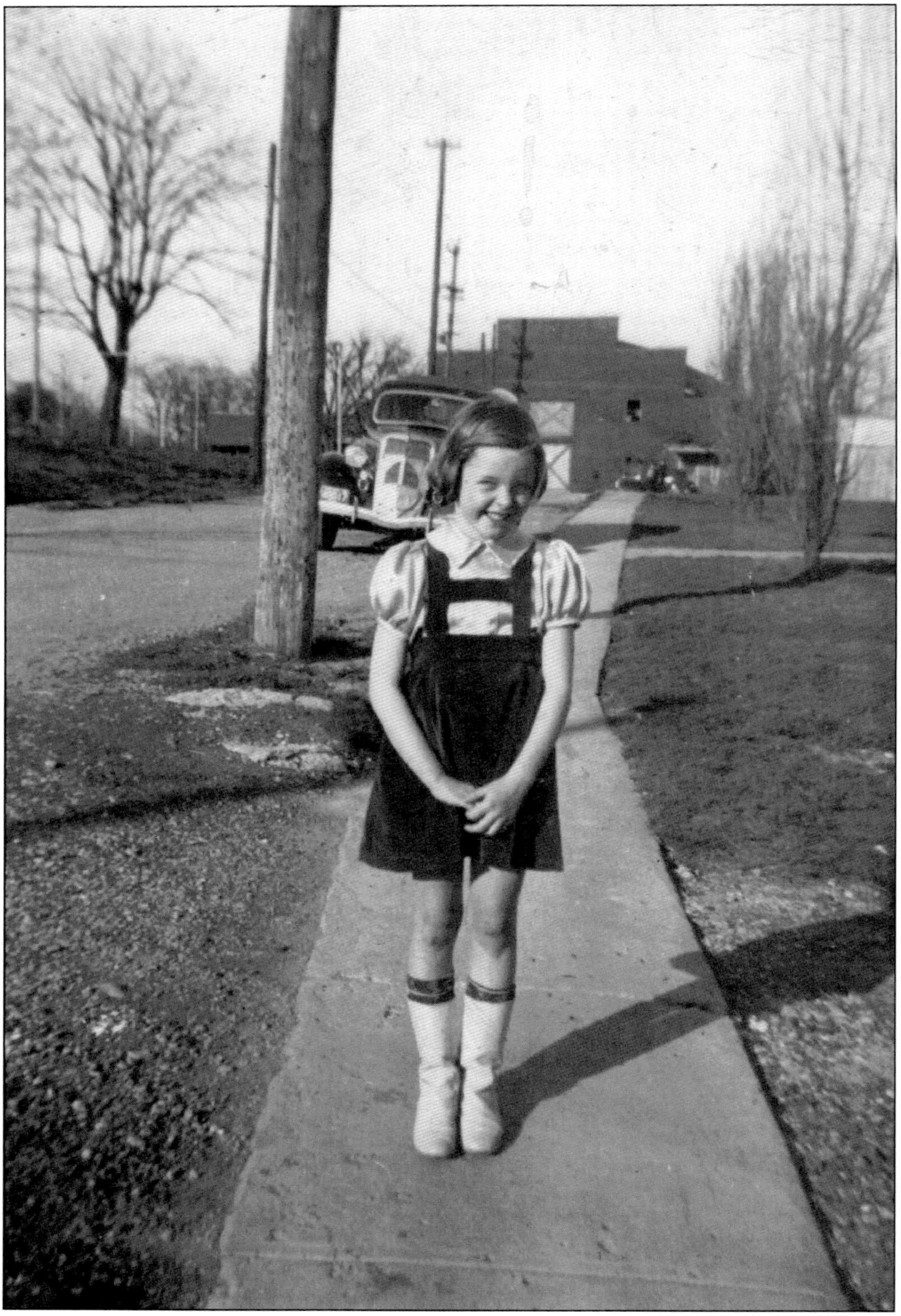

A Big Smile. Faye Brakefield gives a big grin for the camera in this 1940s photograph. Faye is standing on High School Court in front of the high school gymnasium. In the background is Mayhugh Manufacturing Company, and next to Mayhugh's was Groger Truck Line. Faye's father, Cameron Brakefield, owned the Brakefield Drugstore on Main Street in Walton. (Courtesy of Russell Groger.)

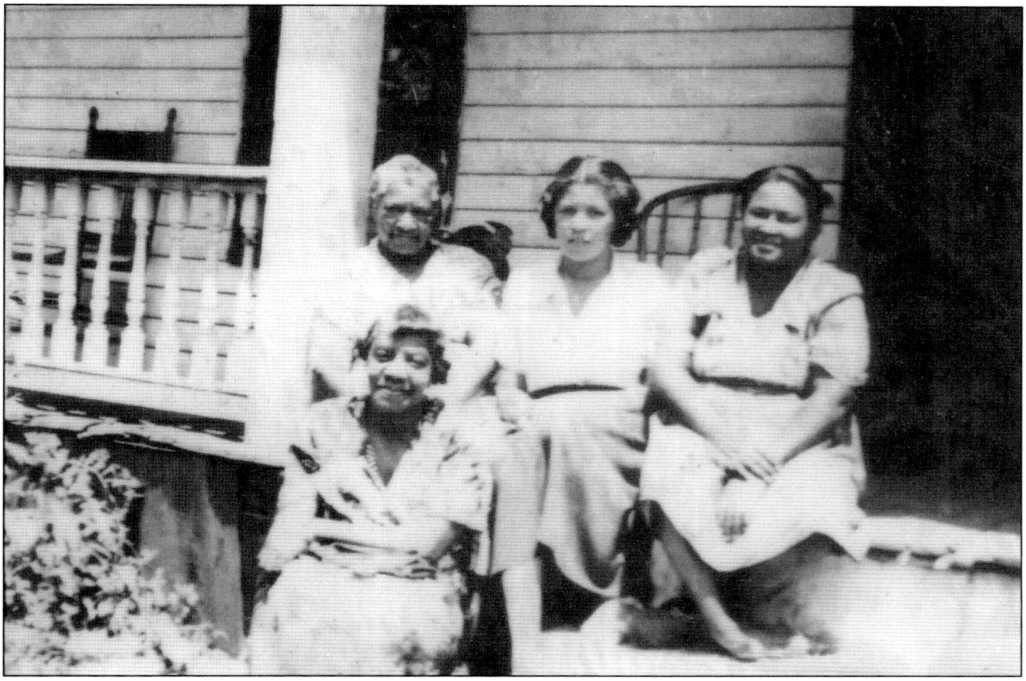

Hanging Out. Aunt Almeda Jones, sister Alice McKay, Matilda Ingram, and sister Joba Christopher enjoy the sunshine while spending time together on a summer afternoon. They were all a part of the close-knit Zion Baptist Church community in Walton. (Courtesy of Zion Baptist Church.)

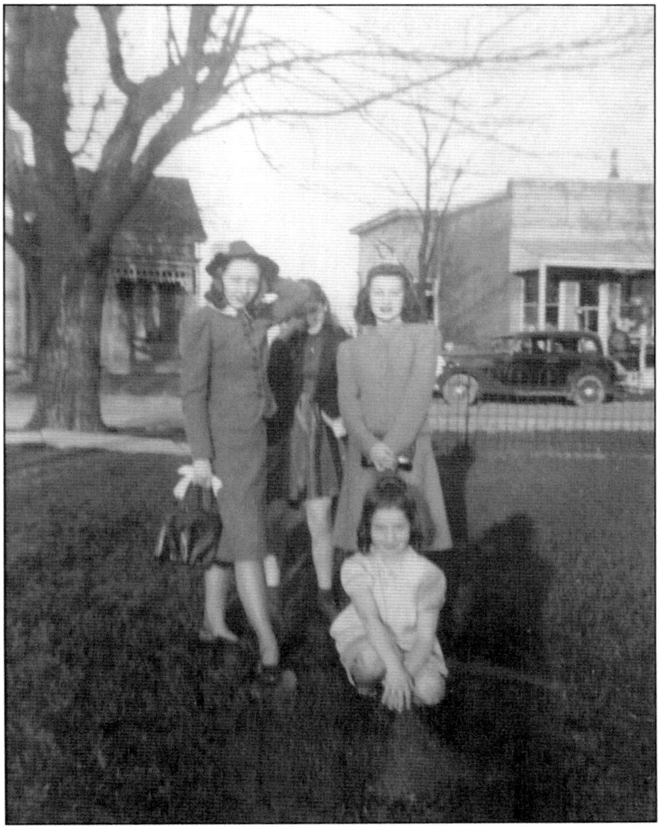

Striking a Pose. These young women are dressed up and out on the town in this 1930s photograph. There was plenty of socializing in Walton, the downtown streets full of pedestrians on their way to shop at the numerous stores, or just to visit friends. The young girl kneeling is Ella Mae Chambers, daughter of C. Scott Chambers. (Courtesy of Russell Groger.)

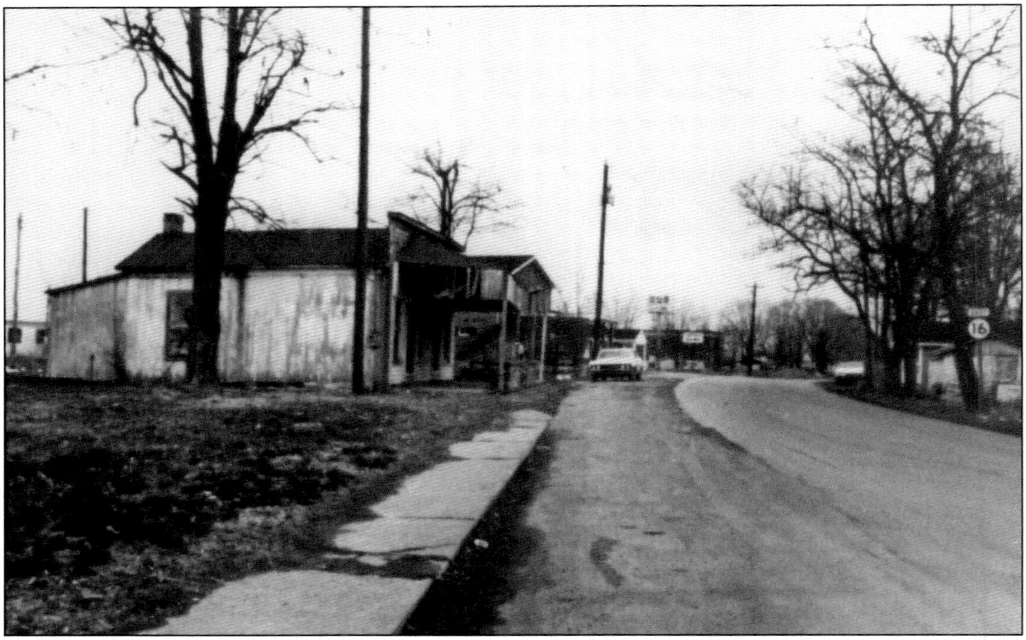

VERONA STREET VIEW. This photograph shows a view of Walton-Verona Road heading out of town. Looking northeast from the crossroads, the old Verona High School is the furthest building on the left, with the Verona Bank and Verona Market beside it. The building closest to the camera is the old A. C. Roberts store. (Courtesy of Paul Webster.)

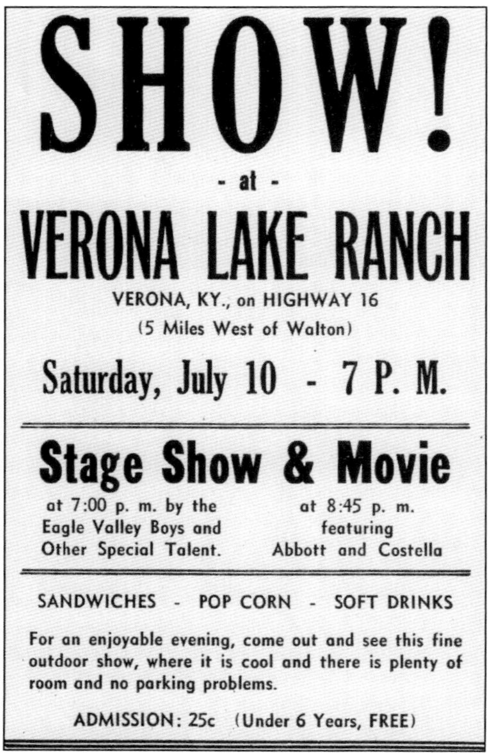

SHOWTIME! During the 1950s, Verona Lake Ranch was a popular venue for entertainment in Boone County. It hosted local beauty pageants and musical shows, becoming so well known that national country stars such as Kitty Wells, Porter Wagoner, Eddie Arnold, and others made the trip to tiny Verona to perform. The ranch was owned by Thurston and Georgie Moore and was located on 100 acres behind the old Verona High School. (Courtesy of Boone County Public Library.)

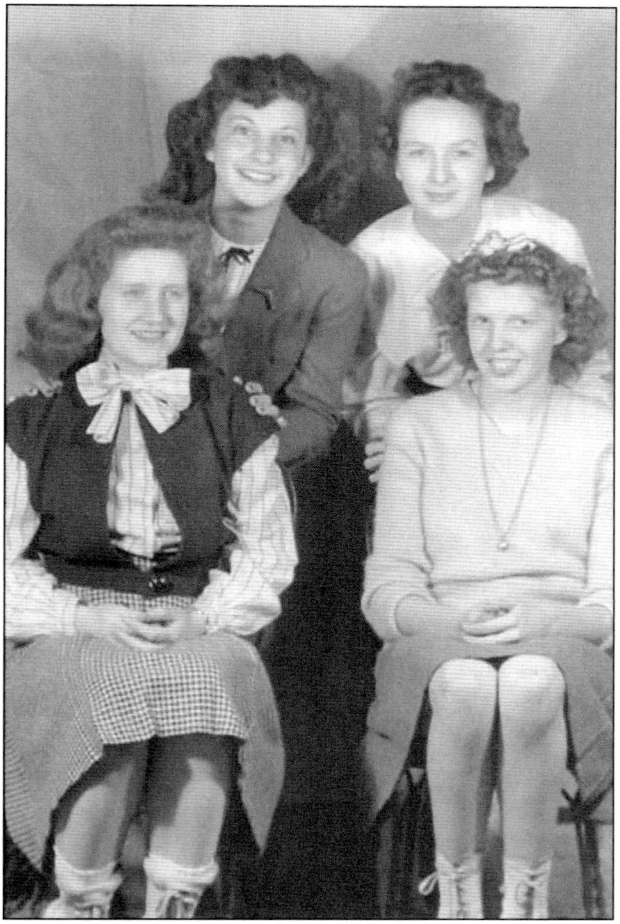

WALTON ROLLER RINK. The Walton Rollerdrome was a popular spot for socializing for the young people in the Walton area. From left to right, Ruth Glenn, Barbara Sebree, Joyce Sullivan, and Beverly Pruitt enjoy an outing in 1947. Pictured below is a ticket stub the girls would have used to gain entrance to the rink. The roller rink was built on the site of the Mayhugh Manufacturing Company across from High School Court. It burned down and was rebuilt, and is currently used as a thrift shop. (Above, courtesy of Bernie Spencer; below, courtesy of Kathleen Wiley.)

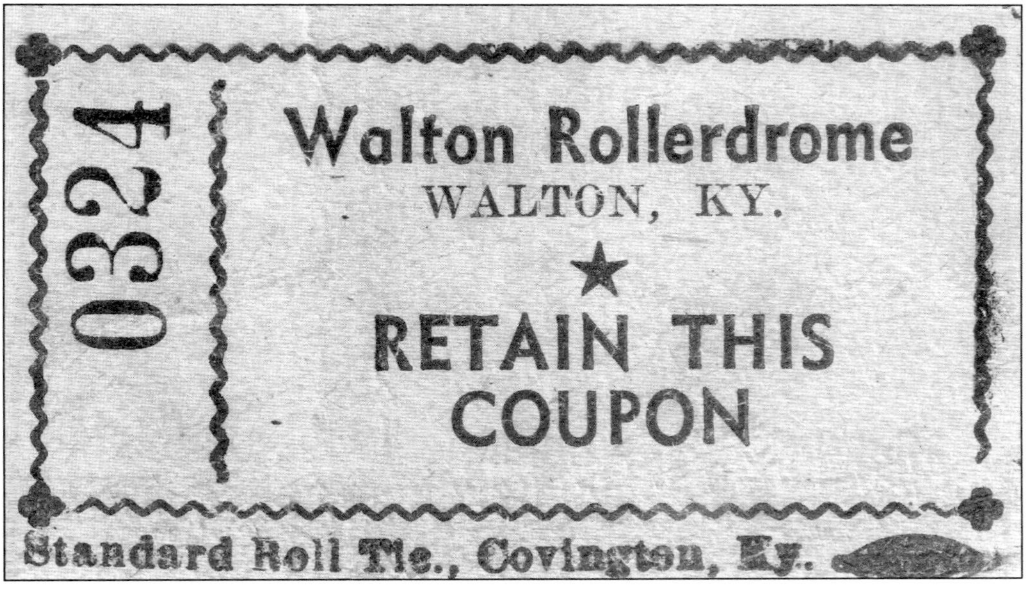

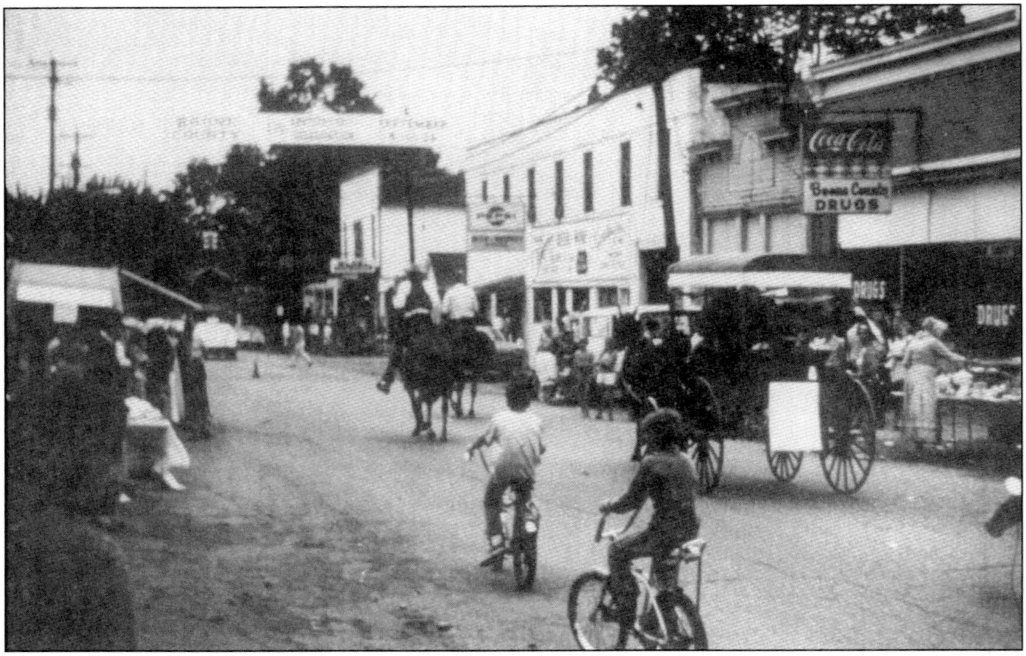

OLD-FASHIONED FUN. In 1973, during Boone County's 175th anniversary, the City of Walton decided to celebrate its own heritage by instituting the first annual Old-Fashioned Day, a day-long festival featuring a parade, music, games, crafts, and square-dancing. Pictured is Main Street looking south from the corner of High Street. Notice the Boone County banner hanging across the street and the Boone County Drugstore (later Steve's Pub, named after jockey Steve Cauthen). The old opera house is the furthest building on the right. Organizers included Wilford Rice (pictured on left) and Mayor Dallas Justice (third from left). They are joined by Anna Mae Simpson, Gilbert Napier, and unidentified children. (Both, courtesy of the City of Walton.)

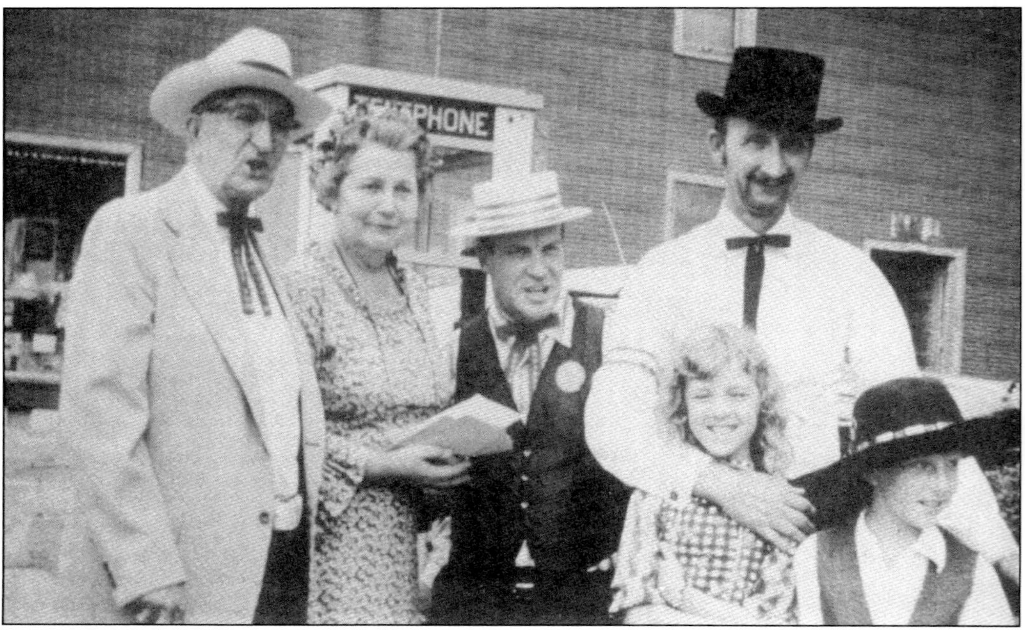

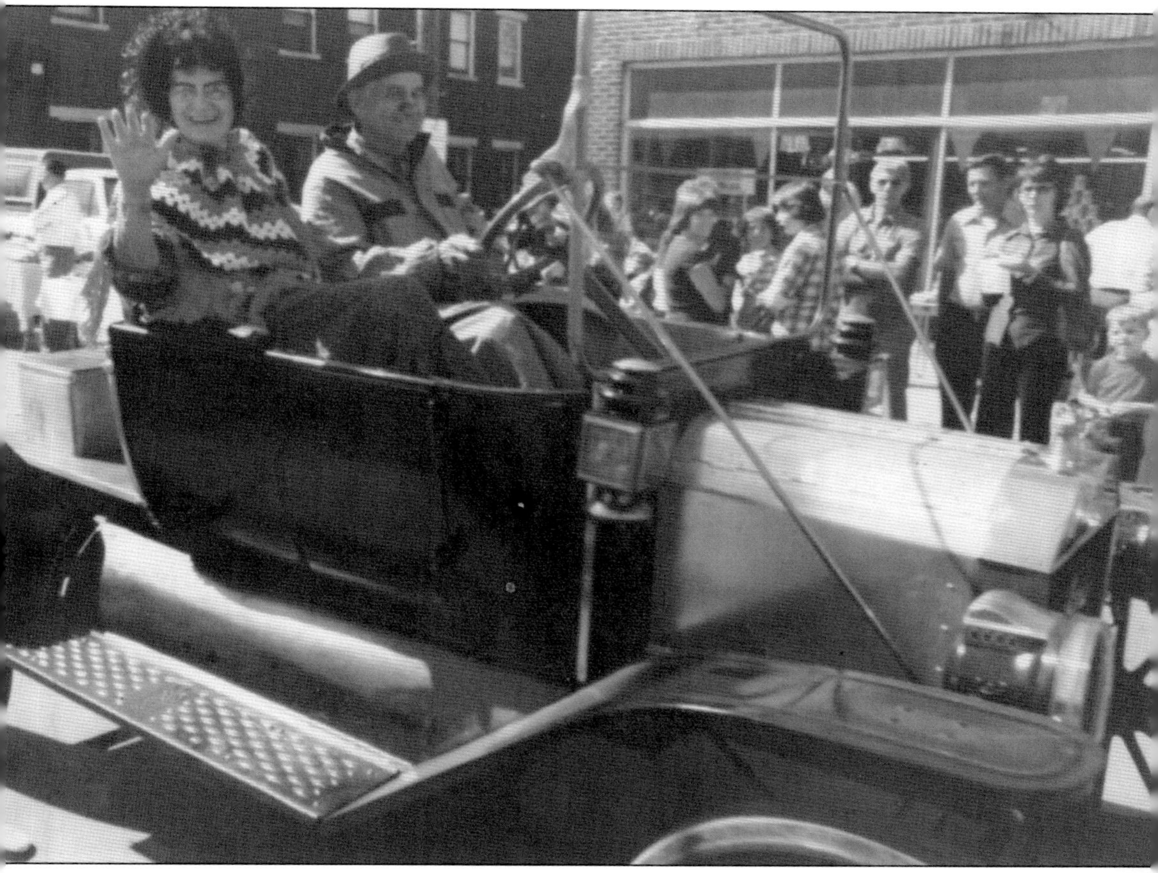

MORE OLD-FASHIONED FUN. Col. John Gault and his wife, Madeline, join in the fun during the annual Old-Fashioned Day Parade. Madeline Gault gets into to the spirit of the day by dressing in period costume and waving to the crowd, while the little boy on the right seems fascinated by the antique car Colonel Gault is driving past him. The initial festival was such a success that it has been held every year since then in September, an event that is not only popular with Walton-Verona residents, but people from the surrounding areas who come to town to enjoy a day of fun. (Courtesy of the City of Walton.)

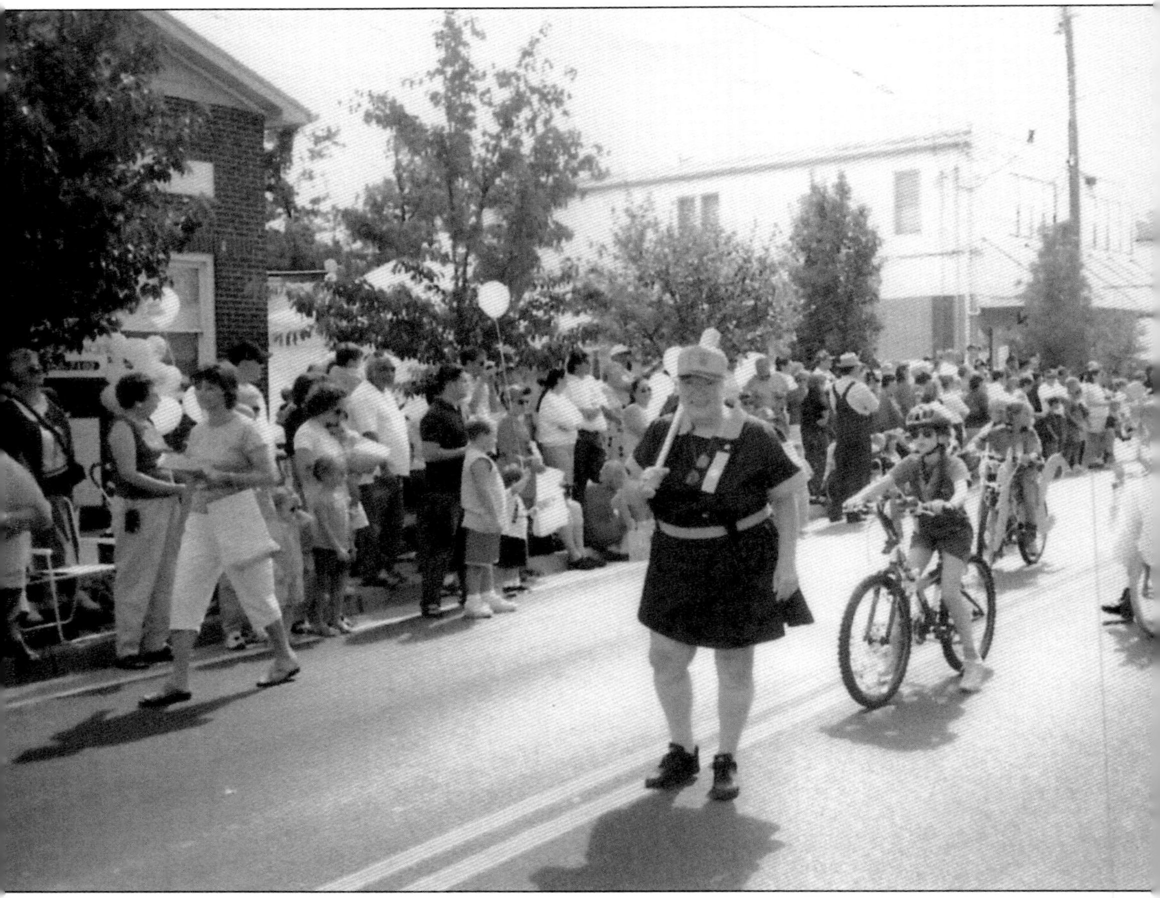

PAT LEADS THE WAY. Pat Scott stops long enough to smile big for the camera during the 2003 Old-Fashioned Day Parade. On this occasion, Pat is dressed in a replica of her All-American baseball uniform to take part in the celebration. She is shown here leading children in the parade on Main Street. The ball field at the Walton Community Park was named in her honor for her contributions to the game of baseball. The AQW, Inc., building is in the background. (Courtesy of Pat Scott.)

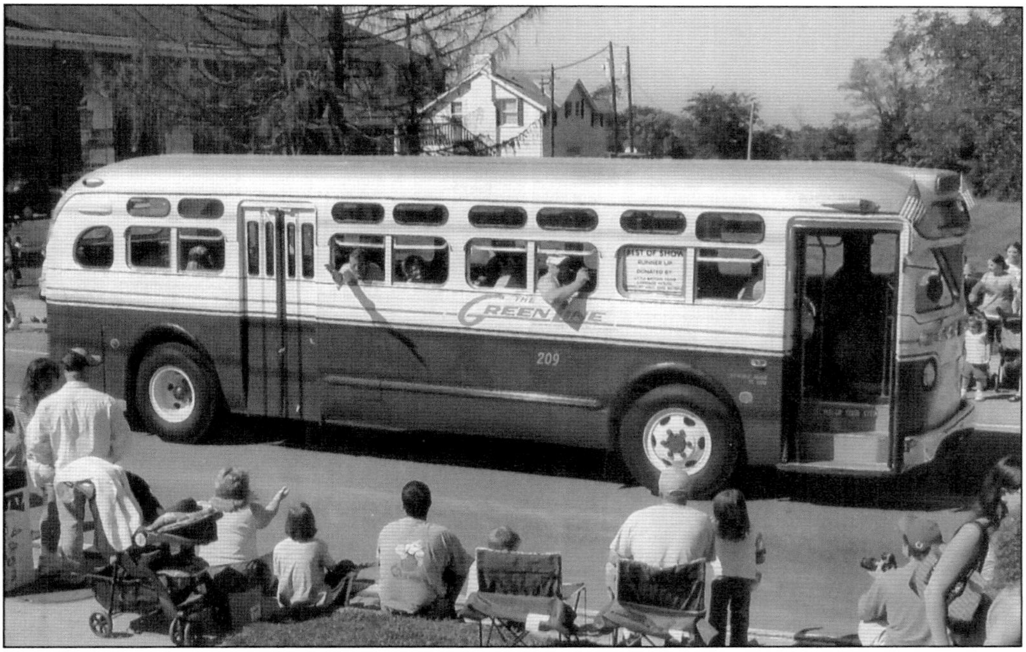

The Green Line Rolls Through Town. The Green Line streetcar line served the Cincinnati and Northern Kentucky area during the early 20th century. By mid-century, streetcars were no longer used, and the Green Line introduced their bus line to continue serving transportation needs. In the above photograph, residents take a trip down memory lane while riding the bus during the 2001 Old-Fashioned Day Parade. In the photograph below, Verona residents Paul and Jeff Webster wave to the crowd as the bus makes its way down Main Street, a reminder of days gone by. (Both, courtesy of Paul Webster.)

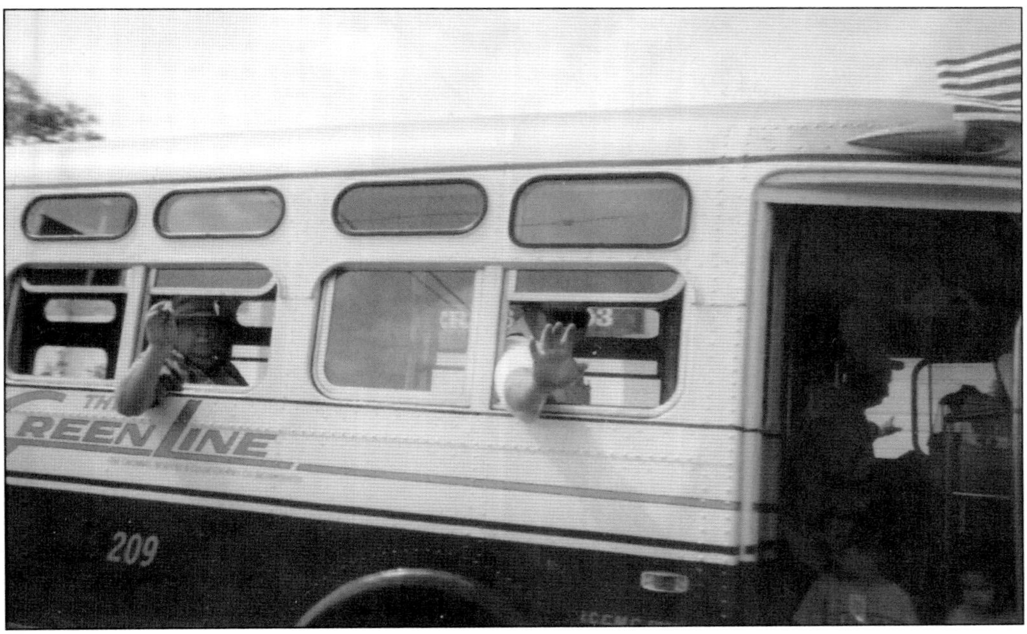